ADVANCE PRAISE FOR *THE BODY IS A DOORWAY*

"This memoir, like all of Sophie's work, defies capture. Reading her is like stepping out of time and into something visceral and haunting and reclaiming. Her prose is a balm that calls me back to myself time and time again into a deeper type of knowing and remembering; this is the kind of book that will make you talk to trees and pray to moths, which to me is an urgent and necessary act."

—**Holly Whitaker, author of** *Quit Like a Woman*

"Full of arresting, luminous, and generative insight. Like a forest spirit gifted with a lyrical pen, Strand shows us the extraordinary connections among bodies, energies, metaphors, and ecologies. Her work brims with wisdom about health and illness, meaning and mystery. A must read."

—**David George Haskell, biologist and author of** *Sounds Wild and Broken,* **The** *Songs of Trees,* **and** *The Forest Unseen*

"Sophie Strand is a poetic thinker, dreamer, and visionary whose words bridge the false divides between the ecological, the political, and the spiritual to present us with a re-membering of the collective body that connects all life. In *The Body Is a Doorway,* Strand inhabits the lyric memoir with seemingly effortless grace, weaving seamlessly from the story of her personal journey through illness, love, and life amidst social and environmental collapse a meditative reflection on humanity's relationship with itself and the rest of the world. Bound together by Strand's delicate prose and shimmering intellect, these threads come together to form a tapestry that offers the reader a map for navigating our world's increasingly uncertain future. Throughout the book, Strand fearlessly plumbs the depth of human society's shadow sides but never gives in to despair, drawing from her characteristic affinity for mythology and archetypal imagination to generate meaning, beauty, and hope. Readers will leave this book with a deeper connection to the numinosity of life, death, and everything in between."

—**Kai Cheng Thom, author of** *Falling Back in Love with Being Human*

"Against the stentorian city sounds screaming the latest new spells to guarantee "healing" and "well-being" to the zealous pilgrim, a whispery song wafts gently across the streets, past the doorways and signs marked by unpronounceable therapies, and through the crevices of our exhausted bodies. Sophie Strand's more-than-human song, her brilliance, her earthbound theology of the body in its gloriously awkward dehiscence, traces out a turn in the fabric of things: a moment when we seem to be recognizing that we are of this earth and we must move and crawl and fall and die and live again at its own pace. Read this book, written lovingly in the lowercase, and you might find yourself scandalized by the spirit of Sophie's sermon: that your body is and always was a doorway, *not the house.*"

—**Bayo Akomolafe, PhD, W. E. B. Du Bois Scholar-in-Residence, Schumacher Center for a New Economics and author of** *These Wilds Beyond Our Fences: Letters to My Daughter on Humanity's Search for Home*

"*The Body Is a Doorway* touched my heart, nurtured my soul, and enchanted my spirit in a way no other book has. Sophie Strand's vulnerable and powerful memoir is a potent reminder that healing is a process of becoming, not an end goal. We are not linear beings; we are ever expansive and interconnected. This rare gem is a must read for anyone on a journey of self-actualization and self-love."

—**Bunny Michael, author of** *Hello, Higher Self*

"*The Body Is a Doorway* is an epic poem of survival—an act of devotion to life itself. While chronic illness lures some victims to abandon their bodies, for Sophie it has been a tether: a calling more deeply into relationship with her body and the living world. Each new mysterious symptom, every medical gatekeeper, even the pathological judgements of the wellness industry are turned into compost by this eloquent writer. From it sprouts the healing metaphors of nature's belonging. This book will feel like a bosom friend to anyone who lives in the lonely land of the sick."

—**Toko-pa Turner, author of** *Belonging: Remembering Ourselves Home*

"When she finds herself grappling with the confounding terrors of chronic illness, one of the most visionary novelists of her generation starts to apprentice herself to the living land, drawing insight and guidance from the other animals, plants, fungal webs, landforms, and inscrutable weather patterns. Using her writing to weave her way, spider-wise, into the polymorphic web of what is, Sophie Strand slowly comes to sense herself as an exuberant expression of the breathing earth, and her body—even in its glitching confusion—as finest medicine."

—**David Abram, author of** *The Spell of the Sensuous* **and** *Becoming Animal*

"Be ready. Here is a graced and feral prophecy, one that breaches our comforting sense of separate skins. With her winged prose, Sophie Strand unweaves outworn binaries of sickness and health, healing and decline, even aliveness and death. Moth wings, woodchuck nibbles, starlight, the fungus beneath our calloused feet—all of these gather to sing a wild new sacrament, baptizing readers in the unruly and beautiful earthen ecologies that make us truly whole."

—**Lyanda Lynn Haupt, author of** *Rooted: Life at the Crossroads of Science, Nature, and Spirit*

"In this prophetic, gorgeously written memoir, Strand tells one young woman's story of confronting mysterious, life-threatening illness, and her efforts to transcend the toxic positivity of the current healing establishment, in which curing equals success. She brings shamanic intensity to her narrative and in a voice that is entirely her own, bridging mythology, medicine, ecology, neuroscience, literature, and cultural commentary in a thoroughly original book that deserves a place on your shelf next to Sontag's *Illness as Metaphor*. Strand is a literary alchemist, a transformer of pain into beauty, capable of revealing profound, brilliant links between the personal and the planetary in language that tears your heart out. *The Body Is a Doorway* brims with passionate complexity. I could not put it down."

—**Mark Matousek, author of** *Sex Death Enlightenment* **and** *Lessons From an American Stoic: How Emerson Can Change Your Life*

"In language as alive as the wind, as sparkling as the river, as wise as the owl, as connected as the fungi, and as illuminating as the mountain, *The Body Is a Doorway* invites us to reimagine ourselves, our bodies, and our humanness beyond the limited narratives we've been given, clearing a path to deeper presence and aliveness. Through expansive, ecological storytelling, Sophie Strand reminds us what becomes possible when we cease the endless quest for wellness and return to the wisdom, wonder, and wildness of our bodies."

—**Lisa Olivera, author of** *Already Enough*

"Sophie Strand is a magnificent weaver of words and worlds. In *The Body Is a Doorway*, she invites us through the portal of her lived experience, and re-earths us of all that we have forgotten. This is no small thing in this distracted world. When I read her, I remember what it is to be truly here. And I feel welcome inside of all of it. This book is yet another revelatory work from this remarkable soul."

—**Jeff Brown, author of** *Hearticulations* **and** *Grounded Spirituality*

"This book is a doorway of no return back into the entangled and enchanted, the pheremonal and phenomenal, the cellular and cosmic, the rhizomatic and territorial. Strand deconstructs and rewrites neoliberal notions of health and well-being through deep personal, multisensory inquiry and physical hardship. She is a somatic and literary cartographer to deeper bodily truths. Those whom society deems "unwell" may be the sentinel species of our times, reminding us of our ignored but unbroken umbilical cord to the broader ecology. The living world is reflecting back to us who we are, and our survival will depend on heeding the omens of our bodies, our embedded communities, and our nesting environments. The human, like the body itself, is not singular. It never has been. It's a cacophony of pluralities, a multiverse of beings negotiating the quicksand of capitalist modernity. No body will be unscathed in the cartographical shuffle of history making. Let this book be a portend and a guide."

—**Alnoor Ladha, cofounder,** *Culture Hack Labs* **and coauthor,** *Post Capitalist Philanthropy: Healing Wealth in the Time of Collapse*

"Sophie Strand once again wrote something that will make you feel enchanted and whole no matter your circumstances. *The Body Is a Doorway* will break your heart and help you put it back together, feeling powerful and connected in even the worst of times. A must read for those of us who are sick, as well as anyone who loves us or might become sick one day."

—**Cassandra Snow, author of** *Queering the Tarot* **and** *Lessons from the Empress*

"Sophie Strand is a living mystic. *The Body Is a Doorway* is a masterpiece—devastating, vast, and gorgeous. So many people find themselves in this dilemma of mysterious unsolvable unresolvable illness that somehow is an affront to North American values of betterment and infinite possibility and self-responsibility. Strand lives and writes herself into a different way with impossible choices that are radically expansive, brutally honest, gutting, and filled with beauty. This book does the work of a thousand therapists."

—**Kimberly Ann Johnson, certified sexological bodyworker, somatic experiencing practitioner, and author of** *Call of the Wild, The Fourth Trimester,* **and** *Reckoning*

"Sophie Strand offers us a poetics of unbecoming. Part ecological analysis, part theodicy, part coming-of-age story, part reckoning with our violent culture, Sophie's book is a magic spell that reconnects the myriad shards of reality with a secret thread. She writes herself back into life—and shows us the way of being whole again through surrendering to the whole, the 'Symbiotic Everything.'"

—**Dr. Andreas Weber, biologist and author of** *The Biology of Wonder* **and** *Matter and Desire*

THE BODY IS A DOORWAY

A MEMOIR

*A Journey Beyond Healing, Hope,
and the Human*

SOPHIE STRAND

RUNNING PRESS
PHILADELPHIA

Copyright © 2025 by Sophie Strand
Cover illustration copyright © 2025 by Jean-Manuel Duvivier
Cover copyright © 2025 by Hachette Book Group, Inc.

Running Press
Hachette Book Group
1290 Avenue of the Americas, New York, NY 10104
www.runningpress.com
@Running_Press

First Edition: March 2025

Published by Running Press, an imprint of Hachette Book Group, Inc. The Running Press
name and logo are trademarks of Hachette Book Group, Inc.

The Hachette Speakers Bureau provides a wide range of authors for speaking events. To find
out more, go to www.hachettespeakersbureau.com or email HachetteSpeakers@hbgusa.com.

Running Press books may be purchased in bulk for business, educational, or promotional
use. For more information, please contact your local bookseller or the Hachette Book Group
Special Markets Department at Special.Markets@hbgusa.com.

The publisher is not responsible for websites (or their content) that are not owned by
the publisher.

Print book cover and interior design by Susan Van Horn

Library of Congress Cataloging-in-Publication Data has been applied for.

ISBNs: 978-0-7624-8741-7 (hardcover), 978-0-7624-8743-1 (ebook)

Printed in the United States of America

LSC-C

Printing 1, 2024

For my parents and for the Hudson Valley

"Life can only be understood backwards; but it must be lived forwards."

—Søren Kierkegaard, from his 1843 journals

"It is as if the land secretes pheromones testifying to its abuse, detectable only by those who are themselves damaged."

—Jan Zita Grover

CONTENTS

THE BODY IS A DOORWAY

CHAPTER 1

Back to the Body

"OH," I THOUGHT AS I LEANED AGAINST A LIMESTONE WALL IN JERUSALEM. My fingers slid against the smooth stone, marked by the slow erosion of two thousand years of hands stroking these walls as they walked the same path Jesus would have taken through the city on his way to his execution. The Via Dolorosa. The Way of Sorrows. "Something is wrong."

I'd been sick for seven days already. Like most people, I was familiar with flus and viruses and infections. But this was different. I was visiting family in Israel, and every day I had woken up feeling worse than the day before. My joints pulsed with discomfort. I couldn't eat without vomiting. Still, I trusted my body. I trusted the promise of my youth.

You get sick and you get better. Sometimes, you need a pill. But usually your body catches you, like when you stumble and recover without falling.

Except sometimes you don't catch yourself. You don't save yourself. You hit the ground hard, and someone else picks up your cross and helps deliver you and the instruments of your murder to their tragic end.

That day, I followed my aunt through the old city.

"Something is wrong. Something is wrong," I mumbled as I stopped in random shops to vomit. Did I mean something was wrong with my body? Did I mean that it was wrong that one man's untimely execution at the hands of empire had been co-opted by that same empire and then used against his own people?

It was odd that my aunt—a secular Israeli Jew—had suggested we follow this path on our visit to Jerusalem. Neither of us were Christian. And yet that day, as I walked into illness, I also walked into ancient wounds, through a city that had known empire after empire, fire, genocide, and bloodshed.

I was dumbstruck by the thickness of time. The air shimmered with heat, with violence that refused to disappear after the bodies had been cleared and the slates of history wiped clean. I shook my head to clear the heat, the sour confusion. My cousin Adam grabbed my arm, peering at me with worry: "Are you okay?"

No. I'm not okay. But I didn't yet have the perspective to be able to say that with confidence. I *should* be okay. I *would* be okay.

Wait. Had I *ever* been okay?

Later that day, as we drove through the desert toward the Dead Sea, I knew something was wrong in my body. It was as if every single one of my cells had shifted counterclockwise. Yes, I looked the same in the sand-scratched mirror outside the showers. I had the same shape. But nothing fit together correctly anymore. There had been a glitch. The matter of me was irrevocably altered.

One day I was well. The next day I was sick. Very sick.

This is the story I told and retold for many years. I told it to myself like a mantra. Perhaps if the words passed through my mouth one more time, I might finally *understand* what had happened. Maybe a clue would finally become visible, unlocking the possibility of a cure and an explanation.

But no matter how many times I told doctors, friends, and, most often, myself the story of "what happened," it was impossible to identify the exact moment when I crossed from the kingdom of the vital into the realm of the unwell. There was no line I stepped across. No visible threshold or doorway. I spent years playing detective, trying to retrace my steps. When did I take a wrong turn? How?

The summer leading up to my illness was dripping with watermelon juice. I was sixteen and interning for the local newspaper, a publication that specialized in harvest festivals, escaped chickens, and contentious debates over renovating the ancient library. Luckily for me, my first day of work coincided with the most dramatic day my hometown had seen in years: the older brother of a classmate robbed a bank and there was a high-speed police chase down the winding mountain roads. I fielded tips and worried calls in the humid little office, feeling like I was a star in some indie coming of age movie.

My life was precisely on time. Yes, as a sensitive child I'd often felt out of step with the world and with my friends. Too precocious. Too attuned to suffering. I couldn't watch movies in which the animal died. I couldn't spend too much time in shopping malls or amusement parks. I was cynical—untrusting of adults—in a way that my peers were not, as if I had been born already battle-worn. But finally, that summer, I felt like my body and my brain had caught up with the culture.

I fit in. I had a new boyfriend. Blond highlights. A group of friends with such intimacy that we coordinated our movements like a swarm of starlings, dancing through parties in abandoned fields, slipping into swimming holes in unison, passing joints and cigarettes, bottles and cans hand to hand so we could all reach the same sparkling level of intoxication at the same moment, as the same extended organism.

One night, my boyfriend, Tom, took me to a secret lookout on Overlook Mountain and we sat in the back of his truck, kissing, watching moonlight shiver like a silver skin across the serpentine Hudson River in the distance. It was impossible to tell where the sky ended and the land began. Fireflies in the forest below us seemed like embroidered stars, coming to sew us back into the cosmos.

I was set to visit relatives in Israel at the end of August. It would be my first big trip out of the country. Yes, I was bummed to miss a final moment with Tom before he left me behind for college in the fall. But I was going to a new country: literally and figuratively. I could feel momentum coiling inside me. The future was a landscape of delicious possibility.

Misfortune and pain have a way of fossilizing the moment that precedes the fall. I think of those empty silhouettes in Pompeii. Women kneeling next to cooking fires. Children playing in the garden. Life becomes a snapshot. The sweetness of whatever came before is remembered as a Garden of Eden from which we've been exiled. When did I eat the apple? When did I damn myself to illness? For one sparkling moment, I stood poised on the brink of healthy young adulthood.

And then I wasn't standing. I was flat on my back, flung into another story entirely.

Stories can be helpful tools for surviving hardship and navigating complexity. That is, when we craft them as sturdy boats, built to our dimensions and desires. But many stories are bigger than our single lives and desires. Many stories are invisible: so big, so culturally ingrained, that we are blind to the ways in which they drive and constrain our lives.

One of those cultural stories we live inside, but have trouble recognizing, is a story about health and personal responsibility. It's a story that's tangled up with theology, anthropocentrism, colonialism, and capitalism. It has very little to do with the happiness and vitality of our actual bodies. The story goes like this: Health belongs to an individual. Health is both a possession and an external reflection of someone's personal achievements or moral failings. Every individual is personally responsible for the ways in which their body changes, misbehaves, and deviates from the norm. The norm is usually measured against white bodies. Young bodies. European bodies. Male bodies.

We all recognize the narrative from the headlines that come up on our newsfeeds daily: Stress linked to cancer. Early trauma linked to obesity. Obesity linked to overeating. Overeating linked to poor impulse control. Ten ways you can detox your system. Ten ways you are harming your heart health. Ten diets that will prevent stroke.

It's not just scientific reports and the medical establishment. This story encompasses both traditional and new age spirituality's obsession with sin and purity. If we are sick, we might have done something wrong in a past life. If we were raped or abused, we probably invited in this "soul contract." If our cancer isn't going away, we are not drinking enough celery juice. If we can't pay for the foods and medicines that might improve our autoimmune issues, it's because we haven't yet manifested enough wealth.

Are you feeling bad? It's probably because somewhere, down the line, you made a mistake. And now everyone knows. Time to prove you can get back on track. Time to pour all your money and energy into *getting better*.

Getting sick, then, isn't just a simple bodily experience. It comes with thousands of years of moral baggage. To get sick is to be impure. To get sick is to fail.

In this story—a story I inherited from the culture at large—my illness represented a personal failing. The impurity in me was too dense, too murky, to allow me to return to health. In this story, that summer is a crime scene. Somewhere in that effervescent adolescent romp, I did something that tipped the scales away from health and toward sickness.

Until the age of sixteen, I was healthy. Then I woke up and I was sick. In that story, I lost my body that summer.

But there is another story. One that is very quiet. But one that strikes me as being closer to the truth.

I did not lose my body that summer. Instead, I finally found it.

Now, I look back on the summer leading up to my illness once more, but I slow down the film reel. I peer deeply into my own younger face. Here I am at the same parties, the same swimming holes, the same mountain summits, but I don't see a healthy young girl anymore. There's a wild glassiness in her eyes. They are unfocused, almost blind.

I see a girl moving so fast, experimenting with so many drugs, taking so many risks, that she might just be able to outrun confronting the pain she's been haunted by since early childhood. I see an animal trying to gnaw its leg off to escape a trap.

At some point in my childhood, I decided to leave my body. My brain seemed to work pretty well. And it was faster, cleaner, and happier when it didn't have to register the unpleasant feelings I associated with my stomach, my legs, my chest, and my throat.

The issue was that no one in my life recognized this dissociation as a problem. In a society that prizes our ability to master our bodies and work against our soft, fleshy needs, my ability to "not feel" my body was rewarded. It was seen as a kind of gift.

"Sophie doesn't feel cold," my mom would tell my friends' parents when I would run outside barefoot, coatless, in the winter, with ice cutting through the soles of my feet.

Brutal cold didn't touch me, and I was always covered in cuts and bruises and burns. I hardly ever wore coats or tights. I completed insane endurance competitions, running long-distance races and setting the presidential fitness record for number of sit-ups in a minute each year. I contorted myself into weird shapes and dislocated my joints to make friends laugh. I pictured my body as an action figure and my self like a balloon on a string, hovering above. What if I could just float up there forever, safe from the messy suffering of everyday life? What if I never had to come down? Everyone seemed to love the show. That summer, I jumped off cliffs into shallow water. I ducked under no-trespassing signs, climbing up through rusted ruins, balancing on the tops of oxidized cranes that hung over open water. I tried any drug offered to me at parties. I smoked cigarettes I convinced older guys to buy for me from the gas station. I snuck out of the house to ride around in my friend's car, seatbelt unbuckled, screaming out the window as we hit a hundred miles per hour on winding mountain roads. I forgot to eat for days at a time. I drank until I passed out. Until I vomited. I ran miles and miles and miles barefoot, until the soles of my feet left bloody footprints on the asphalt.

My parents were terrified. It was tricky. I was a gifted and responsible student. My grades were better than ever. I was doing extracurriculars and winning writing awards. It was hard to pinpoint what was wrong. I was not a classically *bad kid*. In fact, by all superficial metrics, I was doing fantastically. But there was something about my behavior that was increasingly reckless.

Burn me. Fuck me. Humiliate me. I didn't care. I couldn't feel anything. I was invincible.

We live in a society that lionizes warriors, athletes, and heroic individuals who "conquer" their fears. Pop psychology has us complete an inventory of our limiting beliefs as we move along the path toward fulfillment. We must confront our fears and mute the parts of us that register terror. Fear is conflated with weakness. Fear is feminized. Fear is bodily.

The only thing we have to fear is the body itself. That soft, fallible organism, which is not immune to trespass, bullets, rape, and the passage of time.

A lack of fear is rewarded by our culture. But it is also extremely dangerous. Fear is not an accidental feature of being alive. It is an evolutionary gift that developed to help us survive.

Fear is the prickle of adrenaline in our system, telling us that a certain place is unsafe and that predators could be nearby. Fear is the correct knowledge that women feel when they walk home alone at night. To ignore that fear is to risk real danger. Fear is the understanding that our well-being is not guaranteed. Fear is a type of humility. We are animals living alongside other animals. We can be eaten. We can be injured. We must proceed with care and caution. Put very simply, fear keeps us from doing stupid things. It keeps us alert. Disembodiment denies us this somatic intuition. It cuts us off from our ability to smell storms, interact with other species respectfully, and taste for the edibility of wild foods.

When we override our fear, we don't just override our bodies. We override our ability to read and respond to our environments and the messages they are sending us as smells, sounds, and textures.

If we can't feel pain, we also can't access the heights of pleasure. If we don't honor the limitations of a sick body, the body gets sicker. Like walking on a broken leg, refusing to feel can end up making the injury much worse. If you've ever been in an accident, you know that physical pain hits you harder the following day, when your fight-or-flight response has dissipated and you finally deliquesce back into the shape of yourself. After the accident, in your home, in your bed, your body senses that it is safe to assess where the damage has been done. But for some of us, the sense of safety never arrives, and the disembodiment continues in perpetuity.

We keep walking on a broken foot. We keep pretending nothing is wrong because to pause to heal is dangerous. To stop and tune into our body is dangerous. We know there is pain to feel and if we felt it all, it could destroy us.

I look at Western culture and how it has terraformed the world, paving rainforests and marshes and wildflower fields under concrete. I'm struck that the way we live seems like a magnified version of dissociation on a culture-wide scale. Our extractive, ecocidal practices create open wounds in the Earth, escalating extinctions and unbalancing weather systems. We pretend that the Earth we burn for fuel, gash for minerals, and mutilate for capital gain is not connected to us. We live above it. We pretend this Earth is not our own body, extended. Just like I retreated into my head when I experienced pain, hovering like a balloon above my body, so has our culture retreated into the notion of human exceptionalism to avoid feeling the suffering it has inflicted on its own larger body.

But we are not floating above this Earth. We are intimately, materially, metabolically linked with every plant, animal, and ecology that is grappling with unimaginable pain and disruption. We have been numb for so long, we no longer understand that the body we are harming is an extension of our own. When we clear-cut a forest or drive another population of birds to extinction, we do not somatically register that we are twisting a knife in our own side.

What happens when your foot falls asleep and you try to wake it up?

It hurts. It really hurts. There's a reason the sensation is called "pins and needles." As pressure is taken off the sensory nerve and stimuli begin to flow along their proper channel, our body registers pain signals again. The leg was in pain when it was asleep, but we were blithely unaware. Once we wake the leg back up, this feeling rushes back all at once.

Coming back into our bodies isn't always the lubricated pleasure bloom therapists and self-help gurus promise. Mostly it burns and prickles and hurts.

But we *need* to wake the leg back up again to walk, to move, and to survive. We need to wake up to the fact that we live in an intimate relationship with a world that is suffering. The threshold we have to cross is one of extreme discomfort. And most medical and healing paradigms tell us that discomfort should be avoided or medicated. Through force-fed techno-optimism and a constant stream of media distraction, we are encouraged to avoid sitting with silence, with uncertainty, and with howls of pain from the beings that live outside our doors.

But being numb doesn't just mean we avoid discomfort. It means we are equally denied the full spectrum of physical pleasure and intelligence.

There is a world of wild love and bodily creativity just past the doorway of prickles and pins. There is sex without sin. Delicious, incorrect embodiment. Queerness. Interspecies collaboration. There is a community of more-than-human beings with advice on how to navigate climate change and social collapse.

I think back to myself that summer, skating close to death every day. Throwing my body around like it was a prop I could replace. What if I hadn't gotten sick? Would I still be alive? Was that girl really so healthy?

There is another story about how I got sick. One that is harder to hold. One that prickles through me like pins and needles. That summer, lightning struck with illness. I finally had no choice but to come back into my body. Physical pain stitched me back into the physical presence I had been trying to escape my entire life.

I didn't lose my body when I got sick.

No. I finally came back into it. On the Via Dolorosa I came back into my leaky, weeping, feeling body. I could taste my own repressed tears and, deeper than that, under the ancient cobblestones, I could sense a river of older tears that had been forced underground when a human tragedy was turned into religious dogma, stolen, and mistranslated by empire.

There was pain. But there was also pleasure. Finally, there was feeling. Everywhere. There was a big, fat "holy shit!"

CHAPTER 2

Indigestion Is Emergence

MY FIRST SYMPTOM WAS NAUSEA. THE SECOND WAS THE COMPLETE paralysis of my gut, a condition for which I now have a name: gastroparesis. Overnight it became impossible for me to digest food. I'd manage to force down a handful of almonds and, hours of cramping and pain later, the nuts would come back up, undigested. Soon I was starving, feeling my body begin to crumple. But every time I tried to eat, the bloating and nausea would tighten, vicelike, around my midsection. It was as if there was a knot tied in the middle of me, refusing to let anything come in or out.

I lost twenty pounds in a matter of weeks. The thinly cloaked worry on my parents' faces soon transformed into naked terror. I'd been an athlete—a long-distance runner who fueled herself with bagels and pasta—and suddenly I could hardly make it up the stairs to put myself to bed. As I entered my junior year of high school, swaddled in sweaters to keep my newly skeletal frame warm, my parents tossed around the idea that I had picked up a parasite during one of my swimming hole excursions.

"What's wrong with Sophie?" The whispers were hard to ignore. I'd reassure my friends that my doctors would figure it out soon. Probably nothing. A virus. A stomach bug. A food allergy.

But I kept getting sicker in increasingly unpredictable ways. My reactions to food were getting weirder. Not only did my body refuse to digest food, but it also regularly put up a fight the second something touched my tongue, setting off a chain of allergic symptoms. Often, after eating, I'd develop full-body hives, with blood blisters in my mouth and throat. The scariest reaction was the wheezing, which caused my throat to narrow into a slender straw. I was covered in a patchwork of rashes, some scaly, some swollen and hot to the touch. My belly button began to bleed. My joints were swelling and walking was uncomfortable. My brain felt congested. But worst of all was the pain—migratory, cunning in its ability to change location and flavor so quickly that it was impossible to outwit or escape.

Soon my face was familiar to the local ER. And I was familiar with the male doctors who would dismiss my symptoms, belittle me, and yet still suggest invasive physical exams that left me shattered and confused. Were these tests necessary? Was I making this all up? Why did my gastrointestinal symptoms necessitate an intravaginal exam? A breast exam? They would tell me I was anxious. Or they would take my mother into another room to tell her to get me psychiatric help because I was anorexic.

Studies have shown that women who go into ERs with abdominal pain experience a 30 percent longer wait than male patients with the same complaint. Women's pain is chronically undertreated, and women struggle to be taken seriously, often experiencing life-threatening events before they are properly diagnosed. Women's illnesses are much more likely to be diagnosed as psychosomatic than to be connected to an underlying pathology. And given that an initial psychiatric diagnosis dramatically lengthens a diagnostic journey, extending it anywhere from two and a half to fourteen years, we can begin to understand why the correct identification of women's illnesses takes consistently longer on average than that of men's. Women wait longer for every type of cancer diagnosis, and those with female-specific diseases often suffer for ten years before being taken seriously by medical professionals. Women who have been presenting with cardiac symptoms for months, repeatedly going into the ER, die of heart attacks that could have easily been prevented.

In 2018, diagnostic errors were the third leading cause of death in the United States. Whose deaths? That piece of data comes to us loaded with the fact that women and minorities are statistically more likely to receive inadequate care or outright harmful treatment. The sexist gaslighting of modern medicine isn't just a problem. Very often it is a death sentence.

Over the next year, as I grew sicker and more desperate, ferried from specialist to doctor to specialist, I was often instructed to disrobe in front of a doctor.

I would shiver, all bones, feeling like I was about to fail a test. At a moment when my peers were disrobing for each other—experiencing pleasure and play together—my striptease was terrifying and medical and demanded in exchange for the possibility of pain relief and diagnosis.

Often, these male doctors would also suggest they examine me internally—anally and vaginally. And they would perform these tests without a guardian present and without explaining why these tests were necessary. Soon I was shell-shocked, so brittle I was worried I might shatter. I felt my edges blur. I would say yes to anything if it held the potential to help. And this is the reason I quietly assented to exams and tests that felt *wrong*. I wondered if this was what it felt like to be a rat in a lab. Hands were in and out of me, constantly probing.

Maybe this doctor would have the answer. The pill. The treatment. He's older. White. Smug. He has gilded certificates up on his wall. He looks down his nose at me from a distance of years, education, and privilege. He tells me that he's going to need to stick a finger up my anus. He's going to need to inspect my naked body in a dark room while my mother sits anxiously in the waiting room.

Of course I said yes. Of course I didn't understand how inappropriate this behavior was. I wanted to feel better. And doctors were supposed to help with that, right? I was rendered vulnerable by my age, my gender, and, most importantly, by the fact that I was sick and physically fragile.

I was a good student. A good athlete. A good friend. I could be a good patient too.

It is only now, years later, that I understand how common sexual misconduct and abuse are within the practice of medicine. These interactions played upon the power imbalance between patient and doctor, child and adult, woman and older man. I now know that these violations are extraordinarily common. We come to doctors desperate and in pain, and it is that very vulnerability that makes us perfect candidates for assault. We do not know what counts as a standard medical exam. We are ready to do anything to get closer to a cure.

Many of these doctors were famous and well-regarded physicians. They were doctors written up in magazines, with best-selling books about nutrition and chronic illness. And many of them have made these sexually inappropriate interactions a habit. How do they continue to get away with this flagrant abuse of power? The manner in which medical institutions handle misconduct is opaque and lazy. Most doctors never face any repercussions. Patients mistrust themselves and fail to report incidents. And on the rare occasions that these doctors are disciplined, it happens in private. When they return to practice, their history of misconduct is sealed, unavailable to the desperate patients coming to them for care.

First, I was gaslit. I was told that it was all in my head. And I was medically raped. There was a certain relief when, within a month, I was too ill for doctors to pretend I was merely anxious or anorexic. But then, in a state of extreme desperation, I was used as a test rat for experimental medications and treatments for conditions that were a doctor's pet project, rather than related to my specific complaint. Now that I look back, there was little evidence I had any of these conditions.

I was given drugs and antibiotics for parasitic infections I did not have. I was given more than twenty rounds of antibiotics for Lyme disease. Another illness I did not test positive for. When I tentatively asked if these treatments were safe, I was chided.

"Don't manifest a bad outcome," I was told by my parents, who were still relying on simplistic concepts of prayer, purity, sin, and karma, conflating illness with lower vibrations and bad behavior. And yet each treatment made me sicker, ravaging my gut and leaving me covered in hives, my throat tight with thrush.

I couldn't help but feel like I was failing. I hadn't opened myself up to the medicines enough. I hadn't tried to heal hard enough. My doctors were happy to reinforce that sense of failure, rather than admit that their tactics might be at best useless and at worst harmful.

Instead of pausing to assess whether I had been correctly diagnosed with a tick-borne infection and discuss whether it was safe to continue treatments that were obviously killing me, two of my doctors strongly advised running a peripherally inserted central catheter (PICC) line into my heart to receive intravenous antibiotics.

Advise might be too soft a word. They practically threatened me.

"Your brain is going to start going if you don't do IV antibiotics. That's where the Lyme goes to hide. And the coinfections are going to start weakening your heart. You don't want to die, honey? You're young. You should be getting ready for college."

The subtext was: "Don't question us. You'll die if you don't do this."

In the face of all my cultural programming, I was beginning to feel extremely distrustful of my doctors. I was ashamed of this distrust and worried that it might be fear-based.

"You're just scared of the treatments. You need to push through," I would whisper to myself at night, rolled up in a ball, clutching my throbbing knees, swaying on a tide of nausea that was too vast to belong to my body. It felt like an undulating ocean into which I was slowly, cell by cell, melting.

I couldn't differentiate between my failing body and the side effects of all the medications my doctors were throwing at me. One antiparasitic drug put me into something close to a coma for four days. I remember closing my eyes on the couch while playing cards with my mother and emerging days later, in bed, my mouth tasting like asphalt and paint remover.

But every day I was sicker and more desperate. I was literally starving to death. My joints would pop out of their sockets. And my other organs were beginning to glitch: my liver, kidneys, immune markers, and blood numbers began to wobble in ways that perplexed doctors dedicated to the diagnosis of Lyme. No one had the humility to slow down and wonder if something else might be going on.

When do we accept that a painful experience is not going to end or resolve? How do we keep moving? What happens when we cannot digest our fate?

When I did not get better, my friends were frustrated. They didn't know how to include me in their buoyancy, their mischief, and their belief that nothing bad happens to the young. They were busy going to parties, playing in bands, making low-stakes mistakes, visiting potential colleges, and having sex.

They were increasingly uncomfortable with the fact that I was obviously on a different trajectory, so they chose to avoid seeing me rather than confront the brutal reminder that life doesn't always make sense. It's hard being the physical manifestation of other people's anxieties. To be a sick person is to know that you are always, simply by being alive and being unwell, someone else's rude awakening.

My early social media accounts were flooded with other people's prom photos and relationship updates. Meanwhile, I was crawling on the floor to the bathroom to vomit. I was making bargains with myself. *I have to be better by the time my birthday comes. I have to be better by Christmas.* When those deadlines passed and I was even weaker, I'd set another one, feeling my body slip out of time. There was no schedule. No graduation. *I have to be better by the time summer comes along so I can go canoeing with my nature camp up in Canada*, I muttered like a mantra late at night, aware now that this was unlikely to come true.

I would have to figure out a way to survive, or I knew I would die. How could I craft a new life that included the indigestibility of this discomfort, this uncertain disease?

Stuck in bed, I distracted myself from my failing body by following my intellectual curiosity. I researched mythology, the history of religion, evolution, and microbiology. I was surprised when I discovered that a bad case of indigestion was the biological origin of our own bodies. Evolutionary biologist Lynn Margulis popularized the endosymbiotic theory, demonstrating that the complex cells that build our bodies, as well as all mammals today, are likely the product of an ancient symbiotic fusion between simple bacteria. She posits that "bacteria, long ago . . . were partially devoured and trapped inside the bodies of others" becoming the organelles that inhabit our cells. "In both sexual and symbiotic unions, hunger was a likely primordial factor urging the desperate to merge." She repeatedly characterizes the different stages of eukaryotic cell development, a process of infiltration and assimilation, and the subsequent evolution of meiotic sex as a "failure to digest."

With my own body contorted by my attempt to eat plain white rice, I imagined these ancient beings in the steamy confines of a geothermal vent. I breathed through the waves of nausea, imagining that nausea was like a boat, carrying me back through deep time into the shape of one of those hungry and desperate bacteria. What a wild thing to realize—that our bodies were produced by the incomplete cannibalism of ancient microbes. One bacterium's indigestion literally changed the face of the world.

New life grows from failure. Bodies become possible because some other being's body failed to behave correctly. I found this comforting, as I realized that I wasn't going to heal quickly or easily.

My body was not going to simply assimilate the illness or the mistreatment of medical professionals.

Had those first hungry bacteria properly metabolized the other bacteria, nothing new would have been born. The emergence of new life depended on a mistake, an inability to complete a task. What if we rearticulated emergence as the irritant that seeds the pearl? Discomfort that cannot be broken down provokes us into totally new shapes and new modes of body-making.

I stumbled upon the Greek myths of the god Kronus. Kronus, the king of the monstrous Titans, the pantheon that precedes the Olympians, is haunted by a prophecy that his children will usurp his power. He famously eats his own children in an attempt to escape the prophecy of his downfall. But his horrified wife, Rhea, hatches a plan to save her offspring. When she gives birth to Zeus, she creates a counterfeit version of the baby in the form of a stone. She feeds Kronus the stone while hiding Zeus safely in the Cretan mountains. Finally, years later, Zeus disguises himself as his own father's cupbearer, serving him a poisonous emetic. Kronus vomits up his other children, who go on to become the Olympic pantheon. Kronus also brings up the undigested "omphalos" stone that Rhea had switched out for Zeus. Just as indigestion provides the basis for our very bodies, so too it ignites mythic cosmogenesis—the birth of a new cosmic world.

Kronus cannot digest his own children or his own violence. The indigestibility of the omphalos stone creates the possibility for a new mythology. The myth can be read as loosely representative of the historical Greek invasion of the Mediterranean basin, as the Greeks subsumed earlier Bronze Age mythology into their own legends. However, the older gods, the Titans, refuse to be fully digested. Instead, Greek myths read like palimpsests, manuscripts in which one text has been superimposed over an earlier piece of writing. In Greek mythology, the Titans are the undigested residue of the Mediterranean traditions that predated the Greek invasions. The Olympic pantheon that is born is something that, by virtue of unresolved digestion, is generatively plural, straddling geographies, mythic realms, and belief systems. Mythic indigestion is a type of symbiosis. The term for this mythic indigestion is syncretism, referring to the process by which two different religions or schools of thought are amalgamated. Neither paradigm fully digests the other. No one is successfully assimilated. Rather, a new myth or religion occurs by way of messy addition. The indigestion of one pantheon precipitates the emergence of a new pantheon. A stone lodges in a divine gut, and a new world is born.

A more nuanced version of this type of indigestion appears in the biblical story of Genesis, in which Adam and Eve eat the forbidden fruit from the tree of knowledge. We are told that after consuming the apple, "The man and his wife heard the sound of the LORD God as he was walking in the garden in the cool of the day, and they hid from the LORD God among the trees of the garden. But the LORD God called to the man, 'Where are you?'"

This has always struck me as an extraordinary moment. The omnipotent God is suddenly unable to locate his progeny inside the realm of his own creation. The eating of forbidden food has not so much cursed Adam and Eve as it has ruptured the previous cosmological order. Just as Kronus expels the new pantheon, Adam and Eve are expelled from God's garden—vomited out of one cosmic order and into the next. But this expulsion is almost out of God's control. Having eaten the forbidden fruit, Adam and Eve rupture his jurisdiction. They can no longer be located within his domain.

As I read with an eye toward indigestion, I also wondered about the digestion of the "apple" of the tree of knowledge. As I tried, day after day, to consume small amounts of bland food, I wondered about the assumption that eating and digesting were the same thing. I was bodily struggling with the fact that I could eat something but never digest it. In a simple reading of Genesis, we assume that the fruit has been metabolized by Adam and Eve and conceptually integrated. The knowledge for which the fruit tree was named has entered their bodies.

But if we read the actual scripture that sprouts from this apple seed, we do not find people who seem to be infinitely knowledgeable. Rather, they have knowledge lodged in them like Kronus's omphalos stone, undigested and unusable. Most of the Old Testament narratives are composed of profound acts of ravenous spiritual longing, questing, and questioning. If Adam and Eve had fully digested the fruit of knowledge, then why were their offspring asking for visions and spending so much time debating divine rules? Something had been lodged in their systems, but surely it had not been digested and transformed into useful information. Instead, it had forced them into new shapes and new struggles.

The worlds produced by indigestion exceed moral categories. They are difficult to classify as simply good or bad. They are never monistic. They are always monstrously multiple, hungry, and incomplete. For example, the fossil fuels powering climate change today were produced 360 million years ago during the Carboniferous Period, when woody matter accumulated without decomposing, effectively swamping out other lifeforms. It has been speculated that this was a period before white rot had "learned" to break down lignin, the tough component of wood. At a temporal delay of millions of years, an epoch of global indigestion has indeed given birth to a new world—one of industrious smog and ecocidal madness.

And in this coal-smudged, boiling world produced by the anarchic fusion of capitalism and Paleozoic indigestion, it is interesting to note that there is a rise in the incidence of autoimmunity and gastrointestinal illness. More than three million US adults have inflammatory bowel disease, and that number is quickly rising. Like me, millions are grappling with cascading food intolerances. Ravaged by illness, we seek to limit our diets until we arrive at a narrow window of digestibility.

It is easy to pathologize this nutritional limitation. It is obviously painful and physically destructive. But perhaps there is a more interesting story to tell about the ways our bodies fail.

As my list of safe foods dwindled, I stood at a distance from the dominant cultural appetite: for food, for pleasure, for satisfaction, for extraction, for unlimited growth. I wondered why we believe that human beings should be able to eat everything?

There are thousands of books that try to identify the single trait that marks us as uniquely human—everything from our ability to use symbolic language to our ability to change the geological composition of the world. But what if it was much simpler than that?

I have wondered if, perhaps, what makes us distinctly and terribly human is our ability to extract every last calorie from the landscape. We are hell-bent on turning even the most indigestible biota into caloric energy. How is it that grass, incredibly difficult to digest, has become the staple of civilization?

Conversations about overpopulation are often simplistic, giving us a scapegoat when we think about our impact on the environment. But it is important to note that human populations do not take up nearly as much space as we think they do. It is our farm fields that take up the most space, leading to the clear-cutting of forests and the terraforming of biodiverse ecosystems. Our agricultural fields have eaten up the world. Our huge swathes of appetite account for more than half the world's land mass.

In many cultures that predate the rise of colonial capitalism, we regularly see food taboos. We are not, in fact, allowed to eat everything. A very well-documented example of this is the hunting and gathering community of the Ache people in the Paraguayan jungle. Although they inhabit a tropical forest with hundreds and hundreds of edible animals and plants, 98 percent of their calories come from only seventeen food sources. It has been postulated that food taboos and restrictions, while they may be articulated as spiritual, act to conserve biodiversity and keep humans inside a respectful ecological niche. I have found it fascinating that prohibited animals and plants are often characterized as "unclean" within their given tradition. Uncleanness and contamination designate a kind of protection. We conserve and protect what we consider unclean from our appetites.

Uncleanliness is an embrace. A circle of safety. As I knelt in my own vomit, sweating, ashamed of my body's refusal to heal, I found comfort in this reframe. To be unclean, sometimes, is to be safe from the destructive appetites of others. Sometimes it is good that no one wants to eat you.

I wondered what these taboos could teach us about food intolerance and medical dietary restrictions. What if the rise in food intolerances is doing to us physically what we used to enact culturally and spiritually? We are not allowed to digest everything. In fact, looking back to the biological and mythic uses of indigestion, if we are capable of digesting everything, we preclude the possibility of new worlds, new flavors of being. We metabolize away the future.

What if we reframed indigestibility as a sign that something wants to collaborate with us? What if, when something "disagrees" with me, it is actually an invitation to become something absolutely new? While I do not properly metabolize food into a normative body, I do in fact incorporate these foods. I physically change around their immovable matter.

As I entered the second year of my illness with a handful of safe foods and a gut ravaged by medications and inflammation, I needed a story that would keep me afloat. Health was not yet achievable. I couldn't totally digest illness. Or a sense of failure. But I could hold them in my body lightly. I could begin to curve and adapt to their shape. Rather than problematize my indigestion, I started to think of it as an uncomfortable symptom of becoming.

"I'm on the way to being quite different," I whispered, sitting on the hammock with a year of failed treatments behind me. I looked up through humid air at the sky, blurred with clouds, a space where rain refused to fall, balled up into puffs of spun water.

What is indigestibility trying to teach me? What new worlds am I trying to vomit up? What is my omphalos stone?

CHAPTER 3

Ecological Appetites: Hummingbird Lessons

PLUMES OF IRIDESCENT MIST HURRIED DOWN THE RIVER, LIKE SPIRITS late to an appointment with the ocean. Rainwater, translated from the locust leaves, resurrected the storm. But the sky was azurite. The sunlight was dense as butter. Everything had resettled, albeit shifted, glittering, fully transformed. I was catching my breath at the end of my run from my college town down to the water when something cut across my vision. A phosphine streak of citrine and amethyst. A blink. A jewel. The color I imagine lives inside my blind spot.

Ah. Yes. There she was. The hummingbird survived the previous night's thunderstorm and had come to suck sweetness from the honeysuckle trumpets. I watched, transfixed as she danced up, then down, blurred by need and the evaporated heat of sweetness. Her hum was air translated through appetite.

A hummingbird must eat upwards of fifty times a day, visiting between one thousand and two thousand different blossoms. Pollination is incidental. There is literally no time to meditate on the effects of her nourishment. If she goes several hours without feeding, she will die. Every ache for sugar is not an inclination. It is an emergency.

The hummingbird was a living "Yes." Yes to beauty and decoration. Yes to dancing. Yes to the overflowing sugars of spring's floral bouquet. She was an embodied affirmative to appetite and movement and life lived as sensually and immediately as possible.

I tried to reconcile the bright beacon of that yes with how a no had saved my life. I had begun to pray to no with my entire body. No more medicine. No more doctors. No more healers. No more experimental treatments. And recently, no more food. No more appetite.

My last year of high school was a nightmare spent between bed and the hospital. The IV treatment for the Lyme disease I didn't have almost killed me. Over the course of a month, I had a series of life-threatening anaphylactic (allergic) reactions to the IV medication. Absurdly, "an impending sense of doom" is one of the listed symptoms of an anaphylactic reaction. The entire year had felt pregnant with ominous dread. My friends were getting ready to go to college. They were having their hair colored and styled for prom and graduation parties.

I was lying on the floor, drifting in and out of consciousness, having an EpiPen needle stabbed into my thigh in a desperate attempt to open my swollen airways as I wheezed, waiting for an ambulance to arrive.

There were many moments when I thought I was going to die. And there were many moments when I looked to the adults in the room for reassurance and saw that they thought I was going to die too.

By the spring of that year, my immune system was decimated—by the experimental treatments or my mysterious illness, no one could be sure. Not only was I now allergic to all of the medications I had previously tolerated, I was also beginning to experience anaphylaxis when I ate food. Any food. Years of overprescribed antibiotics for a condition I didn't have had weakened my already beleaguered body.

As it became clear that traditional medicine did not have an immediate answer for me, my parents took me to holistic healers, reiki workers, psychics, and experimental nutritionists. I was prayed over and covered in essential oils. I was told to pray better. To detox. To manifest light. To imagine my body filled with golden, vibrating molecules. I was instructed to consume homeopathic dilutions of "viruses" to balance my own system. To sleep with magnets below my pillow. When we are sick and our doctors throw medicine at us that seems to make us sicker, rational orthodoxy fades away. Yes, give me magical cures. Tell me this sickness is karma from a past lifetime, and if I cut the final cords and do the rituals, I might finally experience pain relief and recovery.

Please, anything. I'll do anything.

Here, take one more supplement and we will "clean you out," these healers would say. Your gut is "leaky." Your body is toxic. Your kidneys are full of heavy metals. Your brain is toxic too. Your lymph nodes are swollen because of your low self-worth. Anyone who has ever been life-threateningly ill will know the desperation it breeds. We will try anything. We will do anything. And when treatments fail, and medical doctors, shockingly unskilled in empathy, shrug and suggest this means we will die, we start looking elsewhere—anywhere else—for help.

There's a memory I have that feels so spiderwebbed with sorrow and physical pain it's almost a dream. I can't understand how I allowed it to happen. But it did. It really happened. I'm lying on a giant crystal atop some sort of vibrating instrument in a room padded with purple velvet. A "shamanic healer" informs me that, first, I am a "martyred turtle of great significance," and second, I am deeply unclean. I have karmic baggage. I'm sludged with demons and darkness.

Your illness is dirty. You are polluted. Karmically. Biologically. Emotionally.

"Yes," I tearfully affirmed to my assortment of healers and doctors and guides. "Yes. I knew it. I knew I was contaminated. Tell me, please. How can I live? How can I be purified of this illness I have obviously brought upon myself?"

The answer always cost money. A lot of money. And the answer was always packaged in white light, ascension, purification, and the chlorinated scrub of my gut, my blood, my body, and my soul. And when these treatments, spiritual and medical, not only failed but tended to make me sicker, the healers and doctors would send me a bill and say, "If you're not better yet, it's because you haven't taken this seriously enough or followed the protocols properly. Maybe you don't 'want' to get better?"

The doctors wanted to clean me out, and so did the healers. By the spring of my senior year in high school, I was fully indoctrinated in purity jargon: Christian theology's sneaky way of repackaging itself as both rational enlightenment and new age healing paradigms. And while I was certain they were correct—that I was physically and psychologically toxic—I couldn't ignore that these treatments were not making me better. It was obvious they were making me worse.

"I want to stop for a while," I announced one night, shivering at the bottom of my parents' bed. After another series of allergic events, I was being given a "break" by my doctors before pursuing a new treatment. "I don't think I can take one more medicine. I just want to try to go to college, and if I just get sicker . . . I'll come home. And I promise I'll try a different IV antibiotic."

"You could live at home, and we could drive you to classes . . ." My mother's lips trembled as she trailed off. Then she reached out to squeeze my hand. "You do whatever you want. We'll make it happen."

The assumption of my parents, my therapist, and my cornucopia of doctors and healers was that this attempt to go to school would fail. I was just too sick.

Still, I'd convinced the poetry professors at Bard College, across the river from my hometown, to let me take classes as a high school student—and now I was determined to enroll full-time.

Raised by writers, I'd always known I had both a passion and a talent for writing. I handwrote thousand-page fantasy novels in grade school and spent my adolescence pouring out poetry and stories and journal entries. I dreamed of one day writing my own intensely researched version of my favorite romance, Tristan and Isolde. I'd won awards and accolades for my poems. But in these college classes, among much older students, I finally had the pleasurable experience of exercising a creative muscle, receiving thoughtful critique, applying new techniques, and feeling the "muscle" strengthen. My professors validated this by inviting me into upper-level college seminars as a high school student. I learned about craft and meter and composition. While my body grew weaker and weaker, I compensated by focusing on the strengthening of my mind and my creative pursuits. I produced hundreds of poems and short stories. I devoured the poetry and philosophy books my professors lent me.

But I had been sick for two years. The doctors' attempts to "clean" me had left me as vulnerable and barren as a tree farm is to fungus and forest fires. My body was plagued by infections and viruses. If I could hardly make it to the bathroom sometimes, how could I possibly live on my own, juggling classes and the everyday complexities of college life? Was I just prolonging the next crisis, the inevitable decline of my body into some undiagnosable decrepitude?

I can do this, I bargained with myself in the summer leading up to college. I did an inventory of what *had* provided me with some relief. Most of it was self-discovered and dietary. I'd had some relief from gastroparesis, neurological symptoms, and asthma when I cut out dairy and gluten and sugar. So, I decided to cut out more foods. In fact, the less I ate, the less my gastric symptoms plagued me. The clearer my thinking. I fasted for most of the day, restricting my eating to a small window of time. And, taking a cue from the Bard students who were becoming my closest friends, I began smoking. The smoking was so antithetical to the healing rituals and the handfuls of pills and supplements that had been my religion that it felt like heresy. But I needed a little bad behavior. Illness had trapped me in a sense of constant moral whiplash. Every wrong food or missed pill was a sin expressed through my own body's continued decline.

Smoking was bad. It was wrong. And it felt like it belonged wholly to me. It was my little rebellion. When my parents were out of the house, I would wander into the wildflower-studded backyard and lie back, watching crows stitch forest to sky, sky to forest with their inky wings, smelling the powdery exhalations of dried grass and dirt below me, and flick my lighter, watching the flame catch the paper.

My body was a fire that no one could put out. Why not control my own little fire? Why not burn myself down on purpose?

Paradoxically, it was my death rituals—my smoking and disordered eating—that gave me the life force to make it to college. They propelled me into an adrenaline-fueled approach to survival. My doctors practically washed their hands of me.

"I'm confident you will come back when you realize that IV antibiotics are your only option," one man said smugly.

My parents disagreed with my choice to discontinue treatment, but they knew there wasn't much they could do to sway me.

As a lifelong runner, I pivoted from the measured rhythm of the marathon to the manic energy of the sprint. If I moved fast enough, I might outpace my broken body. The point was not sustainability. The focus of all my new health protocols was to put a Band-Aid on a mortal wound so that I could, at all costs, keep moving. And the allergic reactions I was having to food were terrifying. Each one seemed to validate my sense that I must limit food, limit toxins. I must do another cleanse to see if I could reset my gut and my immune system.

College was lifesaving. I met the feral, artistic oddkin I'd always longed to find. My best friends, Ilana and Hannah and Nora. People with whom I could share the depths of my fear and the heights of my creative aspirations. Herbalists who read Sanskrit. Ancient poets who wanted to mentor me in mystical lyricism. Medievalists with pet snakes and penchants for clove cigarettes. These were friends who wanted to stay up all night discussing literature, making music, and arguing about existentialism while passing around the liquors they had fermented themselves. And while I suppressed my physical hunger as a way of managing my failing body, I satisfied my hunger for literary theory, medieval history, philosophy, and intellectual achievement. Here was a way of externalizing the success I was denied by my body. Here, on the covers of the classics I carted in a heavy backpack across campus, were thin, severe men, overflowing with ideas as knifelike as their countenances, who told me to reject the shadows and walk out of the cave. To reject the body and prize the mind. To find the real forms.

Yes. The real forms were beyond this physical agony. If I could perfect my mind, whittle my physical needs down to the smallest splinter, maybe I could reach peace and purity.

"Such a fragile thing you are. What a beauty," one of my poetry professors praised me, brushing a brittle strand of hair away from my face. The sicker and thinner I got, the more my professors rewarded and fetishized my "perseverance" and "asceticism."

One of the insidious parts of losing weight unintentionally is that, even if you are obviously sick, the dominant culture will congratulate you on your emaciation. I did not have an eating disorder in high school. I loved to bake elaborate English pastries, to experiment with my mom's recipe books, to fuel my long cross-country runs with calorie-dense carbs. But I experienced a strange dissonance when I started to get complimented on my obvious starvation.

When I realized I would no longer be able to digest most foods and experienced dangerous allergic reactions to others, I began to survive on what can only be called "prana"—Sanskrit for invisible life force. Sometimes I wonder how I stayed alive. Unfortunately, this forced, life-threatening asceticism coincided with the adolescent realization that women with appetites are considered unruly and unattractive. I experienced a disorienting dissonance between my dying body and the strangely congratulatory compliments from adults and peers. I was "taught" that my sick body was a controlled body. A fascination. I'd always been naturally athletic and slender, but I'd never given much thought to the size of my body. As it shrank down to right angles and spikes, though, I realized that people found its fragility compelling. Through a complex blend of early childhood trauma, chronic digestive illness, and cultural pressure, I developed an extraordinarily intense fear of both food and appetite.

Was a sick body a beautiful body? Was I supposed to look sick?

Eating less helped. It helped curb the symptoms for which no one had an explanation or a cure. Sure, it didn't seem like a sustainable habit. But I wasn't planning years out at this point. I was looking down at my skeletal feet. I just wanted to experience college as fully as possible.

Survival mechanisms save us in the moment. They are badly built bridges that support one brief, harrowing trip. But they cannot be used again and again, indefinitely. The problem becomes when these survival mechanisms outlive their usefulness.

What is appetite? The word derives from the Latin *appetitus* for "to long, to desire toward, to strive for, to yearn." But appetite is older than Latin, and older than human beings. It is metabolism itself, the chemical reactions whereby a fuel substance is converted into life-giving energy, looping us into an intimate, appetitive relationship with the world around us. The "central pathways" of chemical metabolism were present as far back as the last universal common ancestor four billion years ago. Every seven or so years, our cells undergo a set change, fully replaced by our desire to take in otherness and build our bodies from other bodies. *Metabole*, the root of metabolism, derives from the Greek word for "change." Our bodies stay alive by changing. Our bodies are metamorphizing monuments, changed and reconstituted by our yearnings for certain sugars, flickering spices, tart nectarines.

"Take. Eat. This is my body," Jesus instructs in the Gospel of John, offering the disciples bread. There is a deep biological mysticism in that offering. What we hunger for, we become. By eating bread, we transform ourselves not into sons and daughters of God, but into looped, interpenetrative companions of barley and yeast and salt and sunshine.

True, food had made me increasingly ill. But it also kept me alive. What was I denying myself as I created more and more ascetical rules to keep my body running just long enough to win another essay contest, or take another class on medieval manuscripts? What intimacies was I unconsciously saying no to again and again?

I was deeply embedded in the philosophy and literature departments of my college. All the religious and philosophical texts I studied stressed abstraction and self-control. Within the hypercompetitive academic world with which I was falling in love, female thinness was conflated with psychological mastery and a rigid suppression of appetite through intellectual vigor. The thinner you were, the smarter you probably were. The less you ate, the more you read and wrote.

By year three, it was clear that I was, in fact, sicker. After another round of specialists and doctors failed to give me any clues or cures; after a nutritionist instructed me to live on eggs and rice; after a hematologist convinced me to let him give me a breast exam; after a serious allergic reaction to anesthesia from a routine colonoscopy gave me months of cardiac symptoms, recurrent anaphylaxis, and debilitating asthma; after all of this, I decided to take things into my own hands.

I wouldn't just eat cleanly and carefully. I'd stop eating entirely.

I'm not sure if it was a conscious decision. All I knew was that I desperately loved college and my friends and my studies. I knew that there was no cure for my failing body. I knew that while I didn't have a cure, I did have certain ways of escaping discomfort and pushing past pain that helped me steal another day of lucidity and energy, another month of attending college. I'd just push my body a little more.

The first two or so months were a complete high. I ate handfuls of prunes and lettuce when I felt like I might pass out. I chain-smoked. I ran miles and miles every day.

I now know that anorexia is particularly dangerous because it is addictive, quickly changing your brain chemistry so that starvation becomes a dopamine rush that is hard to quit. I dropped ten pounds. Then fifteen. I was getting compliments all the time.

The less I ate, the more manic I became. The more manic I grew with hunger, the less I was able to sleep. Of course, this meant I had more hours to produce spare experimental poetry and essays on medieval martyrs. I wrote forty-page papers on Heidegger's *Being and Time*. I read the entire canon of mid-century Japanese literature. And I started to lose my hair. And my eyelashes. I lost my period. Just as I was receiving academic accolades, just as I was accepted into a Latin program in the city to further my interest in medieval romances, I realized I was about to die, not from the disease that was supposed to kill me, but from the illness I was being rewarded for academically and culturally. The disease I had unwittingly adopted to survive.

"A culture fixated on female thinness is not an obsession about female beauty, but an obsession about female obedience. Dieting is the most potent political sedative in women's history; a quietly mad population is a tractable one," Naomi Wolf famously wrote in her book *The Beauty Myth*. Unsatisfied hunger prevents us from accessing our full embodied power. It deranges us. It removes the hormones from our bodies that chemically and poetically catalyze a yearning to ripen, to procreate, to love bodily and fully, to let ourselves be transformed by what we taste. To stop eating is to stop participating in the world. To demonize appetite is to demonize the metabolic alchemy of our very cells. If we are rivers of carbon and matter, breathing in microbiome, drinking in pollen and sugar, releasing heat and carbon dioxide, and created by movement, then the suppression of appetite is like a dam. It says, *I would like to be still and stagnant. I would like to stop becoming.*

Legend has it that the Buddha almost died after six years of spiritually unsatisfying asceticism. After finally reaching Enlightenment, sitting under the bodhi tree, he was nursed back to health by Sujata the milkmaid. She was so worried about his emaciation that she brought him a bowl of rice pudding. The Buddha's teachings about nonattachment are, paradoxically, only possible because he finally let himself become intimately attached again: to Sujata, to appetite, to sweet nourishment. I always think of my English grandmother when I hear this story. We would share rice pudding and tea every afternoon, during the brief period before her death when she lived with my family. She was a glorious, imperious woman who loved beautiful clothing and good food.

Perhaps it was lucky that I was studying the history of martyrdom that spring. I read at length about saints who had starved themselves to death for a God that refused to intervene when they were raped and tortured. Women who went seeking their own annihilation. The parallels to my own life were hard to avoid.

I was going to die of a starvation-induced heart attack. I was so thin that I had callouses on my tailbone from sitting on hard classroom chairs. I'd perch in the wide expanse of farm field behind the old house I was renting with friends, jealously watching the moon rise: replete with light, with fecundity, with enoughness. It was a gleaming pupil in the inky blackness of the night's eye.

"I want to live," I would murmur like a spell to the velveteen wings of bats, swinging softly through the pollen-laden air. When had I given up on healing and begun this downward spiral? Why was I punishing my body when it was already doing a good enough job of that on its own?

I thought of the softness of my grandmother. Her lap had been a place wide and loving enough to hold me, to let me fully relax. I was not a safe place to land. Not for me. Not for anyone. I was unintentionally martyring myself.

Sitting at the river after my morning run, I examined the past months of starvation for what they truly were: a slow-motion suicidal impulse. And then I wondered how it was that most beings follow their hunger like a compass. Like a map. I thought of the bumblebee purring with desire, pursuing a hunger for nectar into the flower and incidentally pollinating plants along the way. I remembered splitting open a rotting reishi mushroom and gasping to see beetles living inside, eating the mushroom while also calling it home. The beetles knew that appetite was a home. They knew that to yearn for the mushroom, to seek it out, was to yearn for a community, the place where they would be able to rest and mate and feast.

It was in this meditation that I spotted the phosphine streak of the hummingbird.

"Teach me how to say *yes* again," I asked the hummingbird. Yes to life, to food, to real healing, to joy, to love, to pleasure.

She dipped her beak into a bloodred trumpet honeysuckle blossom. I followed.

While a hummingbird's copulation lasts only four seconds, the hummingbird will spend her life guided by another, interspecies penetration—a stronger, weirder intimacy. Beak into blossom. Her relationship to flowers is an ancient orchestration of appetite, vision, metabolism, and form.

It is generally agreed that hummingbirds coevolved—mutualistically embedded themselves—with ornithophilous flowers. Hummingbirds, noseblind, navigate by color and are sensitized to reds and oranges and bright pinks. The flowers that rely almost solely on a specific species of hummingbird tend to blossom inside the color spectrum of that hummingbird's desire. In fact, it has been noticed that flowers pollinated by hummingbirds display a narrow color spectrum, rendering them invisible to other pollinating insects and birds. But just as a hummingbird can fly forward and backward, mutualisms flow both ways. The morphological characteristics of hummingbirds are specifically tailored to the flowers they penetrate for nectar. The shape, curvature, and length of their bills are keratinized odes to particular blossoms.

But hummingbirds are not only miraculous for their dazzling plumage and saccharine passions. As I watched her slide up and down the hillside leading to the river, zooming backward, forward, hovering, looping through ivy, I realized that they wonderfully problematize my ideas of frugality and time and pleasure. Hummingbirds are the only birds that can fly backward and hover, correcting and maintaining homeostasis, even inside experiments with wind tunnels. They need to eat constantly. And, though costumed in feathers, they are as light as one, hardly topping 0.16 ounces. Surprisingly, these warm handfuls of appetite migrate unimaginable distances, following the summer south, inspired to impossible feats by sweetness and cross-species desire. Hummingbirds can travel more than twenty-three miles in a day. They fly solo, without stopping, sometimes traveling all the way from Canada to Mexico in a matter of days. Once their energy is spent, they fall out of time into a state called "torpor," in which their body repairs itself enough to begin the journey back into frenetic dance, heat dissipation, and nectar-seeking.

The hummingbird shows me that matter tends to flow rather than stay still in a single person, in a body of water, or even in a cell. How well-tricked we have been into ideas of solidity by the skin silhouettes that we call a human self. But what powers our bodies, our speech, our very brains, is the metabolic process of energy conversion. Food is converted to energy and waste is excreted, only to become something else's food. When we remove ourselves from the metabolic exchanges that weave the world together, we are trying to protect ourselves from changing. But within the deep time of evolution, refusing to adapt is a surefire way to go extinct.

Metabolism is a dance reminiscent of the hummingbird's unusual figure-eight wing pattern, which churns the air rather than pushing it downward. It depends on a delicate interplay of release and consumption. In catabolic actions, compounds are broken down into usable forms. For example, in cellular respiration, glucose is transformed into pyruvate. And then anabolic reactions create new compounds, like proteins and carbohydrates, that nourish our biological needs, rebuild cells and bodies, and make sure we are rivers of carbon and matter. Every day our cells are replaced, nourished, and reconstituted by our hunger.

Hummingbirds almost seem to squander embodiment. They flap their wings more than fifty times a second, requiring an enormous amount of food to continue their movement. And yet the movement itself is choreographed toward and for the food. Metabolism loops. It stitches us into intimacies. The hummingbird draws this into exquisite, vibratory focus. No sooner is a desire met than it explodes into dissipated heat. The wings churn the air, the beak seeks a flower, and the hummingbird is almost a porthole into how quickly matter moves through us, alchemically transformed into the glitter of feathers, the purr and hum of wings, the match-strike of flight upward and beyond, southward, always drawn by every yearning, metabolic cell toward summer.

Life does not have a savings account. It has an appetite. An appetite for dancing and for sweetness and for interpenetration. Life does not stay still. Every cell is a constant influx and outflow of matter.

You saved yourself by saying no, I realized. *But to keep living you must learn how to say yes again.*

I quit smoking that day. And I vowed to follow my appetite back into life. Even if it was painful. Maybe there were medicines that could still help me. Sweet medicines. Flower medicines. Movement medicines.

"To enter life, be food," writes poet Linda Hogan. But I also believe, "To enter life, want food, seek food, become food." One day we, too, will be eaten. But until then, let us pollinate flowers, spread spores, open up fields, graze grass, and create meadows with our seeking tongues, our heat-generating desires, our wild, life-giving appetites.

CHAPTER 4

The Animate Everything

IN THE YEARS FOLLOWING THE ONSET OF MY ILLNESS, I EXPERIENCED many medical emergencies. In particular, the severity and speed with which an allergic reaction could stop my breathing and drop my blood pressure delivered me into claustrophobic confrontations with mortality. Would the medics get there in time? Would the epinephrine work? If my consciousness fully narrowed, would I wake up on the other side? Every wheezing breath was tighter than the last, acting like a bottleneck on all those superficial worries I'd been entertaining only moments before.

I found myself praying in these moments. But not with words and not to any gods or goddesses. No. When my life was on the line, I called on the beings with whom I had actual intimacy.

The doves. The foxes. The mugwort. The raccoons. The mountains. The velvet-headed mushrooms.

I was raised by writer parents whose primary areas of research were ecology and the history of religion. We adopted any stray cat that appeared at our door. Or goose. Or chipmunk. Our house was an unofficial animal rescue operation. The dining room was filled with squawking, meowing animals, and seated at the actual dinner table were often monks, environmentalists, rabbis, and anthropologists. The human and the "more-than-human" were always intermingled in our home, with cats hopping onto laptops and adding their gnostic typos to my parents' manuscripts. That, along with a steady diet of

Zen folktales, Miyazaki films, Beatrix Potter, and Tolkien, provided a strong foundation for a relational worldview that is now popularly characterized as "animism"—a belief system that views all beings, be they rock or water or animal or plant, as animate and alive. Inspired by his years as head monk at a Zen Buddhist monastery, my father had my younger brother and me leave a portion of our food for the ancestors and hungry ghosts each night. We'd place these morsels on the back porch and, sure enough, raccoons and possums would soon arrive to gobble up leftovers.

"Those are the ancestors. Those are your family." My mother made sure we didn't think of this as a mistake. The animals and plants that lived outside our home were an extension of our family. They were our ancestors.

My father, a haiku poet, took me on long walks through the mountains, teaching me to count the traditional five-seven-five syllables on my fingers. He taught me that poetry was tactile, written with handfuls of birdsong and moss. Poetry was not a solitary and still activity. It was kinetic and relational: a direct dialogue, written while moving, with your hands reaching out to stroke bark and lichen, rain-licked stone, and the hard syllables of fallen acorns. You found poetry in the speaking world and then let your hands feel into the rhythm. It was not your possession. It was a territory you explored with your animal body.

Perhaps because I spent so much time outside, strangely wary of what could happen indoors under adult supervision, I frequently had intense encounters with the wild ones—snakes, bears, owls, insects. I would burst into my parents' writing study (the dining room table), chattering about how a snapping turtle had laid her eggs in front of me. They would bring out our book of animal lore, flipping to the "turtle" entry, before explaining that this turtle might have a message for me encoded deep in its folkloric history. We read Lenape stories about turtles, scientific studies about turtles, poems about turtles.

Growing up, my world scintillated with aliveness. It spoke with every scent, star, and swarm of starlings dancing like a storm cloud over the field. This feeling never went away. And I continued to take the coordinates of my life from big animal encounters, choosing to interpret these moments of contact as holy "redirections" at critical junctures. I hesitate to characterize this view as one of enchantment, as it was deeply tied to knowledge that violence existed in the world past comprehension, past our simplistic human ideas of fairness and justice. It was more a matter of *volume*. The world was always speaking—with every plant, every shifting molecule, every curling tendril of moisture. When I was younger, I had the volume turned all the way up, my ears open to the polyphonic ecstasy of every landscape. But as I grew older and tried to fit into the dominant culture, I unconsciously turned this music down, voice by voice, until the grass no longer whispered and the stars were mute and mouthless.

Instead of praying to turtles and mountains, I spent hours reading philosophy and postmodern literature. The only words worth reading, the only voices worth registering, belonged to human beings—and not even human beings generally, but the elite class who had mastered theory and grace, rhetorical craft and composure.

Is it little surprise that these new role models were usually scholarly white men?

My freshman year of college, the world was full of human voices—rational and male. It was sterile and controlled.

And then, just when things in my life felt tightly managed, exquisitely intellectualized, I got pregnant. Despite using birth control and being told that my history of ovarian cysts and endometriosis might render me infertile.

Even though I'd turned down the volume on my animistic sensibilities, I knew immediately. As I wandered through the forest paths of Bard College, my hand trailing along the thick waists of sycamores and honey locusts, I startled at a flash of blue light ahead of me. It was the shape and height of a small child.

I've had visual migraines my whole life. They manifest as mirrored puddles obscuring the center of my vision, or bright flashes of luminescence that is sometimes silver, or often a deep, unearthly indigo. Modern science tells us that these flashes, zigzags, and visual disturbances are just that—disturbances. Neurological glitches. But as a child, tormented by terrible nightmares, I had initially thought these lights had come to protect and soothe me. I thought these flashes were "fairies." They would dance across the dark ceiling like neon sprites. It wasn't until much later, as I explained these fairies to a kindergarten teacher, that they were pathologized as migraines. Yes, they did obviously accompany pain, pressure, and vertigo. Sometimes they blocked out my vision for an entire day. But couldn't they also, simultaneously, be some magical messenger, hijacking my own mind to give me a neon-bright kiss of magic?

Our symptoms can be plainly symptoms, downriver manifestations of bodily malfunction. And they can also exist within an animistic cosmology—a world where everything speaks. Our symptoms can be entities of their own with messages that can't be sent on human lips in the form of human words.

I saw the blue light, and I knew a week before the line even became visible on the test. And as if the bodily experience of becoming plural was mirrored sympathetically in the world, I once again noticed that everything was pregnant with meaning. Every *thing* was really every *being*. And every being was speaking.

Still, the news devastated me. I felt guilty and ashamed. How had this happened? I'd taken all the right precautions. I had to finish college. I had to figure out why I was so sick. I knew I wanted an abortion.

"I had one too. In college," my mother explained gently, on the phone, when I called her with the news. "We'll figure it out together." At that point it was still highly taboo for girls to share their experience with abortion. I hid it from all but my closest friends.

By whatever unfortunate cosmic timing, the abortion landed the day before my December birthday. I bled so heavily afterward that I had to immediately go to the hospital.

A few days after the procedure, shell-shocked and confused by a grief I had not been expecting, I let my friends know that I needed help.

"Let's go to the bar," suggested my friends Hannah and Nora. We knew upperclassmen boys would be there. I let my friends apply makeup to my face like medicine, pressing love as blue eyeshadow around my tear-raw eyes. We called a cab to take us to the local bar that notoriously served underage girls.

"Black swan," it was called at the time, named for a theory developed by Nassim Nicholas Taleb in 2001 to describe the outsized role of "high profile, hard-to-predict, and rare events that are beyond the realm of normal expectations in history, science, finance, and technology." A black swan event interrupts our expected reality and reorganizes everything that comes before and follows after. And, most importantly, black swan events cannot be accurately predicted using the standard scientific method.

It was a fitting name for the location of my own such event.

That night, the Black Swan Bar was packed so tightly with college students that I couldn't inhale without feeling my rib cage pinched by someone's elbows. My nervous system was lit up like a Christmas tree, sparkling with every accidental touch of another body. I felt raw, exposed, and alien. I wasn't sure which hurt more: my womb or my heart. But I knew that a drink might help numb it.

"Are you okay?" Ilana, my beautiful sprite of a friend, spotted me through the sea of people. "Weren't you just in the hospital? Let's go back to the dorm."

I hugged her and laughed with as much raucous nonchalance as I could muster. "No, no. I'm fine. I promise."

I swam through the crowd, cradling my vodka seltzer, making brief, shouted contact with friends over the techno music. My friend Hannah worriedly kept her eye on me. She'd been there with jokes, hugs, and bad TV the day before the abortion, when my boyfriend had broken up with me.

"Are you in my Hinduism course?" A short, ginger-haired man shouted in my ear.

"No!" I lied, ducking under someone's arm. Sufficiently woozy and sad, I leaned against a free space of wall when the clock struck midnight, that instant enshrined in fairy-tale temporality.

It was like a scene out of a movie. All at once, five undercover cops pulled out their badges and began a huge sting operation on the bar.

It was mayhem. College students were running for the door, shoving each other over the bar countertop. The smell of beer carbonated the sweat-thick air as people dropped their drinks at their feet.

Hannah was suddenly by my side, tugging at my hand as we tried to escape the insanity.

"Line up so we can Breathalyze you!" shouted a cop, blocking the exit. I swore under my breath. I would *definitely* fail the Breathalyzer. My parents would hear. Somehow, I was convinced that the incident would find its way to my academic record, a record I envisioned as a stone tablet, engraved with only my best cerebral self.

I was running through these panicked thoughts when someone interrupted me. A small, unremarkable-looking man with a slightly receding hairline had his hand at my elbow.

"You've had a hard time. I thought you might need this," he whispered and slipped something heavy into my hand. Then he disappeared into the crowd.

I looked down, befuddled, to see that I was holding a golden rose, with details so fine that it must have been fashioned with a microscope in hand. '

Something about the weight of the rose in my hand dropped me back into sober clarity. In that moment, I knew what I had to do. Pulling Hannah and my friend Nora into the bar's kitchen, I hastily unlatched a window above the sink. We shimmied through, racing down the sidewalk until we could hide behind a tree and call a cab.

"How did you know to do that?" Hannah asked, breathlessly, as the cab carried us through the country roads that led back to our campus.

"I don't know. I just did. Like magic," I answered.

Not *like* magic. It was magic. A black swan event of my own.

Later, I examined the golden rose. It must be covered in gilt paint, I figured. Cheap. I asked everyone I knew about the man. I tried to describe him and struggled with words that felt flat and unspecific. "Short. Short hair. A . . . normal face?"

No one had seen him but Hannah. She had witnessed the interaction but found that she couldn't remember what he looked like.

I put the rose next to my bed. Later that summer, I had it looked at by some jeweler and sculptor friends.

"I have no idea how this was made. This is real gold, and I think it's been directly poured over a rose to produce details that fine," my jeweler friend offered, her eyes wide in confusion.

"Yes. Definitely gold. A lot of gold," another craft-savvy friend confirmed.

In the years since, I've had the rose examined by many people and, still, no one can understand how it was made.

Who was the man? How had he sensed my need for a miracle? Why had he given me the rose?

"It is at any rate essential to a genuine fairy-story, as distinct from the employment of this form for lesser or debased purposes, that it should be presented as 'true,'" wrote J. R. R. Tolkien in my favorite of his essays, "On Fairy Stories." It didn't matter how that rose was made. It mattered that it felt like the truest, brightest thing that had ever happened to me. It was my own black swan event, reminding me that on the flip side of every anguished moment is an animate world of magic that is imbued with a sense of humor. The fairy wasn't tall and handsome. He was small and average. He fit into the logic of my reality—its texture—while also offering a flower from the other side.

Magic, for Tolkien, was the opposite of the "supernatural." He argued that human beings, in our false sense of superiority, are the real supernatural element in every story, always believing we can explain and control the elements. He offers, instead, that fairies are "far more natural than he." They are the natural miracle of swarming locusts, starling murmurations, rainbows, mushroom "fairy" rings. Yes, if we work hard enough to explain them, like the rose, maybe we can create a hypothesis for how they arrive, fully formed and already dancing. But the truth is, we cannot recreate the recipe. We cannot manufacture or plan for magic. The black swan event laughs at our standardized scientific predictions.

Magic, for me, is closest to Tolkien's idea of eucatastrophe: the happy disaster that arrives inconceivably in the nick of time. The eagles save the hobbits from Mount Doom. Aslan arrives in Narnia, and a world of winter relaxes into springtime. The golden rose inspires me to climb out through the kitchen window.

Magic is often a story that, when you share it with other people, threatens to make you look insane. But then, like me, you hold out the gold rose and say, "Feel this. Look at this. Tell me how it's made?"

We can't predict these magical interruptions. But when we relax our expectations about what is alive and what is truly "real," magic starts happening all the time. It is "a sudden and miraculous grace." It is the open window in the kitchen. The escape from this world and into this world. Magic doesn't take us out of our ecosystems; it roots us more deeply into them. It gifts you a gold rose and says, "Silly girl. This wasn't made. It was grown."

In the months following my abortion, I found myself taking many long walks, trying to move through emotions so dense and wide it was easier to imagine them as a landscape external to my body rather than as some sort of emotional weather that lived inside me. I was deeply relieved I'd had an abortion. But I also didn't feel like it had been *nothing*. The experience registered as a loss. But I had no rituals or guidance on how to honor that feeling.

What is it actually like to have an abortion? There is no one right answer. There is a biodiversity of answers. A teeming forest of songs. When you choose to have an abortion, I like to think you are choosing to open up space in the world where a child would have stood. That empty space is a generosity. It is a space where birds and frogs and trees and flowers can find haven. An abortion leaves behind fertile soil where your life can grow into new shapes. And it leaves open soil where other species can thrive.

I felt like a tidal being, made up of liquid mixed with profound relief and grief. And calling back on my early animist beliefs, I felt personally that I had indeed gestated a brief life, a small seed. This was a deeply personal sense: a bodily feeling, not a statement of fact. Everyone experiences birth and abortion and miscarriage differently. A weather system had passed through my body. I was changed, and I was desperate to honor that change in a way that wasn't articulated in the highly polemical world of politics.

It was on those long walks through the country roads that myceliate out from the nucleus of Bard's campus that I arrived at a practice of my own making, scraped together from the Tibetan Buddhism that had permeated an early childhood spent with a Tibetan babysitter. Within certain strands of Tibetan Buddhism, there is a belief that, between lives, a soul passes through liminal realms or "bardos." It is customary for those still living to pray for the departed for forty-nine days, ensuring safe passage into the next life.

Little seed, I thought, placing my hand on the generosity of my empty womb, the soil of space, *I have decided not to plant you in my body, but I will plant you in the world.*

I resolved to "plant" my released child for forty-nine days: in forty-nine poems and in forty-nine other beings. I wanted to see my abortion not as a meaningless blip or a death, but as a gift of life. That seed didn't become a human. Because I had an abortion, that seed became the gift of vitality for other beings.

I planted my abortion in the nuthatches picking berries outside my dorm room. I planted my abortion in the lilac bushes, grown scrubby midwinter. I planted my abortion in the fungal networks dancing under each of my footsteps. "Live a life as a bluebird, a virus, a raccoon. Be safe inside fur, inside snakeskin. Inside this wide, welcoming world," I whispered, pressing my hands and my prayers into the soil, the trunks of trees, the gentle curlicues of winds coming in through my window.

The ritual made me realize that the sexism of our political atmosphere conflates fertility with pregnancy and birth.

Contrary to popular conceptions about abortion, my abortion was a womb that gave birth to *me*.

It also planted me back into the singing, speaking world. On day forty-nine of my self-made ritual, I felt solid again. My internal shorelines had thickened. I hiked down to my favorite rock that looked out over the Hudson River, and a red fox darted in front of my path. "It's you!" I thought.

And then I saw a vulture. "It's you!" I thought again. I breathed in and felt the chill blue of winter air swimming in my blood. I put my hand to my belly. I didn't need to give birth to that child to be that child's mother. I could mother it every day by honoring and greeting the world around me.

It was this simple practice of greeting the world that I called on when I quit smoking and the rituals of anorexia. I poured all my resurfaced anxiety and depression that smoking had kept at bay into miles of walking. Waking at dawn, I'd head down past the train tracks, greeting the river and the mountains across the water, the shore fringed with daylilies. Then I would wind my way up through a patchwork of farm fields. Ten or twelve miles a day. While my peers were still drinking and smoking, snorting lines of Adderall between library sessions, I was walking, trying to put physical distance between myself and the survival mechanisms I knew were obsolete.

Soon I knew where the heron flew at first light. Where mist curled up like a house cat in a gully. Where the red-tailed hawks pierced the sky with the needle of their morning cries. I knew the willows and the knotweed and the tides of phlox in spring. I knew the stray cats. I knew the baker who woke with the dawn, like me, to get his pastries into the oven, often offering me a piping hot cup of coffee on my way through town. Within a ten-mile radius, I walked thousands of miles. I didn't travel far. But I traveled deep. I thought bittersweetly, "Well, I've poured myself into that field. I've been more intimate with that land than with any lover. That field is walked, grooved, deeply rooted in my heart."

A year after quitting smoking, I sat on a hill overlooking that small college town, the river, and the mountains beyond.

A crow beat its wings with such rapidity it rippled into liquid. Sunlight streaked across the dawn sky, warping through the wind's weft, weaving a tapestry of breath, pollen, smoke from forest fires a whole country away, carbon excreted as saccharine heat from a hummingbird, dull threads of exhaust braided into a heron's exhalations. Smoke had turned the sun flat and red as one drawn by a child with a crayon. The sky was the blue of accumulation, built of layer after layer of pollution, smog, pollen, refracted light, and reproductive matter: spores, pheromones, funk. The train screamed as it cut through the greenery, dragging its mournful cry and black exhalations across the springtime. I was reminded of the words of Chilean poet Raúl Zurita as he wrote after his torture at the hands of Pinochet's military dictatorship: "Life is very beautiful, even now."

Life is soup. Life is compost. Life is contaminated. And life is very alive.

I glanced from the sky down to my toes, tucked into the fine, ashy dirt, and spotted a spider, a tumbleweed of silver wire, glittering against my foot. And below that, mycorrhizal threads wove together the locust trees, the Russula mushrooms, the ghost pipe, and the grass with the trees, enfleshing the soil itself so it could hold steady when the rains slid out of the smog-swollen sky. Deeper still was an underworld biosphere of carbon held together by archaea and bacteria and fungi. I knew that pulsing through the soil was the spilled blood of the Munsee Lenape, their stories all but erased, who lived continuously next to the river for thousands of years before the genocidal Dutch and French arrived. I reached down and pinched the dirt, inhaling its waxy, mildewed perfume.

No. Divine feminine or divine masculine wouldn't carry me through pain and addiction. God wasn't wide enough for this unruly dawn. There were yellowjackets already looping through the clover, gorgeous from a distance and deadly to my immune system if they happened to puncture my skin. Even the bacteria carefully cushioned in my gut were precarious. One internal shift and they could poison my blood.

Everything is connected to something. But not everything is connected to everything. The differences are vital. The smoke that coated my tongue that morning did not belong to me. It was wind-buffeted, from a fire burning across the country.

The miracle isn't that everything is the same—infused with a pearly, universal "source"—but that everything is being. Being differently. Being chaotically. Panpsychism is the Eurocentric academic framework for what Indigenous cultures have long believed: consciousness is inherent in all matter. Of course, there is debate over the definition of consciousness. Is thinking different from simply experiencing something? Does proto-consciousness exist in elementary particles, slowly accumulating into emergent minds like human brains?

A squirrel dropped a hickory nut on my head. Somewhere, a dog barked. An ambulance drew its long, nervous song through the empty morning roads. Someone was dying. Someone was melting out of being a someone, transforming into a patchy, heterogenous everything.

Is that death? Is that inanimate? It seemed to me that when someone died, their body became even more alive, an aliveness that was plural, polyphonous—suddenly an ecosystem of bacteria and fungi and beetles and beings all feasting, decaying, making love, making soil, making connections.

I sighed. I didn't need to write another academic essay proving that world was alive. It didn't matter if I could prove an electron was having an experience.

What mattered was that the world was speaking again. Songs and psalms and riddles that didn't depend on language. Stories that didn't issue from single mouths, but that happened interstitially, linking beings in the fertile, friction-prickled boundaries between differences.

It was the differences that seemed crucial to me. Without difference, there was no room for conversation. There was no need for the tender questions that catalyzed storytelling and generated the gradient of landscapes. I knew from my childhood of hiking that it was the gradient of the mountain that allowed the snowmelt and rain to braid into a stream that carved and curved down through stone into the valley. The difference between the summit and the valley created this nourishing thread of water that irrigated the fields, filled the rock pools, and woke up leathery lichen on the side of a stone that had been thrown awkwardly into a field, millions of years before, by a glacier.

Audre Lorde writes in her essay "The Master's Tools Will Never Dismantle the Master's House": "Within the interdependence of mutual (nondominant) differences lies that security which enables us to descend into the chaos of knowledge and return with true visions of our future, along with the concomitant power to effect those changes which can bring that future into being. Difference is that raw and powerful connection from which our personal power is forged."

When I was a child, I didn't have a word for my multispecies view of the sacred. But as I returned to it, years later, I came up again with the term animism.

The animism that saved me again and again was not one of enchantment and preciousness. It was an animism of chaotic difference. Of woven contamination. It was an understanding that just because I was alive, that did not mean I should assume that the aliveness of the hill or the river or the wild roses was the same flavor as my own. Knowing that a stone was alive kept me alive. But most importantly, knowing that a stone was alive *differently* than me kept me asking questions—humble and curious and available to surprise.

I opened my arms up on the hill to the Animate Everything. The illness. The pain. The heartbreak. The joy. The birds and microplastics and trains and mushrooms and confusion. The black swans and the migraine fairies. The differences that stung and pricked and decayed and fermented and sometimes wove together to create a dense, polluted, gorgeous periwinkle sky.

CHAPTER 5

Tying Our Roots Together

MY BODY SPARKLED WITH PAIN. I TRIED NOT TO MOVE, NOT TO BREATHE, instead focusing on the places where my back connected with the large, sun-baked rock beneath me. The flat slab of bluestone lay in the middle of my favorite stream, embraced on either side by water still chilled by its descent from the Catskill peaks. I tried to feel the stone's steadiness soothe the unsteadiness in my *own* body: the places in my spine that, like the stream water, overflowed the line and meandered out of linearity. *Make my herniated discs a silted streambank*, I prayed. *Make them a question mark of water curving into the forest.*

I inhaled carefully, imagining the stream as a splint against my spine, correcting me not into straightness, but into its own cursive intelligence. What if my spine was *not* incorrect, but rather liquid, making love with the landscape? The summer sky pressed its blue flesh against my face, sunlight pooling at the bottom of my irises, creating a tidal pool of my eyes: a place for crustaceans and lichen to congregate. Despite my deliberate stillness, my left hip rolled, making a noise like a door unlocking. I rested my hands over these bone parentheses that could not keep me contained.

I was falling apart. Overflowing my shorelines.

Without the distractions of anorexia and smoking, I was forced to confront the fact that I was too sick to delay treatment any longer. My allergies were worsening, each anaphylactic event taking me closer to the cliff's edge of my own mortality. Migraines came on like monsoons and then overstayed their welcome, distorting my vision and squeezing my brain. One lasted thirty days. By the end of this ordeal, I felt I'd been on a very long, nonconsensual psychedelic trip. Yes, my ego had been erased, but not in the way that left me feeling renewed and rewired. Every day my hips and shoulders slid in and out of their sockets. Without the crutch of starvation-aided dissociation, I could no longer ignore the chorus of pain drifting through my body. Something was wrong with my spine, my vascular system, my bladder, my liver. My heartbeat raced and my blood pressure dipped when I changed positions. I went through periods of time when, inexplicably, I could not swallow, choking even on water.

The summer after I quit smoking, I spent hours horizontal, on river stones or the ground, trying to listen to the place in me that shared a root system with the slower, larger body of my ecosystem. The Hudson Valley was skilled at holding stormy weather. It had survived the weight of ancient glaciers, the pummel of hurricanes, and the clear-cutting of ancient forests by colonizing Dutch farmers. Maybe it could teach me how to hold my own internal tempests, my own changing climate.

I was removing my armor, piece by piece, coping mechanism by coping mechanism. I chose to attend my parents' pagan prayer fellowship instead of going out to party with friends and celebrate our senior year of college. I wrote my final college essays in the early morning, preferring to avoid the late-night, Adderall-fueled library hours when students competed over who was more exhausted and manic. I stayed slow and sober and low to the ground. Off came the shield of anorexia and the metal breastplate of neurotic self-denial. But absent that hard exoskeleton, it turned out I was melting into something formless.

My popping joints and degrading spine made me feel like a Frankenstein assemblage of nuts and bolts and random bones, none of which fit together correctly.

It was time to stop saying no to medicine and doctors. If I was saying *yes* to life again, I needed to also open myself up to the possibility that there was a diagnosis and a cure for my mysterious ailments.

Initially, I went back to the Lyme doctors, but I was no longer a compliant teenager, impatient for any cure. I knew that a quick fix often caused more problems than it solved. I asked these doctors to rerun their tests and was confused when none came back positive for tickborne illness. I was even more suspicious when, despite these negative tests, the doctors once again suggested putting me on four different antibiotics simultaneously. When I balked at this, I was labeled "noncompliant."

Instead of continuing to believe in a diagnosis that neither fit my bloodwork nor my symptoms, I decided to follow the clue of my life-threatening allergies. A kind gastroenterologist who'd given me a colonoscopy a year before had noted that the severe inflammation in my gut paired with these allergic reactions could indicate something called mast cell disease. "It's very rare, but you never know. I'd check it out." He recommended a specific immunologist near New York City. I'd pocketed the name, too overwhelmed at the time to add another doctor to my already bloated retinue of healers, specialists, and nutritionists. Almost none of these people were covered by insurance, and money was tight. My parents were living with financial uncertainty between freelance projects, and I was juggling several jobs on top of college and poor health: bartending, babysitting, setting up sound equipment for lectures, editing other people's work. My stomach dropped when I saw the immunologist's out-of-network fee, but I was desperate enough to call and get on her six-month waiting list. I was curious and frantic for help, but cynical about the likelihood that she might have anything new to offer me.

Thankfully, my studies were a lifeline. I'd finally found my footing again—literally—as I walked hundreds of miles and translated those walks into pages of eco-poetry. My professor Robert Weston, seeing my love of philosophy and ecology, supplied me with the writing of Deleuze and Guattari, Donna Haraway, Lynn Margulis, and a slew of other science writers. My poetry mentor Ann Lauterbach, who shared my love of cats, fierce feminism, and wildflowers, was generous enough to let my work stray from academic sterility into more feral realms. I wrote poems constelled with the beings I encountered on my walks: salamanders and chestnut trees, wild primroses and waxcaps. I'd always loved science, and now I found that it offered a deeper, magical layer to my explorations into the tangled world of ecosystems. This magic wasn't supernatural. It was *completely* natural. I discovered that there were beings composed of multiple species, cohabiting bodies. Our own bodies owed their origins to ancient bacteria. The Earth itself was like a giant body—each ecosystem operating like an organ does in a human body, regulating the larger biosphere. I'd always felt deeply allied to mushrooms—to the way in which they refused easy classification, twinkling between angel and demon, medicine and poison. As a child I'd spent hours lying on the ground, following snakes of white rot through tree trunks, delighting in dew-polished mower's mushrooms that popped up like punctuation marks overnight across the backyard. *Puhpowee*—I learned the Potawatomi word used to describe the force that drove these mushrooms up with miraculous speed. The word felt like a spell. *Help me, mushroom up from the underworld. Help me emerge.*

I dove back into fungal science, trying to train myself in terminology that was at once foreign and mesmerizing: rhizome, hyphae, septa, lamellae, anastomose.

One night, in the middle of my final year of college and amid my renewed quest for healing, I had a powerful dream.

In it, I was walking down the country road that cuts like a knave through the cast shadow of Overlook Mountain. The time of day was indistinct: the mauve sky was stippled with stars, and the moon hung sated and swollen just above the mountain's summit. My body felt almost unsteady as I moved forward. It took me a moment of walking to realize that the physical sensation of shakiness was not so much unsteadiness as it was *ease*. My body had released its tense posture, so long torqued by injury and pain. My body felt *healthy*.

It was this sudden realization that made me pause, looking down. But my eyes dropped immediately below my feet. I gasped.

The ground below me was glassy, its smoky translucence revealing a great depth that stretched for miles into the Earth. Except I was not standing on emptiness. No, the depths below me scintillated with movement—a vast soil ocean of connectivity. Millions of lines spangled the ground, too thin for tree roots, each exactly one cell thick. They looked like sewing thread. Or solid starlight webbing its way between the oaks and ironwoods, the grasses and the wild rose bushes, the body of a dead raccoon softening into decay somewhere in the barberry thicket. Someone had been weaving the forest together. A giant spider? How did I not know that an entire world was teeming right below my feet?

Months later, as I spent hours researching fungi, I stumbled on something that brought the dream back with exquisite clarity. My dream vision of an underwebbing of connectivity was not fanciful. In fact, it was the biological intelligence underpinning the evolution and continued existence of 90 percent of all plants. Except that this intelligence was *not* plants. It was fungi—mycorrhizal fungi to be exact.

While you may be familiar with the moist, dome-headed mushrooms that pop up after a rainstorm, the lacquered bracket mushrooms peeking out of tree trunks, and the classic, red-freckled *Amanita muscaria*, mushrooms are not individuals. They are fungal reproductive events that "fruit" up from much larger, distributed bodies that live belowground, inside of wood, and in decaying matter. Mostly, fungal lifestyles are conducted by hyphae, the branching filamentous threads like the ones I saw in my dream, which weave together to create a dispersed mycelial body. These breath-slender tendrils don't just weave through soil. They actually "create" the soil, acting as the connective fascial tissue that keeps the earth from eroding, captures carbon, releases minerals, ferries bacteria to pockets of decay, and breaks down waste to generate more nutritious humus.

Most plants and trees depend intimately on a specific type of fungi—mycorrhizal fungi—to plug them into the underworld of water, nutrients, and interspecies communication.

As I studied these fungi, I was simultaneously deepening my study of religion and myth.

I'd been particularly drawn to myths of descent that promised an eventual ascent and return to springtime, health, and love.

"On this day I will descend to the underworld. When I have arrived in the underworld, make a lament for me on the ruin mounds. Beat the drum for me in the sanctuary. Make the rounds of the houses of the gods for me," reads the ancient Mesopotamian myth of the goddess Inanna. She removes her adornments and finally her ego itself as she is transformed into a hunk of rotting meat, hung on a hook. Her final ascent back into the world of the living is made possible only by the help of others: a fly, whom she declares sacred and gifts "the beer house and the tavern"; her underworld sister, Ereshkigal;

and finally the sacrifice of her lover, Dumuzi. The underworld is not the land of the individual. Inanna is forced to shed every piece of jewelry and clothing that identifies her as special in order to enter the depths.

It seemed to me, as I read of Innana and Persephone, that the underworld was not a land of the dead so much as it was the beginning of life: a soil womb where the world above was gestated. This was perfectly mirrored by Persephone's creation of the seasons, with her own body stitching cycles of decay and regrowth together. The harvest depended on her ability to follow the seeds deep into the ground each year.

I'd been in my own underworld for a long time, wrestling demons, trying to answer the riddle that would let me once again ascend back into the sunlight. There was a part of me that felt like the key to my own healing might be stowed in one of these archetypal journeys.

It felt fitting when I discovered my favorite underworld myth—not in the annals of human history—but pressed between the stratigraphic layers of deep time itself.

The earliest underworld myth predates human heroes. It even predates trees. Five hundred million years ago, early plants first migrated from the sea to dry land. Today, you would find these early plants unrecognizable. They were closer to chlorophyll puddles or tumbleweeds. They had no root systems. Luckily enough, fungi were already intimate with the soil and rhizomatic behavior. Over a period of tens of millions of years, fungi acted as surrogate root systems for the plants that have slowly developed into the forests and food-bearing crops with which our metabolisms are so interwoven. While plants now develop their own rhizomatic networks, they are still only able to access water and nutrients within a tight radius. Fungal mycorrhizal systems that enter into plant roots extend these networks, connecting older trees with kin and uniting diverse arrays of vegetal, fungal, and microbial communities. They seem to embody what poet David Whyte calls "the conversational nature of reality," queering our idea of where to draw the species lines, the sex line, the boundary line of an individual. When a tree constituted by mutualistic fungi that is involved with five other plant species mates with another tree constituted by a similar entanglement of dependencies, how many beings are included in the reproductive act? How many beings are having a conversation? The connection between plants and fungi is so strong that endophytic fungi are vertically transferred to the newer generation through seeds. When the fungi live in the very seed that will become a tree, their role becomes something between midwife, parent, lover, and friend, helping the tree tap into the rich nutrients of the soil and the community of other beings that constitute an ecosystem. Put more simply, fungi introduced plants to the underworld. And it was only in the underworld that plants learned how to make community. Community that bridges differences: in species, in age, in biosemiotic language. Fungi taught plants that survival isn't about individuation. It's about becoming radically involved—so involved that you let your friends into your very genetics, into your root systems.

Mycorrhizal fungi taught me that giving didn't always abide by human concepts of fair transaction. It was more concerned with the connectivity itself. Mycorrhizal fungi were living verbs, ferrying nutrients from tree to tree, decomposing dead matter, constituting the very structural integrity of the soil. These fungi acted for trees like bodily connective tissue does for people, holding our organs in place, giving us our physical elasticity and ability to move and adapt, shuttling nutrients from place to place. These fungal systems seemed to whisper that a self wasn't a single body. It was a *movement*, flowing on mycelial threads between species. Between worlds. A self could plant itself in another being's seed. A self didn't stay still. It fruited up into the world above as a mushroom, pretending individuality, only to sporulate, seed clouds, fall as rain, and sink back into the underworld of the dirt to weave the world, invisibly, quietly, back together.

I had been writing "mycorrhizal" poems for months when my appointment with the immunologist finally arrived. I was trying to construct poems that were nonlinear, with multiple doors of entry. What if you read them backward or sideways? What if you started in the middle?

My father drove me to the appointment, and we talked about other things rather than dwelling on the inevitable disappointment that these doctor's appointments usually produced. We talked about how I wanted to go to grad school for medieval studies after I graduated, focusing on the study of manuscripts. Maybe I'd take a year off and try to work for one of the environmental magazines I'd so admired. I was torn between my desire for academic success and the knowledge that I was happiest outside, barefoot, deep in the forest. Left unspoken behind all of this was my fragility, my escalating symptoms. How could I really achieve *any* of these dreams? I was on my last reserves of physical energy, trying to finish college with as much grace as I could before my body gave out.

There is a common new age maxim that says, "What's meant for you will never miss you." Maxims like this are also known as "thought-terminating clichés." They are used to shut down curiosity, end arguments, and pacify cognitive dissonance. As someone with an illness that had resisted explanation or treatment, I'd become highly cynical of phrases like this. They erased the complexity of our individual struggles.

And yet that spring, what was meant for me arrived just on time. I think of all the delicate pieces that had to fall into place to put me in the immunologist's waiting room, sitting as I usually did with my legs twisted together, my hand resting on my cheek, staring at a gruesome diagram of the sinuses on the opposite wall.

"Do you always sit like that?" the immunologist said sharply when she came out to check something with the secretary, staring at me with intense interest.

"Yeah. I do. Why?" I was confused.

"Come into my office. I want to run a test on you quickly."

The small, keen-eyed woman had me bend over, stretch out my arms, and bend back my thumbs, my elbows.

"What does this have to do with my allergies?"

Instead of answering my question, she responded with one of her own.

"Have you been flexible your whole life? Do you dislocate joints?"

"I pop out my joints all the time! I used to be known in my friend group for being able to put myself into pretzel shapes . . ." I laughed, remembering the first time my friend Ilana had happened on me sitting in the same odd position I'd adopted in the waiting room. "I love you, but that is *not* normal, Sophie."

"I thought so," the immunologist's face tightened. She sat down, looking through my charts and tests. "Slipping rib syndrome, postural orthostatic tachycardia, gastroparesis, herniated spine . . ."

"What did you think? What is it?" I felt my chest constrict with anticipation. I felt myself being categorized, captured within a diagnostic embrace. *Please tell me this has a name*, I thought. *Please explain this.*

"I just gave you something called the Beighton test. It confirmed my suspicion. I believe you have a genetic connective tissue disease: Ehlers-Danlos syndrome."

It turned out that the immunologist had been surprised to find that patients coming to her for mysterious anaphylaxis and mast cell disease were also showing signs of a rare connective tissue disease. Researchers hadn't been able to explain the correlation yet, but it was definitely connected, and the doctor had been primed to spot the telltale signs in me: velvety skin, abnormal posture, extreme flexibility.

I called in my father, and the immunologist began to lay out the symptoms. They fit me like a glove. And then she listed the specialists I needed to see and the tests I needed to have performed *immediately*. Cardiologists to check for the threat of aortic dissection. An evaluation for vascular abnormalities. A neurosurgeon to discuss intervention for Chiari malformation, a structural defect that causes the skull to sag into a degrading spine. A gastroenterologist. The list went on and on.

"Wait," I asked, dumbfounded. "So this means I have an issue with the connective tissue in my body?"

"Yes, that's correct." She nodded, then continued. "Your body doesn't produce collagen correctly, so it implicates all your bodily systems, making them too elastic. This can be extremely dangerous, especially when it comes to your vascular system."

It did not escape me that while I had been devoted to the connective tissue of ecosystems for years, my own body was suffering from an insufficiency of its own connective tissue. What a weird synchronicity. It was as if the dysfunction in my body had been a compass, guiding me out of human concerns and into the underworld of fungal systems.

I listened, as if from a great distance, while the doctor explained all the ways Ehlers-Danlos impacted my body. The hereditary condition was rare, with several different subtypes, and was estimated to affect one in five thousand births. It caused cataracts, joint dislocations, cardiac issues, aneurysms, internal bleeding, gastrointestinal dysfunction, obstructive pulmonary disease, spinal deformities . . . the list went on and on, and I felt each symptom hit me like a wave. She mentioned that for reasons that had yet to be proven, Ehlers-Danlos seemed to predispose someone to mast cell disease, endometriosis, and a host of other strange immunological diseases. It was considered one of the most painful conditions in the world, ranked next to complex regional pain syndrome and bone cancer.

"What can I do? What's the cure?" I asked desperately, trying not to dissociate.

The doctor finally stopped her frantic recitation of facts. She let her fingers steeple together, looking down her narrow nose at me with impersonal pity.

"As of today, there is no cure. Only symptom management. It is degenerative, so you must be proactive with appointments and care."

"What do you mean?" I gasped. "No cure? What's my life expectancy?"

"Well. It varies from subtype to subtype. We need to get you to a geneticist. You could live a long life. We don't know yet."

She should have known I could easily google this question for myself on the ride home.

I'd finally gotten a diagnosis that seemed to accurately explain years of disease. But what happens when the answer to your prayer feels like a curse? Because that diagnosis didn't come with a cure. With a happy ending. Instead, it seemed to come with a death sentence. A decay sentence. A punctuation mark in a story I did not want to live out.

Over the next month—as my body seemed to live out the diagnosis, the discs in my neck herniating so badly I had to wear a neck brace to all my final classes, almost unable to move at all—I poured myself into my love of fungal systems.

If I couldn't find a cure for my body and condition, maybe I could find what I was seeking in my web of connections instead. It didn't feel random that mycorrhizal fungi had asserted themselves so loudly in my field of consciousness at the very moment when I'd been gifted with this tricky diagnosis.

The ways my body rejected unity—dislocating, rupturing, decaying—seemed to affirm the generative difference that made up the forests and meadows and mountains I loved so much. My body was an ecosystem. I thought of those ancient plants, struggling on dry land, reaching out to the fungal systems belowground. If I was going to survive, I was going to need to tie my roots to other roots. While researching resilience ecology, I learned that landscapes with more biodiversity, more overall connectivity, are better able to withstand natural disasters and climatological pressures. Maybe Ehlers-Danlos was asking me to drop below human exceptionalism into the underworld of symbiotic co-creation?

I wandered deep into the pine tree–furred trails leading up Overlook and found a mossy patch of ground. I lay down and whispered secretly to the mycelial threads spooling out below me: "Come and weave through me. If there's too much open space in my body, maybe that space was left open for you." If I couldn't have properly working human connective tissue, then perhaps mycelial connective tissue could do. Perhaps there was a way that the absent connective tissue in me opened up interstices in the body where other species might slip in.

I asked the fungi to teach me like they taught plants five hundred million years ago.

Teach me how to root into a specific place. Teach me how to create connections so feral and far-reaching they make me resilient with otherness. Teach me how to flow into the whole forest.

CHAPTER 6

Becoming a Ruin

ALTHOUGH I DID NOT KNOW IT FOR MANY YEARS, LOVE STORIES SAVED my life. In early childhood, I was introduced to the 1997 *Cinderella* musical movie starring Brandy and Whoopi Goldberg as I grappled with an inchoate experience that ruptured my sense of the world's goodness.

When I felt I might disintegrate completely, I would ask someone to play my cassette tape of the songs from the movie. I would sing "Ten Minutes Ago" or "In My Own Little Corner" and rock myself back and forth, doing what I now know animals do to move through experiences of terror. They shake and rock and move. They dance their nervous systems back into balance. Love stories danced me back into a world where magic was still possible. Terrible injustices could be set right with a kiss.

I lived on fairy tales, medieval romances, bodice-rippers, popular vampire series, and smutty paperbacks I found at library book sales.

And yet, as I was inoculated with heteronormative romance, I felt certain that heteronormative romance didn't want me. All the protagonists possessed something I didn't have. Purity. Innocence. Beauty. When I found Hans Christian Andersen's didactic *The Little Mermaid*, I met something that felt better matched to the feelings of shame and secrecy that were interminably tangled with my desire for love. Here, I finally recognized myself.

"Is there anything I can do to win an immortal soul?" she asks.

> "No," said the old woman, "unless a man were to love you so
> much that you were more to him than his father or mother . . .
> He would give a soul to you and retain his own as well . . ."

In *The Little Mermaid*, a soulless girl—a girl with the incorrect body—desperately seeks the attention of a human prince as a means of achieving an immortal soul and spiritual perfection. That was closer to what I felt. So was the idea of lack. I could only be saved from the darkness I was desperately trying to keep a secret if someone else "fixed upon" me and let some of their goodness and purity—their immortal soul—flow into me. The message in the classic tale is bleak. A girl needs a man to achieve spiritual wholeness, and she is damned if she can't win his fancy. And yet the Little Mermaid's desire for ascension and her unsatisfying trials were more familiar to me than the easy romance of *Cinderella* or *Sleeping Beauty*.

The Little Mermaid sacrifices her voice, her body, her family—and, finally, even her life—and still the prince chooses another girl. And yet, she does eventually achieve spiritual purity in an act of selfless sacrifice, melting to seafoam on the dawn waves. She ascends, out of the sea, her body, and her desires, into suicidal spiritual steam.

Yup, I thought. *That feels closer.*

I was an undersea creature longing for the dry land legs that would let me walk into normalcy and love.

It was much later that I learned the background behind *The Little Mermaid* and understood that the experience of queer longing and alienation I'd resonated with in the story had not been a projection. In 1836, Hans Christian Andersen was obsessed with Edvard Collin, the son of his wealthy patron. Andersen sent the young man letters that overtly declared the homosexual passion he knew was dangerous to profess: "I long for you as though you were a beautiful Calabrian girl . . . my sentiments for you are those of a woman." In another, he waxed poetic: "Rosebud, so firm and round / Lovely as a young girl's mouth! / I kiss you as my bride!"

Collin was perplexed by his young friend's advances and mostly ignored them. Later in life, Collin would confess in his own memoir: "I found myself unable to respond to this love, and this caused the author much suffering."

After hearing that Edvard Collin was to be married to a young woman in 1837, Andersen quickly produced what would become *The Little Mermaid*, a tale of unrequited love and incorrect embodiment. I longed for romance, but as I grew up, it was impossible to ignore that I was queerer and dirtier than classical romance wanted me to be. I grew into the frustrated longing of Andersen's Little Mermaid. It didn't escape me that he wrote an allegory about the queer experience of being without a voice, and I, too, was struggling with the curse of silence. There were parts of my life I could not give voice to—even around those to whom I felt closest. Like Andersen and the Little Mermaid, I knew that to speak was to potentially put myself in danger. I was able to pass for "human" just like the Little Mermaid—able to convince my friends and family that I was happy and normal—but this illusion was kept in place by all that went unsaid. The vocal cords that held my rage and sorrow had been frayed in the dark oceans of my early childhood.

Like Andersen, I found that writing stories was a way of navigating my feelings of alienation and pain. I did not believe I was pure enough for an immortal soul, for a prince, or for my own love story, but at least I could write one. I could participate in romance by way of my pen.

In high school, my friends would "hire" me to write them personalized love stories—essentially real-life fan fiction featuring my friends and their crushes as characters. They'd give me a person and a scenario: the hot drummer dude from our gym class and a summer party up in the mountains. I'd gained some internet notoriety in early fan-fiction chat rooms for my wild, queer versions of popular fantasy novels. My core group of girlfriends were my first readers of these chaotic, gender-bending romances. And eventually, after confronting the violence of a pornography-literate teen sex culture, they asked me to write them into the love stories they were finding hard to attain.

Fan fiction has traditionally been a landscape populated by those who *don't* get included in the stories. The marginalized—the queer, the disabled, the nonwhite, the nonmales—cast themselves in their beloved literature by literally writing in the margins—making books wider, fleshier, and weirder by writing over and into the original text. We must not forget that Shakespeare, the son of an impoverished glover, wrote himself into the court of

England and literary acclaim not by imagining original stories, but by retelling popular contemporary plots. *Romeo and Juliet*, *Othello*, *The Winter's Tale*, *Much Ado About Nothing*, and *As You Like It* are all essentially fan fiction of earlier authors.

Fan fiction and marginalia are often downplayed as the silly pastimes of the amateur and the untalented. But fan fiction is much more than doodling on the edges of stories. Fan fiction can be a revolutionary act of rupture, puncturing the artificial boundaries that decide who can speak and who must remain silent under the sea. *The Little Mermaid* is essentially a story of a girl who punctures boundaries: between the sea and the land, then the land and the heavens. Her story leaks past the margin of one world and into the next. And Andersen himself was engaging in a radical act of marginalia. *The Little Mermaid* does not originate with Andersen but was instead inspired by the earlier *Undine* by Friedrich de la Motte Fouqué.

The sexual stories being given to me and the rest of my young female friends felt too narrow, too unfulfilling. The myth of heteronormativity didn't fit our mermaid tails. And so, I started to tell and then to write these "real-life fan fictions."

What began as a playful game soon took on mythical proportions when several of these stories subsequently came true—right down to minute details. It was as if the story, once spoken, had taken on some sort of magical property, calling into being its desired fulfillment in the real world.

"You should try it for yourself," my friend Ilana urged me our freshman year of college when I was mooning over a graduate student with a southern drawl. She called him Professor Americano and was cynical of his polished style and smug superiority. She preferred the vegan guitar players and dirty punks. As a joke, I finally turned the storytelling back on myself and wrote out a laughably specific scenario to entertain her, Hannah, and Nora. It included glasses of chilled sake, walks under the moonlight, and a conversation about Andy Goldsworthy, my favorite sculptor.

Within a month the situation took place, right down to the Andy Goldsworthy book opened on the coffee table. Had I seen into the future? Or drawn the future toward me? Was storytelling like a stitch, drawing two disconnected patches of time together?

Unfortunately, the man I'd cast as the main character was the only part of the story I didn't enjoy, as he complained about his ex-girlfriend for hours while descending into maudlin drunkenness. But the experience did ignite a playful superstition about my own stories. Sometimes they slipped off my tongue and began to write the real world into being.

We must remember that the word "spell" means alternatively to speak, to make happen, to write out, and to magically summon into being. These feral love stories seemed to be etymological unions of all these spells. Once spoken, these stories took on the power to summon new worlds, new realities.

As Anaïs Nin wrote, "I believe one writes because one has to create a world in which one can live. I could not live in any of the worlds offered to me. . . . I had to create a world of my own, like a climate, a country, an atmosphere in which I could breathe, reign, and recreate myself when destroyed by living." Fan fiction is incantatory, the magical spelling of the witches, the hedge-riders, the homosexuals, the mermaids, the exiled storytellers. It widens the margins imposed by sexism, by racism, by expertism, and makes room for new worlds: both on the page and in our very lives.

My margins were dilated by the wild and often queer romances of Mary Renault, Anne Rice, and Octavia Butler. These authors gave me permission to write stranger worlds and to compost bad tropes into good soil. They gave me permission to use language against itself, to write fan fiction of worlds that said they didn't want me.

I tried my best to write myself into love. But as hard as I tried, I didn't quite feel like I deserved it. I was still an undersea girl with a secret tail and a stifled voice. I was always going to watch from the sidelines while other people found happiness and partnership. The best I could hope for was to finally ascend like the Little Mermaid into an eternal soul. I saw my version of Andersen's ascent as one that led to intellectual and creative acclaim.

I had boyfriends and girlfriends. But I tended to pick ones I knew were safe. People who couldn't break my heart. I didn't feel like I deserved "the real thing." Instead, I studied medieval romances, in particular the story of Tristan and Isolde, chasing on the page what I wouldn't allow myself to quest for in my own life.

Spells can also be curses. Once a story is spoken aloud, it takes on power, even if it is a bad story.

I received a very different type of incantation when I was finally diagnosed. Suddenly, I was no longer headed toward the certainty of a cure or a happy ending. And strangely, once my new team of specialists started rattling off the symptoms and complications I should expect to encounter, I started to rapidly decline. Within months of my diagnosis, I had spinal issues so bad that I could hardly walk. My safe foods dwindled down to a list I could count on the fingers of one hand.

What was happening? Who did this story belong to?

Instead of moving to the city like my peers or immediately heading on to grad school for medieval studies like I was planning, I was forced to move back in with my parents the month after I graduated from college. I could hardly eat, hardly sleep, hardly walk.

"The new apartment is gorgeous. I can't wait for you to visit," Ilana gushed after moving to Philadelphia with a cohort of my college friends. I shivered, wondering how I could even survive the train ride down to see her.

I was experiencing a new symptom every day. Itching so bad I felt I might tear off my skin. Something was wrong with my liver and kidneys. Numbness and neuropathy on the right side of my body. The worst symptom started to occur regularly around five or so at night, regardless of whether I had eaten anything. I would be fine until suddenly I'd feel a wave of dizziness. Then a wall of nausea would hit me so acutely that it erased my mind. I'd wake to find myself a lost hour later, curled up next to the toilet, feeling like I'd been scrubbed internally with steel wool.

"What comes next?"

Maybe what came next was being less able: to think, to write, to walk, to be.

I needed to spend my life with utmost care. Every moment of mental clarity was a priceless treasure I might never touch again. I sat on the hammock behind my parents' home, strung between two oaks that had parented me as surely as my own parents had. I lay back and watched the sky bruise into dusk, shimmering with stars and fireflies.

I wanted desperately to find a miracle cure. I wanted to feel better. I wanted to write books. I wanted to fall in love.

But at this point, exhausted and captured by the term "incurable," what could I possibly orient myself toward?

I was reminded of a line from one of my favorite Robinson Jeffers poems: "Life is good, be it stubbornly long or / suddenly / A mortal splendor: meteors are not needed less than mountains."

What did it mean to stop deferring my life? If I wasn't going to get better—if, in fact, I was probably going to get a lot sicker—then it was better to live life as a "mortal splendor" and claim my desires before it was too late. Life was a sandcastle. It was time for me to explore its rooms and terraces and turrets while it still stood, knowing there was no way to prevent the oncoming waves. My brain was not going to last forever. My body was not going to last forever. I'd always looked up to my favorite writers as being older, wiser than myself. I'd always thought I'd have years to steep in my own juices, honing my craft before writing the stories I so desperately wanted to make into novels.

My doctor's recitation of oncoming decay indicated that I might not have much time to perfect my craft.

It wasn't completely true that I was waiting to write novels. I'd written several, but I considered them all private practice attempts. In elementary school, I'd drafted and revised by hand several blousy fantasy novels when my parents were going through financial insecurity and I was convinced I might be able to write us a way to more stability. I wrote young adult novels in high school that I outgrew as I wrote them, constantly revising them to age my characters up to my new level of maturity.

But there were stories I'd buried inside my heart like a squirrel caching acorns for spring.

Except that each spring, I deferred digging up these stories, writing them down, giving them a shape. Those acorn stories, buried for too long, decided to become useful anyway. They decided to become trees.

The day after yet another anaphylactic reaction and trip to the ER in an ambulance, I sat down and asked myself, "If you knew you had only one year left to live, what is the most important story you would want to tell? What is the story you care most?" The question wasn't hypothetical. It felt like a sober way of assessing how to make my life a "mortal splendor."

If I am a meteor and not a mountain, how do I learn to accept the speed, the movement, the ecstatic arc across the heavens?

I was coming to believe that stories preceded our arrival. Mineral stories. Deep-time stories. We were authored by geological stories with scales too vast for us to ever grasp. We were infected with fungal stories that altered our consciousness, with civilization-changing consequences. What if civilization itself was a nonhuman narrative, authored by fermentation yeasts using humans as mere characters?

I wanted to write stories that were as textured, entangled, and biodiverse as an old-growth forest. As feral and involuted as a spoonful of dirt holding one billion bacteria, up to ten miles of mycelial fungi, and thousands of protozoa.

I decided I would bring these questions to the altar of a love story. I would make a love story that was bigger than a human couple.

Something about falling ill in Jerusalem had stitched me into the land of Judea and Galilee and to the tragedy of a storytelling healer killed by empire. The Gospels, it turned out, were a sort of fan fiction. But it wasn't the kind written by marginalized communities. Instead, they represented the dominant paradigm coming in and co-opting the story of a person they had oppressed and executed. What did that initial mistranslation of the story obscure? What was behind the ascetical, white Jesus who, although he invited women to the table, had become a figurehead for ecocide, colonialism, and sexism? I was obsessed with the women who scintillated just below the surface of the Gospels—financing the ministry, witnessing the horrors of crucifixion and empire up close, then going on to teach and preach themselves in the early Christian communities the Roman Empire eventually deemed heretical. In particular, I was drawn to Mary Magdalene, one of the main characters of both canonical and extra-canonical accounts of the life of Jesus. Jesus "loves her best," calls her "the apostle of the apostles," and kisses her on the mouth in the Gospel of Philip. She is the one to whom he first appears resurrected.

I'd long desired to write the story of Mary Magdalene, but with the texture and research of some of my favorite historical fiction authors. I was increasingly suspicious of human beings' need to assert ownership over narrative and speech. Did stories really belong to us? What would it look like to write ecosystems instead of anthropocentric heroes' journeys? I wanted to bring back to life not just the erased people—the women, the sick, the abused, the enslaved, and the servants—but also the ecosystem that had inspired the nature-based teachings of Jesus.

Miriam—the Aramaic version of Mary—arrived all at once. I could smell her, taste her, feel her frustration and anger and sorrow like a second skin growing over mine.

I wrote a hundred pages in two months. The experience was like falling in love. Characters arrived in dreams, and then I'd wake up feeling as if I'd lost someone I desperately cared about. The only way to assuage this grief was to *write* them and give them a new life. I stayed up late, wandering back roads in a meditative state and asking my characters what they wanted. Yes, I plotted and planned, but very often my characters would interrupt a scene and demand something different from the narrative arc. I left appointments early to spend time with them. I dreamed about the fields and rivers and houses that were blooming from my fingertips. Writing is always close to magic—to spelling. There is the author, and then there is "something else." Ursula K. Le Guin explains, "All makers must leave room for the acts of the spirit. But they have to work hard and carefully, and wait patiently to deserve them."

In the summer of 2016, my heart was all open space. All soil. It was left mulched and uncluttered enough for that spirit to burst its seed coat and sprout. If I was going to die, I would at least write the best love story I could before I went out. I didn't have to be perfect or well-studied to write. I didn't have time to fix myself before I began.

During this time, I often climbed the nearby Overlook Mountain up to the abandoned hotel and the fire tower, letting the physical exertion act as internal leverage, moving plot pieces and narrative questions around in my head as I physically ascended.

How could I bring the sensual and ecological reality of Second Temple period Palestine to life? How could I create not a single human narrative, but a teeming ecosystem of voices all striving to survive the Roman Empire? I was lucky that my whole life had been preparatory research. My parents wrote about the history of religion and, in recent years, had focused on the pagan root system underlying Catholicism. For some strange reason, I'd been fascinated with the story of Jesus since childhood, much to the confusion and amusement of my animistic parents. I'd drawn pictures of a crying Mary at the foot of the cross as a child, wondering how this tragedy was turned into a miracle. How did a Galilean healer with a penchant for nature-based storytelling get mistranslated by empire and co-opted by patriarchy? How did a healer get used to create so many wounds? I thought of my feet tracing the path of the Via Dolorosa in Jerusalem as I grew sicker with each step. Why did we worship his untimely death rather than grieving the unfulfilled promise of his wild storytelling? Of course, as I began to plot the book and write the first chapters, I saw that there was more research to do. I love research more than anything: exploring primary documents, searching through dusty tomes, discovering an old academic monograph no one has read in years. But I was already deep enough in the material that I couldn't make the excuse that I needed more time to prepare.

Reaching the top of Overlook, I came around the bend to the view of the Overlook Mountain House at an elevation of 2,920 feet. It is, in fact, the third version of the hotel, which first began in 1833 during the wave of European tourism into the Hudson Valley that was inspired by Thomas Cole and other landscape painters. But the mountain, sliced open for stone and then built upon with her own body, was never comfortable with the inn. The hotel, made to accommodate more than three hundred guests, burned down three times over the last century.

I ducked under a fringe of ivy trailing down from a stone entryway that had once held a door. Someone had camped on the mountain, setting a fire in the blown-out remains of the hearth. Peppery drafts of ash and pollen streaked through the roofless ballroom. Spiderwebs laced up the windows, long and glassless. Peppermint starbursts of mountain laurel hovered like pink clouds at the top of a staircase that led into open air. A yellow birch stood like a shaft of moonlight, uniting two rooms without floors, their shapes suggested only by the remaining stone walls.

I grew up in the shadow of Overlook and knew its body—its ruts and curves and cut trunks—like the scarred, mottled hide of my own body. I knew that hundreds of timber rattlers bred in that small area near the hotel and the summit.

From what lore and information still exists, I've gathered that the Indigenous Mahican and Lenape people of the Hudson Valley never lived on the mountain and only ever climbed up for serious ceremonial purposes. They used a word, "manitou," to denote the powerful energy of the Great Wall or Catskill escarpment of mountains, of which Overlook is the first summit. Manitou can loosely be taken to mean a being of reverence, something outside of simplistic human dualisms of good or bad. Manitou meant, *I am bigger than you, small human, and extremely powerful.*

Sitting in the ruins—smelling the honeysuckle beginning to unfurl its interrogative perfume under the morning sun, feeling those scent questions tickle my tongue and wake up my song, my desire to move and dance—I finally felt at home, geographically and in my own body. Each window blasted open by fire was a picture frame for a better painting than anything I've ever seen in a museum: sky and leaf and clamorous green.

I thought about the diagnosis that had come like an answer to a prayer before clamping around me like a prison. I thought of the secret, thistle-spiked shards of trauma lodged in my nervous system, the scars that healed like wet tissue paper in my collagen-deficient skin.

I knew what it was like to be the Overlook Mountain House. I was also a ruin. Once, in an imagined past, I had also housed dancing parties and groups of artists who lit candles and walked down to Echo Lake just over my summit, drinking champagne next to beavers and watching the moon curve over the ancient grooves of glaciers. My body had once been a locus of celebration.

I thought of those times when I had come close to love.

A man with a boyish face and wild curls on the banks of a river after a week spent canoeing, his hand hovering over my thigh like a thundercloud over a tree-furred valley. A friend coming to visit me after many years, roasting a chicken, walking under the chill light of the stars, and staying up till the wolf hour, a candle between us, our unspoken significant others like plexiglass between us, asking, "Why didn't it happen between us? Why didn't we get together?"

I had never been whole. Or if I had been, it was before I had the word for whole. I'd never been pure enough for a love story. And then I'd gotten sick, and the sense of inadequacy and alienation had increased. I could write love stories. But my own body and heart were too ruined to house anything but rattlesnakes and blackbirds.

A wind stirred a high-pitched smell from somewhere. It was honey-sweet, surprising me back into the softness.

The mountain's silent scent tongue told me, "I prefer the ruins."

The mountain made sure that the hotel burned down not once, but three times. The hotel was never supposed to be enclosed and habitable. It was always destined for porousness. For open communication with the entire ecosystem of the Hudson Valley. Its cracks and fissures made it a perfect landscape for snakes and trees and ivy and the occasional intrepid wild turkey. It became a skeleton that was embraced and enfleshed by a green body: the vegetal manitou presence of Overlook Mountain itself.

Sitting inside the hotel's open body, I felt something release in me.

What if I accepted the ruin? What if I accepted my porousness and the power of the fires that opened all my windows and let the greenery inside? The point, for me, was no longer to struggle toward some unattainable, isolated perfection, but to accept that the ruin was the point.

Let seeds fly inside and root into the floors of my body. Let the birch trees push off the roof of my bounded stories about selfhood. Let me become a window, a frame for a green world. I prayed.

Some spore must have lodged in me and spread its mycelial mischief deep into my tissue because soon after that day, I decided to date again, despite having already exhausted online apps and the local pool of single people.

If there wasn't a cure for my body, maybe there was a cure for my heart? Maybe somebody would love my snake-entwined, ivy-gilded ruins?

"Bring me my person," I said aloud to the full moon, giving my spell breath and volume.

Within a week I'd met Jason. A tall, flaxen-haired artist with big hands who liked to walk silently through the woods. Who liked to read long, dry books about local history. Who bought flowers every time he left the house. He wanted a big farmhouse and a family. He wanted to grow plants and learn their names. Our first date left me extremely nervous. I could feel that I'd met someone who had the potential to upend my life. All my instincts told me to run.

I didn't run. I let the story tell itself. I surrendered to being a character in a love story rather than its author. The loss of control was equally terrifying and delicious.

Still wary of being ghosted by someone I genuinely liked, I held off on telling Hannah or Ilana. But after he took me on a hike through old mines in the mountains, kissing the side of my mouth as I peered in the gaping stone caverns that exhaled chill air, I knew I had to jump. I called Ilana as soon as I got home.

"I've met *him*. The person. The right person."

When Jason found out about my illness, he told me he loved the ruins: snakes and vines and symptoms and uncertainty. He took me to my favorite lake and gave me a rose. He kissed me and asked, "Can we live together? Can we make a home together?"

"Yes," I said. "Yes," I spelled out to the universe, feeling my future dilate and explode its original margins.

I was finally living my own fan fiction.

"Look!" He grasped my shoulder and pointed overhead. A bald eagle swept the sky clean of mist from an earlier rain, curving around us. I could feel its wings crown us, its flight creating a ring of safety within which we could build a shared life, a shared vision.

Yes. If this is possible, then maybe it means I've been wrong about every-thing, I thought. *Maybe miracles are possible.*

CHAPTER 7

Smell Your Way Home: Phlox, Foe, Friend

I'VE ALWAYS HAD A PROBLEMATICALLY SENSITIVE NOSE. AND IT'S BEEN made more sensitive by years of food and chemical sensitivities. Often, I can tell when someone close to me is sick before they know it, just by their body odor. There are certain mycelial systems I know by a taste I experience as I walk over their hidden underground bodies, which is only confirmed later in the season by their visible fruiting mushrooms. I love perfumes, carrying several in my pocketbook at once not necessarily to wear, but to uncork like portable memories, letting them slip me back into the sensory shape of a lost summer afternoon spent on a violet-studded riverbank. A bag of smells is a bag of songs. A bag of smells is a bag of time machines, transporting you back to people you've lost and ecosystems long since clear-cut and developed.

For years, I harbored a suspicion that like dogs scenting truffles, I would know I had found a home for my heart when my nose told me. My nose would know better than my mind ever would. In fact, every spring, the limerent glimmer of lilac drawing me out of the house and up into the mountain roads affirmed that my nose was my most direct connection to my heart. Smells could move me, literally, out the door and into the forest, as I was suddenly hijacked by a pheromonal behavior-scape bigger than my single body.

Swarming bees locate a new hive and attract the rest of the colony through a pheromone called Nasanov, which includes such familiar terpenoids as geraniol, nerolic acid, and citral acid. Beekeepers have noted that the Nasanov pheromone, produced by glands placed parenthetically around a worker bee's stinger, can be detected by a naked human nose and smells of lemongrass. This is a fact that beekeepers take advantage of when they use lemongrass essential oil to trap bees or introduce them to a new "hive." In fact, bees' lives are intimately orchestrated by smells. The smells of flowers and, most importantly, the pheromones secreted by their queen.

The queen coordinates behavior, hive-building, defensive techniques, and nectar-collecting strategies via her pheromones. Fascinatingly, if you remove a queen and wait for her "smell" to blow away and then insert another queen, you can drastically alter the collective behavior of the hive. The bees live in the queen's smell, her atmospheric aroma, like we live inside culture, unwittingly letting it orchestrate and organize our tasks and lives. Beekeepers have observed that when dealing with an aggressive hive, if you remove the queen and let her pheromones fade before adding in a "gentle" queen substitute, you can create the conditions for a "calm" colony.

Imagine. A razzle of citrus. Cut grass. Spike of bergamot crushed between dogteeth. Star scent. Shiver musk. Your antennae quiver with sparkling electrons. You hum and skim through oak trees, singing with your whole body until you reach it: the hollowed-out oak trunk. The place your brother and sister bees have been covering with a perfume called "home."

Ever since I learned about the Nasanov pheromone, I have wondered what it would be like to smell my way home.

Smell shows us that our behavior is never a solitary event, locked inside singular selves. Smell leaks between bodies and it leads us home, tying us into community. Smell is a vital sense across a variety of species. And it is often the sensory communication that translates most easily between disparate species. Truffles exude gases up through the soil to entice animals to dig them up and help the fungi reproduce. Lodgepole pines that are attacked by beetles send a smell "scream" out into the forest, warning other trees to prepare for attack. Dogs are the most popular smell superstars, scenting oncoming seizures in human owners, unearthing Iron Age corpses, and locating prized truffles blooming darkly below the duff. In Texas, cadaver compound was injected into oil pipes, and the pipes were observed for vulture activity to locate where they had sprung a leak. The vultures homed in on the smell of corpse emanating from the broken pipes. Elephants choose the most nutritious, highest-sugar fruit by way of a scent evaluation. Recent studies at Oxford University's Department of Zoology demonstrated that Scopoli's shearwater birds navigate great distances across water via "olfactory maps." The study shows that many other birds find their way home by smell too. The ocean is an odoriferous landscape. It is a series of perfumed songlines.

The idea of songlines might not be that much of a stretch. The vibration theory of smell posits that just as smell is, in a manner, touch—an interaction between scent molecules "touching" the olfactory cleft of our nose and setting off a domino chain of electrons—so smell might also be sound. First formulated by Malcolm Dyson in 1928, the theory suggests that a molecule's smell is due to its vibration frequency. The theory has received pushback from the "shape" theory, which posits that molecular shape is more important than vibration, but as a poet, I am drawn to the lyrical nature of smell as song. Perhaps that's why, faced with impoverished smell vocabulary, we rely on phrases like "chord" or "note" or "symphony" when describing perfumes and complex aromas.

Humans, although we live in a culture biased toward visual and auditory stimuli, receive a remarkable amount of information via smell. Recent research has upended the myth that humans are smell-deficient. The human nose is capable of distinguishing more than a trillion distinct odors. A Scottish woman named Joy Milne can accurately make a diagnosis of Parkinson's disease with her nose. In fact, her nose is a finer diagnostic tool than any technology, picking up the disease years before it even registers on traditional tests. It may be that this skill isn't just her superpower. We are all making subconscious decisions based on smell all the time, like the worker bees inside the pheromonal ocean of the queen's influence.

In a famous study nicknamed the "sweaty T-shirt" experiment, Swiss scientist Claus Wedekind showed that people exposed to T-shirts soaked in different people's body odor unknowingly and consistently picked the T-shirt from the person with the histocompatibility gene (MHC) that was most different from their own. The MHC gene is responsible for the growth of a healthy immune system in a fetus, and it has been shown that mates who represent a diverse combination of MHC genes produce healthier, more immunologically robust children. Studies aside, most people have had the experience, at least once in their life, of smelling a lover's body odor and knowing deeply, somatically, that there is chemistry. What if we didn't date via visual cues, but dated via smell? Would we make better choices of partners?

We smell events before they happen. Cut grass blows downwind. Bad smells shepherd us away from fire, from pollutants, from eating rotten food. We smell events that have already happened. A ghost of perfume tells us our friend has just left the room. And memory is intimately entangled with smell. A perfect blend of lily and gardenia summons my grandmother with such vivacity that the rest of her easily materializes: I see her powder blue dress, her dove brooch, her mischievous eyes. Though she is long dead, I open her old perfume jar and suddenly I can touch her again, speak to her. Smell is often the doorway into other sensory experiences.

As I researched scripture for my book, I was struck by the preponderance of perfumes and unguents. The Song of Songs, one of the most popular sections of the Hebrew Bible, is a sensual glossary of erotic smells. The scents of spikenard and aloes and myrrh lead us through the Gospels. Jesus is constantly anointed, washed, and articulated by smell. I have observed that smell is one of the most effective ways to build an embodied world when I am writing fiction. We know that most of taste is really smell. The first mouthful of wine on a summer night. The dark cherry of black coffee, sipped as the sun spills into your living room. Like the bees following Nasanov to their new hive, smell can help us find a foothold in a world of abstract words. Smell can build the scaffolding for a story that doesn't just live in our heads—it enters our organisms and coordinates cascades of hormones and the activation of certain memories.

The artist Kate McLean was interested in the relationship between smell and biosemiotics—a study defined as the exchange of sensory signals between animals and their environments. McLean created a project called Sensory Maps. She would lead people in "mapping" their cities by smell and creating complex "smellscape" maps with the aggregate information she received from participants. With her focus primarily on urban environments, McLean has suggested these maps can be utilized by urban planners and developments.

Where should smells be preserved? Where should we decide not to develop due to a bad odor? Diving into her work, I was immediately reminded of Bernie Krause and his acoustic niche hypothesis in relationship to soundscape ecology. The theory is that animals in a shared ecosystem develop different tones and rhythms that work together, like an orchestra. Each sound finds its perfect channel so that it doesn't "interrupt" anyone else's song. Thinking poetically, with the vibration theory of smell as being related to sound, I wonder what an aroma niche hypothesis would look like? Do ecosystems evolve complex symphonies of smell—fungal, vegetal, animal, elemental—that all cooperate and combine into a perfect sensual symphony? And if this is true, what of anthropogenic smell? What about smell pollution that is so pervasive it almost, especially in the smell maps of Kate McLean, overwhelms any other biological, environmentally excreted perfumes? What if birds can't find their song/smell lines across the ocean? I thought of my own desperate attempts to find a partner, swiping through profiles on apps, looking around at local coffee shops for other solitary writers and artists. The truth was that I wouldn't know my right partner as a pixelated picture on a screen. I'd know it with my nose. What if we were all wearing so much synthetic perfume that we couldn't make a correct olfactory assessment of potential mates?

Diane Ackerman writes memorably in her incredible book *A Natural History of the Senses*: "Our sense of smell can be extraordinarily precise, yet it's almost impossible to describe how something smells to someone who hasn't smelled it. . . . We see only where there is light enough, taste only when we put things into our mouths, touch only when we make contact with someone or something, hear only sounds that are loud enough to hear. But we smell always and with every breath. Cover your eyes and you will stop seeing, cover your ears and you will stop hearing, but if you cover your nose and stop smelling, you will die." Smell requires our bodily attention while refusing our cognitive capture. It insists we close our eyes and open our noses.

I decided after years inside academia trying to *answer* questions, I would rather *smell* them. *Lead me home. Show me where to go.*

When I first met Jason, I let my nose lead the way. He smelled right. Like meadow grass heating up under the sun. Like cardamom and leather.

"I like how you smell too." He would chuckle, sticking his nose in my armpit, causing me to squeal with delight and mischief. He encouraged me not to wear deodorant, saying he liked my natural body odor.

And we smelled our way home literally, arriving in late spring to see an eighteenth-century inn for rent deep in the mountains. We were greeted by a burnt sugar sigh on the wind, like the world was just finished baking, releasing almondy curls I could almost see as yellow steam rising alongside the pollen. A British woman who reminded me of my own British grandmother owned the property and showed us the giant planks of wood, the living room that had originally been a taproom and bar when the house had been a carriage stop. The house was nestled right at the confluence of Beaverkill Creek and Esopus Creek, right at the four corners created by the two oldest roads in the area. It was painted elephant blue and had enough yard space to grow herbs and tomatoes. But it was none of this visual charm that sold me. Instead, it was the smell that hung like a scent corona around Mount Tremper and the blue inn: delicate mountain flowers, almost milky, like they were exuding the nutritive element of springtime's secret, pink body.

"There are so many plants to work with . . ." Jason wondered out loud as we explored the neighborhood, crawling under a no-trespassing sign to access an abandoned ivy-digested bridge that spanned the Esopus, which gave the best unobstructed view of the mountains in the area. Jason was an artist who, when I met him, was interested in cyanotypes and plant morphology. He never failed to bring flowers and weeds inside, photographing them against white backdrops, zooming in and using his computer to trace their minuscule bristles and sepals. "And it smells like a flower shop," he added.

What I didn't know was that we were smelling phlox and that by the time we'd move into the house in early July, the vibrant flowers would have withered back to stalks among the sedge and clover. That first summer we'd be lulled into a sense of floral security, enchanted by the waves of late summer aster and goldenrod. What I didn't know was that the smell we had found so inviting would, only a year later, almost kill me.

Wild *Phlox paniculata* is one of the sixty-five members of the Polemoniaceae family. If you gave a kid a box of paints and asked them to decorate the forest, you would get phlox: huge neon splashes of purple, pink, pearly white, and red stochastically sprawled across the landscape. They are bright as sunspots burned into your retina. And their perfume is sweet and powdery. What I originally enjoyed as delicate now reminds me of the cloying, synthetic sprays young girls would wear in high school to mask the animal funk of their pheromones.

I'd always been vaguely allergic to phlox. It runs in the family. Growing up, every year my dad's eyes would water, and he would start to sneeze the day the first bright phlox flowers surfaced on the roadside. But my own allergy had been relatively mild. A sneeze or two. Maybe my eyes would feel itchy on their peak pollen day in mid-June. My allergy was never bad enough that it dissuaded me from approaching the flowers, sometimes even accenting a foraged bouquet with a magenta spray. A sneeze was well worth the delight of the smell and the color.

By the time we moved into the blue inn, my body was in a state of over-reaction. Since my diagnosis of mast cell disease in combination with Ehlers-Danlos, I'd been compelled to try new allergy drugs. Paradoxically, these treatments left me sicker and more allergic than before. My system seemed to always be on high alert, ready to break out in immunological hysteria at any surprise encounter. Suddenly dust and mold, substances that had previously only triggered mild sneezing, were liable to throw me into a life-threatening asthma attack. My parents' cats triggered hives and wheezing.

But I was making a home with a partner for the first time. And I made a home with smells. I baked gluten-free bread, lit beeswax candles, and tucked palo santo sticks into the corners of windows. Although my own diet was dwindling, I tried to enjoy food through its spices and exudations, preparing elaborate dinner parties for my friends and enjoying the way the dining room warmed up with shared breath, uncorked wine, and a rosemary-dusted chicken roasting in the oven. My favorite moments were in late summer, with our porch door flung open to let the moss-bright exhale of a thunderstorm pour into the kitchen. Home wasn't just a place. It was a collection of smells that communicated warmth, sustenance, and friendship.

I was also busy ghostwriting children's novels and was overworked to the point that it was easy to ignore smaller warning signs and smells wafting in from the winds of the future, foretelling weather I was ill-prepared to face.

When I first sneezed, I didn't think much of it. I walked past a fuchsia bundle of phlox on my walk home from my favorite coffee shop. "Hello, you beautiful spring stars," I thought almost affectionately, mulling how they constellated the meadows and roadside like a brightly colored cosmos.

Two days into phlox season, though, I had to admit something was different. For one, it turned out that the smell that had initially drawn me to the blue inn was due, in part, to the fact that the house was encircled by the densest phlox clusters I'd ever seen. I was overdosing on phlox pollen every time I opened a window or stepped outside. And I was no longer just sneezing when a particularly pollen-rich wind reached me. No, I was soon breathing through a swollen straw of a throat, wheezing and struggling for air. I felt like I was at altitude. I was a serious runner who suddenly could hardly scale a flight of stairs, my brain cottony and bruised in a skull that felt too tight. I woke up on the third morning and screeched when I looked in the bathroom mirror and saw that overnight I had turned beet red from head to foot.

I started to pass blood in my urine, and my kidneys ached. I had difficulty swallowing. People with long-term health issues will understand the term "treatment fatigue." I was slowly reaching a new type of medical defeat. Nothing I'd done had given me any relief. A belligerent and exhausted version of me insisted that I would not go to the hospital unless there was no other option. I didn't have time to sit in waiting rooms and be told my situation was hopeless. I had books to ghostwrite. I had to try to finish my novel. Surely phlox season would pass. I was resolved to get through it by drinking tons of water. Shutting the open windows. Focusing on the tasks at hand.

I tried to hide the seriousness of this episode from friends and family, avoiding calls from my closest friends, Ilana and Edith, and putting off my best friend, Hannah, whom I'd been planning to have over with her boyfriend, Marty. We'd been enjoying settling into coupledom alongside each other, meeting up for hikes, adventures, and dinner parties as a foursome. Our boyfriends were both artists and struck up a fast friendship.

"I'm just so busy. Let's try next month?" I croaked as an excuse, glad she couldn't see my blistered face through the phone.

But within a week, I could barely make it down the stairs in the morning or take a full breath. I developed a fever as my hypervigilant immune system decided to cook me alive. My eyes swelled shut. I started to hammer Benadryl, hoping it would at least blunt the worst of the symptoms.

Now I look back and wonder why Jason didn't put me in the car and drive me to the emergency room. Only months prior I'd taken him to the ER for a brown recluse bite and then nursed him back to health.

Hounded by a perfume I had once loved, I took refuge in the one air-conditioned room in the old house: the taproom turned living room. I camped out with books and blankets but found that I was too sick to even write or read.

What was the spark?

I think the spark was phlox itself. The name for the flower actually originates in the Greek, *phloxes*, for flames. The scent that had drawn me to this home began to burn me up from the inside. This was physical, but soon it was also mental. Sitting in the living room, staring out the window at the wafting golden sheets of pollen, I wondered about the ways that plants spoke to one another through smell. I wondered about all those voices I had dimmed out because they didn't arrive as human language. The perfume voices. The vibration voices. The spore voices. The tree and root voices that spoke so slowly, you needed to widen your sense of time to listen.

Unable to read or look at a screen, I found myself listening to hundreds of hours of herbal podcasts, radio shows focused on lore about local plants and cures, and interviews with ethnobotanists and herbal healers. I blinked blearily through my collection of wildflower and local plant identification books, tracing the illustrations of phlox with a hive-blistered finger.

"What am I supposed to be doing?"

The perfume of phlox had led me to choose this strange old carriage inn as my home. But it was leading me home in a deeper, stranger way too. Phlox forced me to sit still enough to realize that I had to change my life. Strangely, I'd strayed off the "path" by staying too firmly on the path. As a child I ate dirt, kept notebooks full of drawings of my favorite plants and mushrooms, and bushwhacked through the forest. But driven by financial desperation and overwork, I'd been moving at a pace not suited to the plants and not suited to my own body.

In other cultures that are still attuned to the wisdom of plants, it is common to engage in plant meditations or plant dialogues by ingesting a small amount and asking questions. The stage for the dialogue is our very own bodies and the way they glitch and change in relation to the vegetal intervention. Vegetalistas in South America will ask for plant dreams. But in our fast-paced, Eurocentric culture, we don't often go to plants and ask for medicine. We've been taught the world doesn't speak.

Sometimes the message has to get loud to get our attention.

Phlox realized I needed to be interrupted. I needed to slow down so I could see the frills and ridges in ferns, the miraculous expansion of the knotweed overnight. So phlox decided to come to meet me. And dream through me. She knew the best lure was smell. She drew me into my home, and then she embraced me with her asphyxiating wake-up scent.

Finally, a week into the trial by flower fire, I dragged myself outside wearing a kerchief around my face and drapes of clothing to protect my skin from the pollen. I hobbled down to the edge of my little kitchen garden, to a spot where phlox was flaming technicolor. Pearl. Purple. Pink. "What do I need to do? What do I need to do next?"

The answer came immediately. And it came in a tumble of smell. A tumble of technicolored voices.

It's time to move at the speed of plants. It's time to study us. To devote yourself to us.

I dragged myself back inside and signed up for every local class on herbalism and plant identification I could find. I gathered all my books on ecology, plants, mycology, herbalism, and trees, and I ordered more. Much to Jason's consternation, I turned the living room into a compost heap of books and pressed flowers and notebooks spread across the floor like fallen leaves. Within a month, I was doing an apprenticeship with a famous herbalist, who advised their students to ask the plants for their message before we looked it up in a book. This was a crucial piece of wisdom. Quite often, our intuition precedes and confirms scientific data. Plants don't need to be measured and studied to reveal their secrets. They just need us to get quiet enough to listen with all our prickling senses.

Within a month, I was addressing small health issues with tinctures and teas I had made myself. After learning the hard way that I was deathly allergic to most antibiotics, I suddenly had another method of treating small infections. I was able to treat a nasty bladder infection herbally rather than by surrendering to a hospital stay. A year later, when I was diagnosed with acute kidney dysfunction, I tapped into the plants before beginning a medical intervention. "What do I need to do next?" I asked, this time more confidently. And they helped me, showing me what to eat and brew and do. When I managed to correct my kidney numbers in a week, my doctors were stunned.

When I look back on that strange moment, I can finally see that the phlox saved me. Phlox set fire to my intimate and collaborative relationship with plants, which had over time burned down to dormant embers. Phlox physically stopped me, reintroducing me to a speed of life more rooted and seasonal, which was much better suited to my own tricky body.

It was their smell that first caught my attention. And it was that smell that convinced me to settle down and breathe deeply—a medicine that far exceeded my idea of how medicine was supposed to act.

It was this floral course correction that eventually guided me to one allergy medicine that did seem to help my mast cell condition: strong nettle infusions. The phlox were an initiatory event, squeezing me until I burst open, flowerlike, into an expanded vegetal awareness.

I'll never forget the second week of phlox season, when I found that I could breathe again. I walked out my front door to see that my new peony bush had recently produced a dew-encrusted, salmon-pink bloom. And below the peony, crown vetch was weaving little purple fairy crowns. Cleavers bordered the walkway down to the road. Poison ivy tentacled up the old oak. Mower's mushrooms bubbled up from below the porch. All that year I'd felt alone, living far away from the bustling towns full of my friends, working so hard I didn't have much time to relax. But now I could see that I'd been crowded around with a community that was speaking with every scent molecule and spore it could muster to reach me.

That is the medicine, phlox said to me. Smelled to me. *Your home is not a house. It is a hive of vibrating smells. A dance of green beings risking their lives to sting you into awareness.*

Inspired by the biosemiotics artist Kate McLean, I began to smell-map my way through my mountain-shadowed home. I followed my nose to a plant and then accepted the greeting, kneeling and getting to know my new friend. I kept a notebook of smell observations that broke the rules of terminology, classifying plants and smells by color, by birdsongs, and by emotions.

Smell is a song of homecoming, vibrating with melodic messages about behavior and mates and environmental hazards. Just as it is for the bees that follow the lemongrass pheromone to their new hive, smell was the link between me and the riotous vegetal world I had accidentally muted.

That summer, kneeling in front of the dried phlox stalks, glad their peak pollen season was finished, I realized that home was not a lover or a place for me. It was not the house or the financial stability I was doggedly trying to create.

Home, for me, was an open state of mind. A state of mind wherein every funky, musty, lusting, loving being could reach me and change me.

I breathed in and I knew I was finally listening, not with my ears or my head. But with my nose, my belly, and my heart.

CHAPTER 8

Storytelling Is an Emergency: Ecological Storytelling and Survival

"WHAT IS YOUR EMERGENCY?" I ASKED THE GROUP OF FEMALE HIGH school students I'd been tasked with mentoring. "What if you only had time to tell one last story? What if your life depended on a story?"

The girls looked at each other knowingly, a spark of flint-bright grief already present in their eyes. It should have been too early for them to know that their ability to tell a good story wasn't about craft so much as it was about survival. But they already knew. Every woman knows that storytelling isn't a hobby. It is vital. A way of staying alive against all odds.

As a child, I'd looked for both temporary escape and proof that it was possible to survive violent rupture. In fantasy and historical fiction, I found the characters that showed me adjacent worlds. There were children who had been hurt and abused who triumphed against adversity, got revenge, and claimed magical powers.

If your world wants to hurt you, read about another world. Write another world. Write yourself a better ending.

Creativity was always tangled up with survival. My parents had early success with book deals in the nineties that encouraged them to leave their stable jobs in the city and move us upstate into the mountains. But after we moved, they struggled to make ends meet. The publishing industry was reorganizing. They were forced to juggle multiple freelancing gigs at once while racing to meet manuscript deadlines, all while raising my brother and me on a shoestring. Writing was always motivated equally by passion and the desperate desire to pay the bills. I'd hover on the stairs late at night, listening to their muffled voices in the kitchen, arguing over whether they could keep the house.

They worked hard to hide this reality from my brother and me. Our house was filled with plants and animals and friends. What we lacked in money we made up for in a joyous community that bridged species and ideologies. But I knew that writing was not just a hobby. It was a job. It was food on the table. It was what just barely kept our family afloat in an ocean of bills and debt and uncertainty.

In sixth grade, sensing our radical financial instability and panicked we would lose our woodland home, I resolved to write a book that would save our family. I fancied myself a new Christopher Paolini, a teenage prodigy who could write a best-selling fantasy novel. When I think about how my writing practice was born, I see that it was not from the gentle promptings of my poetic soul. It was driven by desperation. I wanted to make money to save my family.

And even deeper than that, I wanted to write worlds that were big enough for the difficult questions with which I was struggling.

I wanted to write biodiverse ecosystems, not single-sprout stories. I longed for places that were moss-soft, valley-wide, soil-sturdy enough to catch me and hold me when I could no longer contain my grief and terror. I didn't just love and enjoy the fiction of Anne Rice, Mary Stewart, Octavia Butler, Ursula K. Le Guin, Mary Renault, and J. R. R. Tolkien. I sought refuge in those stories. I stayed alive in and because of those stories.

A good book was a life raft. A parachute. Built to carry my heart and body safely to solid ground.

This creative urgency was sneered at in college. Art was detached and abstract. Cool detachment and deliberate difficulty were prized above narrative propulsion and character development. There were plenty of classes on language poetry and deconstructing the short story, but none on the practicalities of making money as a writer or the dire need for stories that could imagine alternative futures for our flailing culture. God forbid your novel had a plot. God forbid it was a love story. God forbid it had more than three anemic characters living in a monochromatic cityscape.

When we prize books and poems without plot and without heart, we create a feedback loop that encourages writers and readers alike to accept worlds without meaning, without plants and animals, without possibility and love. We were encouraged to write what was novel and cool, rather than the stories that burned in our chests and kept us alive through impossible adversity.

After college, finally liberated from the sterile confines of human achievement, I realized I'd misunderstood literacy as the sole property of human beings. In fact, blinkered by our own thought patterns and stories, we'd become relatively *illiterate*, unable to read our actual environments for information on food, medicine, and weather patterns. Literacy didn't just mean being able to decipher human symbols. It meant being able to read an incoming storm in the pattern of shifting leaves, detecting phenological cascades leading into a season, identifying bird calls tracing the path of a predator through dark undergrowth.

The more time I spent outside, the more I doubted that the best stories were by human beings.

We had not invented storytelling. We had arrived *in medias res*, inside a biodiversity of stories already millions of years deep into a geological drama both too small and too large for our limited sensory apparatus to ever comprehend.

Every story, like every human body, is an ecosystem of other stories: the virus author that "taught" us mammals how to develop wombs, the ancient ecological pressures that molded us into multicellularity, our pulsing microbiome, our fungi-dusted skin, our metabolic reciprocity with every substance we breathe and drink and eat. Every recombinatory miracle of genetics gave birth not to an individual on a hero's journey, but to a biodiversity of competing and converging aliveness. If I was beginning to understand that my body was an ecology, I realized that so should my stories represent textured, relational, sometimes ruptured ecosystems. We are not kept alive by single species or single stories. We are authored and breathed into being by polyphonic, multi-voiced, interspecies epics.

Although I was writing my novel from the perspective of the Magdalene, I used her as a portal out of human narratives. The Gospels were written by people who lived far away from the ecology of Galilee and Judea. It was important to bring back to life the rivers, deserts, gardens, and caves that had held and grown these culture-shaping mythologies. I traveled through the Magdalene's eyes into the complex ecology of Second Temple period Palestine: crows, foxes, fleas, barley, grapevines, spice merchants, Roman centurions, daylilies, sheep, goats, leopards, vultures, pregnant women, sex workers, desperate invalids, and crop-destroying weeds. A character might look singular, but you could write them as a Trojan horse for an entire world—human and more-than-human.

It wasn't my obtuse poetry about existentialism that saved me. It wasn't my academic prose about ecofeminism and language poetry. It was the story that had caused all my academic mentors to grimace when I mentioned it in passing. It was the story my creative peers would think was overly earnest. Unfashionable. It was not the kind of project that would fly at the prestigious MFA programs I had considered attending before my health declined.

When I was asked by my old high school to mentor a group of teen female writers, I knew that I had to be straight with them. I had to show them that writing was a high-stakes activity that didn't just live on the page. Stories were atmospheric and encompassing. There were stories that infused our life like air: invisible until we realized we lived inside of them and thrived or died according to their limitations.

Patriarchy and heteronormativity and capitalism and human supremacy are stories. And they were originally authored by someone with a very specific bias. *It is within these imperceptible yet encompassing narrative structures that we often find ourselves stuck like flies in a spider's web.* The only way out is to unweave and weave as desperately as possible until you, too, become the spider, responsible for sewing together alternative webs of complex connection.

The girls arrived flush with that strange blend of adolescent vitality and the first glimmers of patriarchal self-castigation. They still had those unbridled cackles of preteen girls at a sleepover, exchanging fantasies and wildly inaccurate theories about sex. But they were just on the cusp of internalizing the sexism of the culture. There were moments when I spotted their anguished self-consciousness and recognized a younger version of myself. A girl would reach for her third chocolate chip cookie and then scan all the other girls' plates, doing a quick comparison. Was she too much? Had the other girls eaten as much? Should she limit herself?

After a few sessions, they warmed up enough to share more about their experiences as teens in high school, hesitantly confessing their fear of sexual harassment, body dysmorphia, constant shame, and climate anxiety. Woefully little had changed in the seven years since I'd graduated high school. This was the same fall that Christine Blasey Ford was forced to take a stand to relive her sexual trauma in front of a disbelieving and abusive American public. These girls had all already experienced some degree of sexual violation. They regularly experienced verbal harassment. School administrators labeled them troublemakers and policed their clothing while allowing boys to show up to school wearing practically anything, including T-shirts emblazoned with sexually offensive images. These young girls had already been encouraged by trusted adults in positions of authority to dim their brilliance and trim their dreams. They were already skittish. And rightfully so.

I couldn't lie to them and tell them the world was safe.

But I could give them the same lifeline that had helped me.

"Don't write a story you think will be hip. Write the story that will save your life. If it saves yours, it will probably save someone else's," I explained one autumn afternoon, the sky smoking purple with twilight in the big windows that framed the girls as they sat at my dining room table.

I was thinking of one of my favorite childhood stories: One Thousand and One Nights, or as it was known originally in Arabic, *Alf laylah wa-laylah*. In the frame narrative that acts like a soil foundation for all the other stories-species that weave the epic collection together, we meet King Shahryar. King Shahryar weds thousands of virgins, killing them off one by one after a single night of matrimony. Predictably, the king exhausts his kingdom's supply of virgins and is forced to select his vizier's own daughter, Scheherazade. Scheherazade is described as canny and well-educated. But that does her position a slight disservice. She is in a radical state of emergency. This is not a whimsical night of storytelling for her. This is an adrenaline-fueled, panicked, extraordinary act of self-preservation. One Thousand and One Nights is not a hundred-page novella a graduate student wrote about being young and single in New York City. It is a shiver of air between her neck and the guillotine. It is storytelling as emergency.

And Scheherazade succeeds, somehow, story by story, to save not only her life, but the potential lives of thousands of other virgins, as she reforms the king's psychopathic nature.

For a long time, I read this story from a strictly feminist perspective.

It was a perfect metaphor for the narrative backflips women must perform daily to stay alive. *How do I deescalate a violent man following me home? How do I calm down an abusive lover? What stories do I tell myself to keep myself alive? How do I convince myself that this hardship and this violence will somehow end? How do I force a doctor to hear my story so that I receive the right treatment in the ER? How do I write myself into the story so other people believe that my worlds, my fantasies, and my desires matter?*

But that fall, reading climate reports and prickling with bodily unease as the summer heat pushed well into autumn, I found my initial interpretation of Scheherazade widening.

I became less concerned with the gendered reading of Scheherazade, although it was still compelling. In her story, I was reminded of one of my favorite mythical figures I had studied in college: the boy Merlin. Like Scheherazade, Merlin was faced with a bad story. A murderous story. About to be executed by the warlord Vortigern to fulfill a prophecy about a fatherless child, the young Merlin breaks out into a sort of mantic storytelling, producing the whole history of English kings. His poetic explosion saves his own life and authors the history of a nation. Merlin makes me wonder: How do you distract your executioner? How do you deescalate certain violence? How do you stop a narrative that will destroy you? And Merlin answers that you survive by offering another narrative. In fact, you don't just offer one narrative, you offer a multiplicity of stories. A history of animals and battles and kings. Scheherazade chimes in and agrees. She says you offer a thousand and one of them.

"We are not the only beings trying to save ourselves with stories. We've just forgotten that there are stories that use an ecological syntax rather than a human tongue," I suggested to the girls that eerily hot late autumn day. Outside, the geese that often gathered on the river's edge had not yet migrated. There had been no hard frost, and rot still cooked the ground with as much juicy vigor as was usually reserved for the humid days of late July. I wondered if the bears would know when to head up into the mountains to hibernate.

I offered the girls an ecological reading of Scheherazade. One in which Scheherazade was not a young virgin, but the very Earth itself—that intertangled plenum of nested environments all collaborating to create the dynamic homeostasis of the biosphere.

We have put our ecosystems—our dirt and our animal, insect, vegetal, fungal kin—in a state of emergency. Like King Shahryar, we have incorrectly assumed that resources are unlimited. We will never run out of virgins to slaughter: virgin forests, virgin land, even the virgin cosmos. We foolishly believe that we will never run out of fertile soil, medicinal plants, old-growth trees, and biodiversity. But our narrative is terribly flawed.

What if the Earth's biosphere was Scheherazade, looking at her threatened well-being and beginning an elaborate, life-saving storytelling event? I have begun to view the increasingly unpredictable behavior of climate systems as a mode of storytelling—storytelling that happens on a scale, both temporal and spatial, that does not subscribe to anthropocentric paradigms. This is storytelling that uses forest fires as verbs, melting glaciers as protagonists, and rising temperatures as narrative propulsion.

We are entering into an ecological One Thousand and One Nights of climate change. We are entering into a series of stories that are desperately trying to save their teller: the Earth, Gaia, the biosphere, the Great Mother, whatever word, for you, encompasses the sum total of spherical, gravity-bound life.

Will we, like King Shahryar, halt our violence and begin to listen to a new, nonhuman kind of story? Will we let these stories change us and reform us? Ultimately, it matters not whether we do or do not. This series of stories will not depend on a human scribe. It will be written into the stone mantle of the Earth itself.

CHAPTER 9

Thank You, Black Mold

"IF THE DEFILING MOLD REAPPEARS IN THE HOUSE AFTER THE STONES have been torn out and the house scraped and plastered, the priest is to go and examine it and, if the mold has spread in the house, it is a persistent defiling mold; the house is unclean. It must be torn down—its stones, timbers and all the plaster—and taken out of the town to an unclean place," instructs the Book of Leviticus, documenting the first recorded mention of black mold. In 532 BCE, when Leviticus was committed to writing, fear of house mold was so acute that one stone with mold was cause for serious alarm, deep cleaning, and a quarantine of the house, while two stones called for the demolition of the whole structure.

Black mold, *Stachybotrys chartarum*, is a relatively fragile microfungus composed of filamentous cells that produce spores in slimy heads. It grows slowly and it does not compete well with other fungi. You won't find black mold overtaking a forest or blooming outdoors. Like shame, it flourishes in secrecy and seclusion, in cellulose, in grain, in animal feed, and in moist, dark conditions protected from airflow and other competitive spores. More simply, black mold is parasitic with agricultural settings and modern buildings.

First officially identified by Czech mycologist August Carl Joseph Corda when he found it in a house in Prague, black mold wasn't given much attention until the 1930s, when farm animals and human farmhands began to fall extremely ill and die in eastern Europe after coming in contact with contaminated grain and hay. Russian scientists confirmed that it was the spectral toxin of Leviticus that had caused the serious illness in both the animals and humans. Black mold attracted attention once again after the 1970s, when modern buildings began to incorporate cheap building materials and airtight designs. The lack of competitive spores, sunlight, and air circulation, alongside a proliferation of cheap cellulose building materials, created the ideal conditions for black mold's appetites. People in water-damaged apartment buildings died from respiratory failure and autoimmune disease and were described as having "sick building syndrome." It is now estimated that mold digests and destroys more buildings per year than termites and fire combined. And it is almost impossible to calculate how many deaths and illnesses are due to mold exposure, given the wide range of symptoms it can produce.

In my second summer living with Jason, when heat and rainfall records were being broken in the Hudson Valley, I had my first intimate encounter with black mold—with its ashen taste and its celebratory sporulation in rain-plush air. Slowly, I grew to recognize its particular scent. I clocked its presence through somatic translation: redness in my cheeks, rashes on the soles of my feet, a waterlogged narrowing of my bronchial tubes.

When we'd moved into the old carriage house I'd been love-blind, enchanted by the idea of living with a partner. But over a year into cohabitation, something was mildewing in the cellar, both practically and metaphorically.

The house had a secret basement and so did I. I could feel something coiling, readying for release, just below my consciousness. Often, I would start awake at the wolf hour, a fulvous puddle of moonlight on the blanket above my legs, Jason snoring contentedly beside me. I was filled with the agitated sense that I had forgotten something crucial. Something as important as my own name. Or the existence of an early childhood pet. Not only that, but my relationship with Jason, superficially sunlit and perfect, was flooding below the floorboards.

It started with jealousy. As someone who had struggled with self-worth issues, I was initially flattered by Jason's possessiveness. Someone wanted me all to himself. He was even miffed when I went out with friends and stayed out too late. But he was practically livid if I hung out with my male companions. If he caught me texting a man he viewed as competition, he would give me the cold shoulder for a week, turning from me in bed, pretending not to hear me speak to him. Once, after I caught a ride to a gallery opening with a local artist, he stole my phone and blocked this man's number. I often laughed nervously and tried to explain that if he was so worried about my male friends, he should be equally worried about female friends. I'd dated both men and women in the past. But he was blinkered by his heteronormative programming, only seeing other men as real competition.

"Your relationship is so charmed," my friend Seraphina noted when she came to visit, as Jason brought us espresso out on the porch that faced the mountain. "You really got what you wanted."

I nodded while swallowing, sensing something bucking below me, below the performance of well-being.

I had felt love-starved for so long, and Jason was careful to play the part of doting and caring partner publicly. He was handsome and stylish, taking pains to buy the right workwear outfits that gave him the appearance of a broad-shouldered woodworker. Behind the scenes he refused to do most manual labor, preferring the accessories to the actual activities. Our house was littered with abandoned projects: archery targets and fly-fishing rods. But he looked good on my arm at events. His Midwestern manners and charm won over my family and friends. His performance was so convincing that even I doubted the behavior that happened in the car leaving parties, the yelling and chastisement that happened behind closed doors. I ignored it when suddenly I was paying all the bills and negotiating the complexities of our shared life and household alone. He felt deeply attached to the idea that he was my "protector" and "caretaker," and anything I did to suggest that the power dynamic might flow in the opposite direction sent him into a weeklong rage. I felt sure that his jealousy and anger were somehow *my fault*. I just had to get better at understanding his quirks, understanding how to be a good partner. I was walking on eggshells, suddenly keeping my jaw clenched with anxiety morning and night.

Jason was a puzzle. He was fixable. I was loyal, and with just a little teamwork and therapy we could grow into the happiness that we projected onto social media and within our community.

Black mold is a product of darkness and isolation. Emotional abuse, too, thrives in isolated settings. The simple fact was that our idyllic carriage house was located deep in the mountains, out of service, and a thirty-minute drive from family and community. Our relationship was closed off from the fresh air and sunshine of friendly scrutiny. Sensing something raw and unresolved in my childhood beginning to wake up, I was flooded with ambient shame. Shame that couldn't find its source. I felt sure that the relationship was bad because I wasn't working hard enough. Something nasty started to bloom.

That summer the rain fell, first as clean sheets from muscular clouds. Then the rain no longer fell. Instead, it seemed to burst from the air itself like a thin sheen of sweat that coated everything. No matter how hard we ran our ancient air conditioner, everything was always moist and scummy.

I was in the last stretches of finishing my Magdalene novel while trying to juggle all my ghostwriting gigs. Work became my escape from Jason's unpredictable explosions and antagonistic moods. I reasoned that our isolation was a good thing for my work. Isn't solitude what writers long for? A little cabin in the woods? And yet I craved clamor and community. I'd seek refuge in coffee shops, writing for hours, enjoying how the hubbub acted like a noisy embrace. I often sought noise during that period of frigid silent treatments and hissed criticisms. I loved working while a mother rocked her child on her lap next to me, trying unsuccessfully to keep the babe's wailing quieted while she sipped a frothy cappuccino. Life slipped from my world into my book, inspiring quirks and traits in my characters I would never have arrived at in solitude.

While I worked harder, Jason worked less, relying on his parents' wealth to develop pet art projects he quickly abandoned. But he demanded that we keep up the ruse that he was somehow the more financially responsible one. He was older. His parents understood money, unlike mine.

This fiction was flimsy given that my own parents, feeling bad for Jason, started to hire him for small web design projects. He stormed and raged about this, refusing to see the kindness of this charity from my family, who were trying to welcome him into the fold and support his art. I remember one evening, sitting at our dining room table, I confided to Jason about how I desperately wanted to find a way to spend less time ghostwriting while finishing my own novel. Was there other less creatively draining work I could do on the side? A lover of thrifting, I'd been selling vintage clothing to make ends meet. Maybe that was an option. Writing other people's books to support my own writing was leaving me too burnt out to complete my own novel.

Jason bristled, his nose twitching as it did when he was about to fly into a rage. "Don't expect me to support you. I support you enough already."

I felt like vomiting. I felt ashamed, like a little child who has done something wrong. I was too needy. Too much.

But how did he support me? What did he even mean?

It took me a day to remember that he owed me thousands of dollars in back bills.

In the years we lived together he only accompanied me to one doctor's appointment, ever. And yet I felt sure he was right that I was somehow the needy one. I didn't give him enough back. I didn't take enough care of *him*. I was clearly deficient.

On the days he commuted into the city for work, he expected a hot dinner waiting for him when he arrived home. Even if I had been working all day. And I better not be out with friends, leaving him an empty home. This wasn't explicitly demanded. Instead, I learned by trial and error. When he arrived home and there was no dinner, he would rage, complain he was too exhausted to cook, and dissect something I'd said at a party a week before that he had been sucking on like a poisoned cough drop. If dinner was waiting, he was less likely to berate me. And yet, his resentment that he wasn't more successful and more respected was a constant sore spot. He would stay up seething on our front porch, smoking pot, and then explode at me for judging him.

"I'm not judging you. I'm too tired to care," I pleaded one night, pulling a pillow over my head. "I just want to sleep."

In retrospect, I see there were signs well before the summer of mold. I have a belief that places attract us like magnets and then expertly repel us when our time with them is complete. But we are so limited in what we consider communication to be that we often ignore these increasingly loud signals.

The landscape I loved so much at first blush sent me subtle warnings. In winter we lost power for weeks at a time during blizzards. In the spring the phlox pollen was pernicious, with flaxen drafts billowing out from the sentinel pines that blocked the house from the sun. Still, I wrote and ignored the warning bells that I needed to wake up to my situation: both ecological and interpersonal. Something was stagnating.

By midsummer, the air plush with humidity, the mushrooms arrived. As a mycophile I was initially delighted, throwing on my rain boots and trudging out into the puddles. Violet coral fungi erupted like flames in our makeshift kitchen garden. Honey fungi gilded the mountain trails. Russulas as dusky red as autumn apples pushed through the fabric of fallen leaves. There were varieties I had never seen before. Fairy rings seemed to halo my every footstep. I could ignore the thick, gray cloud of conflict and pain that lived within the house if I just went on another walk, another run, another hike.

But then the fungi were no longer just outside.

They were inside the house.

I noticed the black mold a month before Jason did, and the initial lag in our symptoms led to some of the arguments that would seed the end of our relationship.

"Do you smell that? Do you feel that?" I would ask, and he would criticize me again for being sensitive, for being crazy.

"Do you understand how stressful it is for me that you are sick? Do you understand how much pain it causes me?" Somehow, he always emerged as the main character of my illness. When we had first gotten together, I let him know in sober detail what my health challenges were like on a day-to-day basis. I told him it was fine if this was too much for him, and he could tell me.

"Don't do that. Of course I'm ready. I'll never leave you. I don't care that you're sick," he'd promised gallantly.

But the reality was different. He viewed any sign of illness as some kind of manipulative attempt to make him feel bad or take attention away from his needs and desires. I was somehow conspiring to make his life difficult. He treated my every allergy like a character fault. And then, paradoxically, when I quickly learned to hide physical infirmity from him, he would berate me for withholding information about my health.

That summer, I was hesitant to bring up the mold, trying to deal with it before involving Jason. Growing up in the rainy Hudson Valley, I was familiar with mildew and late-summer must. I cleaned the house from top to bottom with tea tree oil and even bleach. I opened the windows to what little sun made it through the dense weave of pines. I lit candles. I scrubbed the floorboards. Still, my body registered that another being had moved into our home. A being that was immune to my purification rituals.

I would wake up at night and taste it: cinder bitter and yet bumptiously, chaotically alive. I thought of the dust bunnies in my favorite movie, *Totoro*: charcoal black stars streaming up from the ancient cellar our landlord refused to let us open or use. A cellar flooded with a summer's worth of standing water we found out much too late. Finally, Jason felt it too: a constant, low-level flu that refused to clear up. A send-away test confirmed what I had known for months—the house had a third tenant, black mold.

By then it was too late.

The mold had eaten everything. My clothes. My art supplies and years of accumulated collage materials. My old Victorian garments, inherited from my costume designer grandmother. It had eaten my library of hundreds of books, which I had unknowingly positioned right over the ancient cellar that was sending up spores. It had eaten the pieces of artwork Jason had painted for me at the start of our relationship.

Even my plants seemed to be negatively impacted. They drooped, waxen and yellow. The fungi I loved so much had arrived in a much more intimate way than I had initially planned. They were in my bedroom. My bathroom. My lungs. They had inoculated my very body.

It would be inaccurate to say we moved. We were forced to evacuate.

In a whirlwind week, I threw away 90 percent of my belongings. Years prior to the pandemic, we found ourselves wearing masks and gloves. Predictably, I was the person who facilitated the move and found us a light-filled, clean apartment in the small riverside neighborhood of Kingston.

As we unpacked, Jason and I argued and squabbled over whether some item was contaminated. We could still smell it. The mold had followed us, lacing our temples into pressurized migraines. Into the trash went the last material possessions we had jointly shared: art books, an espresso machine, a quilt we had saved from an estate sale. We were left with an apartment so denuded of personal artifacts that it barely existed. But during the precious hours when

I found myself alone in my new home, I lay down in a lemon splash of sunlight on the clean hardwood floor and gave thanks. I didn't understand what had happened, but I had a deep sense of having been saved.

It would take another year for Jason and me to finally break up. But by then I realized with grateful surprise that the hardest job of a breakup had already been catalyzed by the mold. When our relationship finally ended, well past its expiration date, I had already thrown away most of the objects and books and art that represented our shared existence.

It is only now, retrospectively, that I can identify my guardian angel not as an abstraction, but as a capricious and tricky being. Black mold. The sunlight, the constant lymphatic pulse of the nearby river, and the fertile community of friends around my new home highlighted what the dark mountain carriage house had cloaked: my relationship was unhealthy. The mold had come in and eaten away the real rot: the shared possessions and compromises that had kept me tied to something that was bad for me.

Black mold is not a forest being. It is a consequence of sedentary communities and of agriculture.

It is fitting that it shows up in one of the first important written texts, the Old Testament. Black mold seems, to me, a consequence of writing itself. It highlights the issue with ideas and stories that are expected to stay the same and stay still. Stable houses and stories sometimes have secrets below the floorboards. The foundations that look strong are secretly liquid with rot. A text or story that doesn't adapt and change to shifting circumstances is a lot like a dark house. Humans, for many more thousands of years than they have lived in sedentary communities, were nomadic, following herds of animals and shifting climates. And their stories were orally transmitted organisms—flexible, adaptable, and evolving. Our homes and our stories used to move with us, on our backs, in our relationships. Of course, black mold blooms in the stagnant world of alphabetical texts. Civilization stays still: textually and physically. When nothing moves, when nothing gets sunlight, the stale conditions invite mold.

The time in which my novel was set was still dominated by oral culture. Stories and scripture were embodied and adapted to changing circumstances. The Gospels lapse into dogma when they are removed from boats of embodied breath and pinned flat to a page. They no longer continue to evolve or respond creatively to critique. As I grappled with these questions in my novel, I grappled with them in my real life.

Confined as we are by our anthropocentric stories, it is easy to demonize mold. It eats our homes. It beleaguers our bodies. But, for a moment, let us decenter the human perspective. What if mold is telling a more interesting story than one of simple harm. What if it is teaching us something vital? Something lifesaving.

Mold told me to move. Mold forced me to move the lymph in my body to clear it of sticky spores. It pushed me out of the darkness of a bad relationship. It helped me move out of an attachment to physical belongings. Mold showed me how to dance into sunlight. In an age of increasingly unpredictable climate events and social unrest, we will need to get agile. We need to get better at movement, learning to be light on our feet. We need to learn how to drop everything and run. Black mold is a fungal wake-up call to the unsustainability of our lifestyles: agricultural and sedentary.

It was little surprise when, a year later, film developed from the time when I was living with black mold yielded a glittering anomaly. There were silver freckles across every photograph taken in the old farmhouse. I knew at once they were my savior spores. Thank you, mold, for saving me. Thank you for showing me where to go.

CHAPTER 10

The Scream

THE SCREAMING WOKE ME AT THE WOLF HOUR. STILL DREAM-ADDLED,
I was convinced someone was being murdered. It wasn't until I'd rushed to the
window that I could distinguish the obscenities peppered into the woman's
raw howling, cycling up the street parallel to our new riverside apartment like
a human siren.

It was not the scream of someone dying or wounded. It was a scream of
rage. A scream of absolute madness.

I hovered at the window for a long time listening to her, clutching the curtains like they were a thin skin protecting my fleshly uncertainty from the certain anger that lay just a breath's distance away.

Jason was staying overnight in the city between jobs. I was alone in our
new apartment, and I knew that going down to offer help in the middle of the
night was out of the question. Calling the police on a woman in the middle of a
psychotic episode was also a terrible option. They were more likely to hurt or
imprison the woman than they were to aid her.

Instead, I knew that I could quietly and invisibly bear witness to what can
only be described as chthonic rage so unhinged from sense that I could hardly
imagine it being expressed through the fragile tissue of a human body without
destroying its instrument.

I squinted through my curtains, trying to make her out, but could see nothing through threads of icy rain, thrown slanted against my window. No one was
visible. And yet, the air glistered wet and raw, flayed by her rage.

I recognized that scream. I recognized it because I had been contracting around that same scream, struggling to subdue it with my entire physicality since I was a child. That scream kept me from a good night's sleep as I lay terrified by the thought that relaxing too much would allow it to erupt from my sleep-slackened maw. I'd always had a deep, unnamed sense that if I traced the sonic waves of that repressed scream backward, I'd arrive at an original horror that no scream could ever address or convey.

When we moved from the isolation of the Catskill Mountains to our riverside apartment, I relaxed into the safety of sunlight and cleanliness, with friends down the street and a bustling community. I scrubbed the wooden floorboards with the scent of lemon verbena and mint. I kept the windows open to the faintly briny scent of the river as it moved the lymph of the land, pushing water through hurt, diluting pesticide-heavy rainwater with its serpentine insistence. The Rondout was kinetic, always in movement. Unlike the dark stagnation of our Mount Tremper carriage house, here nothing stayed still long enough to rot. Bald eagles and swallows and seagulls circled our second-floor apartment as if weaving a crown of feathers around our life. When it rained, the water pulled the soot and dust and pollen from the streets downward into the pulsing vein of Rondout Creek. Surrounded by friends, by birds, by sinewy locust trees and sentinel sycamores, my body stopped clenching against an unsafe home and an unsafe partner. I finally started *feeling*.

And what I was feeling was surprising: the intense urge to vomit.

As someone plagued with indigestion and chronic nausea, I registered this urge as something that diverged from my normal symptoms. It didn't accompany eating or dietary changes. It didn't resolve with actual vomiting. Instead, this desire to vomit emerged alongside an emotion so opaque and visceral that it only ever rippled the surface of my conscious mind as the faintest wave. Just as the black mold had emerged from under the floorboards of our previous home, so did this strange somatic communication begin to wake up in the deepest crawl spaces of my mind.

It took me a long time to name the urge. I'd felt it before, many years ago. It had emerged occasionally during certain sexual encounters with past partners. I'd always known subconsciously that sex was a complicated place for me. I knew I had been taken there too early. I knew as an adolescent, although I couldn't articulate why, that I'd never be a "virgin." There was nothing to lose. It had already been lost. Sometimes, experimenting with a boy in a dark basement while his parents were out, I'd feel a wave of nausea and then find that I'd blacked out, totally absent for the whole experience. Or my entire body would go numb as if anesthetized. No sensations registered.

I recognized that feeling from doctor's appointments when my body was examined and handled in certain ways. It cropped up in odd moments: entering basements and rooms without windows. It was only when I traced the feeling back to early childhood that the waves grew larger, more definitive, in the ocean of my waking mind. The desire to vomit was not so much a physical symptom as it was an emotion. The emotion was something like disgust. Or shame. Shame so viscous and bitter that it made me want to expel my own internal organs.

As I settled into our new apartment and found my new routines, my new coffee shop for writing, my morning walking route down by the docks, I turned over this somatic emotion like a riddle. Where did this shame originate? And why was it so intimately stitched to my body that it could contort me into actual episodes of illness?

Through some strange luck, the first book I unpacked after the move was one that my friend had encouraged me to read for some time. "It's about the connection between trauma and illness. I think you might find it really interesting."

At the time, I was hosting storytelling dinner events for local Hudson Valley women and was overwhelmed by the hidden reserves of violence, trauma, and abuse they kept hidden beneath carefully polished exteriors. These were women who were also struggling with chronic illness, autoimmunity, and a host of other physical complaints. We would all bemoan the fact that while we spent our hard-earned paychecks and precious free hours on therapy, trying to heal our wounds and relational patterns, our boyfriends and spouses rarely ever invested in self-investigation. We talked about many subjects over soup and wine and candlelight—rape, sexism, medical gaslighting, endometriosis, nonmonogamy. But the one topic that kept coming up was post-traumatic stress disorder (PTSD) and somatics.

Somatics is an alternative therapeutic practice that highlights the entangle-ment of the body with the psyche. There are many different modalities—all of which derive from healing practices that have been developed and maintained outside of the dominant Europatriarchal paradigm for thousands of years—but the central tenet is that the body holds the key to our emotional and psychologi-cal well-being. Vice versa, the body holds on to traumatic events in ways that talk therapy does not readily address. While many of my relatives work in psychology and I'd been in and out of therapy since the age of eleven, the idea that the body was involved in the architecture of the psyche was new to me.

Still, when my friend handed me Bessel van der Kolk's now famous *The Body Keeps the Score*, I felt my spine prickle with nervous electricity. I put off reading the book until we moved. Until we escaped the black mold. Until winter blizzards fleeced the world with snow so soft, so thick, it could cushion all my stumbles and sharp edges, dampening the years of repressed screams ready to burst out of me.

At a school event for the girls I was mentoring in creative writing, there was a moment of silence. For a shooting. A war? I can't even remember. But I do remember wondering, as the strange shame-nausea rose in my throat, if silence was really the best way to honor this nightmare? Thousands of years of patriarchy suppressing the voices of women? Thousands of years of colo-nialism suppressing the scripture and embodied wisdom of other religions? Empires cutting the vocal cords of entire cultures? Was this nightmare of our ecocidal culture—silencing hundreds of species a day, whole forests, whole symphonies of birdsong—really best addressed with more silence?

Silence was making me sick.

It was sedimented deep in my cellars, making my body as toxic as the Mount Tremper house had been.

I held off on screaming and decided to read *The Body Keeps the Score* instead. My body was definitely keeping some type of score, but the question that kept me up at night was: Score of what? What happened? What am I refusing to look at?

Of course, I already knew deep in my cells, well below my intellect. My roil-ing stomach and clenched jaw knew. My hips knew. My shaky nervous system knew. I just wasn't ready to know it in my waking mind. Knowing it had almost destroyed me as a child, and I had a blurred memory—aqueous, as if closer to a dream—of going out on our front porch one starry midsummer night, age ten, and praying to the cosmos.

"Make me forget this ever happened so I can be normal. Erase it. Make it go away. It didn't really happen. I don't want to be broken. I don't want anyone to know this happened. Not even me."

The mind is a powerful thing. I pressed down memories too hot, too terrible, for me to carry into adolescence. And while this act of repression gave me the ability to perform normalcy, the unexpressed screams, the pressurized violence, decided that if I denied it my voice, it would use my body to communicate instead.

Reading *The Body Keeps the Score* was like repeatedly being awakened by a bucket of cold water dumped over my head. Only from a distance of years can I now wonder why a book about trauma needed to, itself, be so traumatizing? Horrific abuse and brutality are recounted in each chapter, alongside many physical and psychological ailments that result from these early violations. Van der Kolk explains how the Adverse Childhood Experiences (ACE) Study showed that those with a higher score of neglect, abuse, and trauma were much more likely to develop disease and mental disorders. He writes, "Being traumatized means continuing to organize your life as if the trauma were still going on—unchanged and immutable—as every new encounter or event is contaminated by the past. . . ." And adds:

> After trauma the world is experienced with a different nervous system. The survivor's energy now becomes focused on suppressing inner chaos, at the expense of spontaneous involvement in their lives. These attempts to maintain control over unbearable physiological reactions can result in a whole range of physical symptoms, including fibromyalgia, chronic fatigue, and other autoimmune diseases. This explains why it is critical for trauma treatment to engage the entire organism, body, mind, and brain.

A 2019 study published in the *Journal of Rheumatology* showed that in a sample of sixty-seven thousand women, those with the highest incidence of childhood abuse were at a threefold greater risk of developing lupus than those who had not experienced abuse. Survivors are also at an increased risk of developing serious autoimmune illness, chemical sensitivity, and allergy disorders. The correlations between early abuse and illness, disability, and neurodivergence are too vast to list. As I read *The Body Keeps the Score* and researched the connection between illness and early trauma, it seemed increasingly clear that early childhood abuse registered not only emotionally but physically, taking a toll on our bodies as much as it did on our minds.

I remember sitting on the floor in my living room, just before Valentine's Day, feeling like my heart was about to enter my mouth. I desperately wanted to heal my physical body. And I had believed strongly that medicines, body-work, doctors, herbs, and nutrition were the key. But what if healing involved something much more terrifying than a new drug? What if it meant traveling under my own floorboards and exploring the darkest recesses of my mind?

I'd always found it curious that my genetic connective tissue disease manifested in me and not my brother. My brother was a tall, broad-shouldered, record-breaking competitive swimmer turned farmer. His tanned, brawny vitality was an extreme contrast to my physical fragility.

Why me and not him? I wondered.

But the answer had been there all along: a horrific, alternative timeline haunting my waking reality, infusing my nervous system with adrenaline and cortisol. Memories of violence that, once I denied them real estate in my mind, took up residence in my immune system, my kidneys, and my spine, exhausting my body to the point of serious illness.

My brother had been born a week before we moved upstate from the city and was raised in the safe confines of a wildflower-constellated backyard, surrounded by cats and dogs and trees and maternal mountains. I, on the other hand, had spent my first three years in the frenetic chaos of the city. I was shocked that this time came up relatively blank when I tried to access it. Yes, I had memories, but when I started to examine them more closely, they revealed themselves to be fake storefronts for a movie set, flimsy façades built from stories my parents had recounted. What were they covering up? What had happened?

"I want to heal. If that means remembering what is hidden, then I'm ready. What am I hiding from myself?" I whispered to the snow pawing softly across the windowsill, the high ceilings licked by the blond tongue of light from a beeswax candle, the strong wooden floorboards of my safe, clean apartment. This space was solid enough to hold me.

The answer came as a deluge of hallucinatory memories so bright, so sensually textured and physically detailed, that I couldn't distinguish them from reality. My body was suddenly back inside the abuse. I was propelled through an embodied movie of events that, given that they started when I was pre-verbal, have none of the decoration or sense-making of language. Their violence is stark and uncreated, written into my body before I learned the words for love or cat or ocean. These brutal montages had no poetry, no plot. They were wilder and bigger than any moral framework I'd ever encountered.

I didn't need to vomit anymore. I needed to scream. I needed to break a silence that had a choke hold on my life force.

"If you say anything, we will kill you."

After the abuse, at three years old, I was shown videos of what would happen to me if I spoke up. I would be gruesomely murdered. My parents would be killed. I can still taste the salty clamp of a hand over my mouth. And although I was canny and smart, the threat settled deeper than sense-making and I found myself, year after year, unable to tell anyone.

It took me twenty-two years to break the curse, but on a dusky February night, I drove to my parents' home and told them what had happened. Suddenly, details and strange events all fell into place.

As a child I had been strangely mistrustful of adults. I often sought solace in other beings: salamanders and snapping turtles, my family's pet cats and dogs, moist fungi unlacing nutrients from a fallen log, nimble-footed garden spiders. I whispered what had "happened" into the silver-silken belly of the old cat Mustafa and knew he would not judge me. I spent hours roaming around the nearby woods, feeling myself held by a network of beings that would not lie to me, would not try to harm me. I was always bewildered when my parents' city friends who visited us would say, "Oh, aren't you scared of the bears? Do you protect yourself when you go out at night?"

Bears? I would scoff, thinking of the muscular shadows, circling berry bushes, emptying out our hummingbird feeders with both paws like they were margaritas. Animals were not scary. *It was the humans that were terrifying.*

Irrational fears I'd had as a young child suddenly made sense. My parents wept. I wept. But there was a sense that, even more so than when I'd received my diagnosis of Ehlers-Danlos syndrome, I'd finally reached the end of the diagnostic road.

I had finally figured out why I was sick. It was the secret seed of the abuse, kept silent until it became a somatic scream.

And, according to *The Body Keeps the Score*, there were plenty of new therapies that helped with PTSD. The body was the doorway to these psychological-somatic knots that talk therapy could not properly untangle. There were ways to integrate these violent memories—to approach them bodily and say, "That's it. You're done. I'm ready to claim wholeness and health. I'm ready to feel safe."

Growing up, I would often wake myself in the middle of the night, mid-scream. According to the numerous family members and friends who were scared witless by this behavior over the years, these were bloodcurdling banshee cries. As I grew older, the screaming bouts decreased in frequency. But it wasn't until that winter, after confronting my parents, that I pulled over on the side of the highway and realized, "It's time to start screaming. If I don't let this out, it's going to kill me." Memories, molten with violence, burst the dam, and, the car muffled by snowflakes, I screamed as I remembered with perfect clarity what had been done to me as a child. I screamed louder when I realized it had taken me this long to realize I had to speak up. After that long-awaited release, I no longer screamed in my sleep.

I screamed out loud. I screamed in waking life, and I screamed on purpose.

Screaming is a way of letting grief and anger move. In somatics, it is understood that shaking and crying and screaming after traumatic events reduces the likelihood of post-traumatic symptoms. The violence doesn't get stuck inside the body. Screaming is also an ode: an acknowledgment of love so raw and powerful it explodes syntax; it cannot be contained by a single word.

In Ireland, sean-nós singing, or keening, is a traditional practice at funerals. While keening draws on melody motifs and Gaelic refrains, it is characterized by spontaneous eruption and "raw unearthly emotion." But the English colonial presence in Ireland worked to stamp out a custom that was deemed pagan and savage. It worked hard to repress the grief of a people it was traumatizing. By the 1950s, keening was in decline. It is no surprise that the English wanted to stop the keening. In thinking about it, I'm reminded of the practice in vivisection and animal experimentation of cutting the animal's vocal cords. The worst violence never makes a noise. It is the mute vacuum created by the conscious erasure of another being's agony.

In fact, we could think of silence as being a signature of human violence. Sound ecologist Bernie Krause reports that every year, while visiting his favorite Sugarloaf Ridge State Park, he finds less noise: less birdsong, less tree-leaf susurrus, less murmuring streams. Industrial extractive agendas cut the vocal cords not just of Indigenous populations and lab animals, but also of entire biophonic ecosystems.

As I made appointments with somatic practitioners and trauma therapists, I listened to an old recording of Irish keening and felt it strike the tuning fork of a memory. Three years before I unearthed my trauma, my gray cat, Sebastian, was hit by a speeding car that then raced off, leaving him to bleed out in my arms. All I could do was scream. And scream. There was no other possible response. It should come as little surprise, then, that for days after, Sebastian's litter sister Rosamund circled the house screaming, looking for her lost brother. It was not a yowl or a meow. It was a sound beyond feline vocalization. I thought she might die from it.

Sociologist John Holloway formulates the scream as the "rejection of a world that we feel to be wrong, negation of a world we feel to be negative." The scream is more than just grief and anger. It is the alchemy of the two into dynamic protest. Holloway writes:

> **In the beginning is the scream. We scream. When we write or when we read, it is easy to forget that the beginning is not the word, but the scream. Faced with the mutilation of human lives by capitalism, a**

scream of sadness, a scream of horror, a scream of anger, a scream of refusal: NO. The starting point of theoretical reflection is opposition, negativity, struggle. It is from rage that thought is born, not from the pose of reason, not from the reasoned-sitting-back-and-reflecting-on-the-mysteries-of-existence that is the conventional image of 'the thinker.' We start from negation, from dissonance. The dissonance can take many shapes. An inarticulate mumble of discontent, tears of frustration, a scream of rage, a confident roar. An unease, a confusion, a longing, a critical vibration.

Holloway calls to my mind the Zapatismo call for "No" or "Ya Basta/Stop" in 1994. The hoarse cry of obstinance was formulated to open a space for "many yeses." A scream that protected an adjacent possible. A world yet to come.

I knew when I started my rewrite of the Magdalene's story that the book had to begin and end with a scream. I had to remind people that the story of Jesus/Yeshua is not the beatific hagiography of a good shepherd. It is the horrendous tragedy of a brilliant man slaughtered in the prime of his life by empire. The man who would have been called Yeshua in his native Aramaic was born into an ecosystem of screams, born between Roman general Varus's crucifixion of two thousand Jews in 4 BCE and the massacre of men, women, and children following the revolt of Judas the Galilean in 6 CE. Although Jesus told playful parables, his life did not end with a parable. It ended with a cry. And what is the crucifixion if not a scream so loud that it shreds time, a vocalized rupture that creates cloven epochs: before and after. "Father, father, why have thou forsaken me?" Jesus cries. Why have we denied him the brute anguish of this call? Why have we denied the despair and muffled the moans of the Madonnas at his feet? Yes, they are gilded, pressed in vellum, inked into twig-thin markings on mute pages. But what does it feel like for a mother to lose her son? A wife her husband? What happens to the screams we silence?

What happens to stories that have their volume turned down? I think, like the story of Jesus, they become easier to misinterpret and co-opt.

Upon moving to the Rondout, I grew interested in the history of the area. I knew that the Munsee Lenape had lived alongside the Hudson and Rondout

Creek. I also knew that early in the morning, down by the water, the spilled sunrise would froth like blood on the river. The air would grow dense and ashen in certain spots, causing me to wonder if I was running through invisible clouds of smoke. The seagulls' queries would drop an octave, turning mournful. I could feel something struggling to be expressed here, using storms and birds and even human bodies to give itself a voice. I wasn't surprised when I discovered that the Rondout in Kingston was where the Esopus Wars were fought in the seventeenth century by the Dutch against the Munsee Lenape people. While little information remains about the specific atrocities that occurred during the wars, we know there were hundreds of Indigenous casualties and that just upriver a contemporary Dutch captain, David Pieterszoon de Vries, is known to have said, "Infants were torn from their mother's breasts, and hacked to pieces in the presence of their parents, and pieces thrown into the fire and in the water, and other sucklings, being bound to small boards, were cut, stuck, and pierced, and miserably massacred in a manner to move a heart of stone. Some were thrown into the river, and when the fathers and mothers endeavored to save them, the soldiers would not let them come on land but made both parents and children drown . . ."

I think it is safe to infer that something similar happened in the Rondout. And when I think of that elided history, those screams ignored and repressed deep into the soma of the land, I am no longer surprised that woman felt the need to trace the all-but-erased agony written into the land with her howling.

Although by all cultural standards she was mad, her screaming seemed to me to be the sanest response of all. What does it mean to sit at the bottom of the cross? To bear witness to the colonial bloodstains in an ecosystem? How do we break the curse of our abusers, who imprinted our childhood brains with shame? I do not think there is an answer. There are no words big enough to hold this. I think sometimes the only thing left to do is scream. In the words of Ursula K. Le Guin: "That's what I want: to hear you erupting, You . . . who do not know the power in you."

That spring I committed myself to noise. To clamor. To movement. I needed to let years of repressed anger move through my body. I underlined a passage in *The Body Keeps the Score* and returned to it after ragged therapy sessions during which I shook so hard I thought I might have a heart attack:

> Beneath the surface of the protective parts of trauma survivors there exists an undamaged essence, a Self that is confident, curious, and calm, a Self that has been sheltered from destruction by the various protectors that have emerged in their efforts to ensure survival. Once those protectors trust that it is safe to separate, the Self will spontaneously emerge, and the parts can be enlisted in the healing process.

I was ready to break the silence that was breaking my body. There was a self that preceded my abuse and my illness. It could still be reached. By wailing and shaking and trembling. And maybe on the other side of that vocal wall—that shredded scream—there would be that original self. I felt the spark of potential healing and wholeness beyond my wildest expectations.

CHAPTER 11

Confessions of a Compost Heap: Make Me Good Soil

WHAT IS HEALING? HOW DO WE KNOW WHEN IT IS DONE? WHAT IS wholeness? What is purity? How much time does it take? How much energy and devotion? Most importantly, how much does it cost? Can I afford it?

Can we fail healing? If we cannot heal—if our illness is incurable or terminal—where do we go? What does it feel like to have a condition that resists diagnoses, treatment, and resolution? If the kingdom of the well permanently bars us entry, where does our story lead? What lands lie beyond that kingdom?

Those who are permanently exiled to the kingdom of the unwell are still expected to perform daily penitential rituals of "wellness," handing over money, time, and physical energy to a process that is closer to haunting than it is to healing. When the cut refuses to close, when the neurological glitch clicks into constancy, sometimes we pause and grow curious. We are not the only organisms that experience unresolvable agony. In fact, most ecosystems are currently contending with pollution and physical disruption. Most species find themselves stranded in a frayed web of symbiotic extinctions.

Resilient ecosystems depend on a healthy foundation of death and decay. Rot is a crucial part of nutrient cycling and soil regeneration. All bodies go back to their original mother: matter. The soul is both a womb and a tomb, gestating future bodies from the decomposing remains of other beings. This womb-tomb of mother-matter between our toes grows our food, our shade, our flowers, our perfume, our verdant countrysides. What if my illness was not a problem, but instead a profound bodily generosity that reminded me that at our most basic, material foundations, we are all just preparing to become food for other beings? When we relax our hold on the hero's journey of an individual life, we can see again that we are all the soil bed for something else to grow.

"And so from hour to hour we ripe and ripe, and then from hour to hour we rot and rot; and thereby hangs a tale," laments the melancholy Jaques in Shakespeare's comedy *As You Like It*, hinting at something the playwright understood intimately: disorder and decay are just as crucial to a narrative as order and fecundity. The story does not exist in a single pole of experience but is articulated between ripeness and rot. The tragic play flows from fertility into rot, while the comedy reverses the causality, sprouting ripeness from initial decay.

What does it mean to become soil? What does it mean to become edible? Are cleanliness and purity really the best stars to navigate by as we attempt to heal our bodies and psyches?

While researching Jesus for my novel, I was struck by how regularly a man mistranslated and neutered by empire who becomes the epitome of ascetical purity, repeatedly drawing his metaphors from "the dung heap." Jesus most often compares the kingdom to something culturally impure or blatantly revolutionary: leaven, Samaritans, ravens, women, weeds, thieves, children. Draw a fishing net through Jesus's metaphors, and we come back with more than fish. We come back with the real rejects of society, not the ones deemed attractive enough for the charity photo op.

The folk magician's real teaching was not purification. He ultimately even rejected his mentor John the Baptist's water immersions. In a moment when people were traumatized by Roman imperialism, diseased, and obsessed with purity rituals as a way of taking some small control of their lives, he offered something radical. His offering was to brush off the question of purity altogether. "Who cares? Come and eat with me. Come and share a meal." He purified not by cleaning, but by including everyone in communal healing, storytelling, and food-sharing. Everyone was invited. No one was exiled.

As I dove into the healing traditions that had informed the historical Galilean magician, I was always struck by the thought that these healings were not the antiseptic scrub of modern medicine. They were much more like a probiotic for an antibiotic-blitzed gut. It was more microbes, not less. More ideas. More food. More modalities. It was a messy process of addition, rather than a fine-tuned process of subtraction.

In the months following my realization that my illness and trauma were interconnected, I poured thousands of dollars into the modalities recommended by trauma specialists: EMDR (eye movement desensitization and reprocessing therapy) and a wide variety of somatic (body)–based therapies, mixed with more classic talk therapy. With this new litany of professionals added on top of the nutritionists, healers, and out-of-pocket specialists I was seeing for my genetic condition, my life had little space for anything besides healing and then working to afford those healing modalities. I had to work *more*, in fact. I found myself so exhausted and emotionally dysregulated by all the trauma therapy that whenever I got a free hour, I mostly spent it lying on the ground or staring blankly out the window.

After having managed serious migraines with diet changes, I was suddenly getting migraines again—curiously, after every therapy session. I was reassured that this was a normal stage of recovering and integrating violent memories. My friend who had recommended Mary, the trauma specialist I was paying an exorbitant amount of money to see weekly, nodded knowingly, confessing, "I would get back spasms and feel nauseated after sessions where we did EMDR about my childhood. And I even forgot how to operate my car one day."

"Do you feel better now?" I asked with trepidation.

"Oh. Well . . . I mean there is still a LOT to process," she responded gravely. "But Mary says I'm doing really well."

Mary loved to pull the focus from the positive sprouts in my soil back to the barren zones that refused to support life. She insisted we return to my most traumatic memories again and again until I could hardly remember all the beauty from my childhood—rehabilitating possums, camping on crystalline mountain lakes, baking complicated confectionaries alongside my kitchen witch mother.

I spent six months with one therapist who insisted we continue with EMDR even when I went into severe renal injury. We even discussed the possibility that my kidneys, responsible for removing toxins from my blood, were overwhelmed with the psychological toxins I was supposedly expelling and neutralizing.

Then my hands started to shake. My kidneys kept malfunctioning and my liver numbers jumped. My bodily proprioception—my body's ability to sense my own movement and actions—was off. I felt as if I couldn't properly orient myself in space. I was unsure of how big I was, how swiftly I was moving. I started to hit my head on open cabinet drawers and car doors.

And I was increasingly worried about money. Because all of this cost a lot of money. I was taking any odd job I could. I sold vintage denim online. I ghostwrote another author's social media. Often, I'd wake in the night to find I'd been clenching my jaw so hard that a wire of nerve pain was needling down into my throat and up into my temples.

"And Jesus took him aside from the crowd, by himself, and put His fingers in his ears, and after spitting, He touched his tongue with the saliva," the Gospel of Mark tells us. Apparently, a little spit, a little belief, a little embodied mess, was all it took to activate the immunological potential of Second Temple period invalids. As I wrote about these miraculous healings, I felt envious of the miracle mind that allowed for these spontaneous remissions. I often wished it was as easy for me. How could I activate my own placebo potential and begin to *heal*? Were there rituals or spiritual practices that could help me heal my "shadow"?

Alongside my expensive and time-consuming trauma therapy, to which I was devoted, I ate up spiritual and holistic healing podcasts, searching for some sort of foothold in the unyielding cliff face of illness and PTSD. Plenty of spiritual traditions have equated moral failing, sin, and violence to physical ailments. Surprisingly, new age revisions of sin and karma and manifestation fit well into the psychological and trauma models I was pursuing. If I was suffering, it was because I had pushed my trauma deep into my body. Just as some Christian paradigms believe that sin pollutes the body, causing everything from leprosy to madness, so did childhood trauma beleaguer my bodily systems like a poison. I needed to detox. To scrub my psyche and my gut. I could "atone" financially and practically by going to therapy, reading self-help books, and attending another Holotropic Breathwork workshop. Instagram videos of beatific blond women in Costa Rica talking about their transformative "plant medicine" breakthroughs and regulated nervous systems left me feeling constantly inadequate. Holistic doctors with neon-bright smiles advised me to order their boutique supplements and detox teas.

Friends who had healed relatively minor health issues advised me to try a celery juice cleanse, try veganism again, try to meditate more, to pray more, to dance more, to focus on the positive more. I really needed to focus on lifting my vibration.

My vibes were off. So were my genetics and my nervous system. But I kept the wild hope alive that if I wasn't getting better, I just wasn't trying hard enough to heal.

I just needed to try harder.

One of the interesting similarities between revealing that you are chronically ill and revealing that you are a survivor of childhood sexual abuse is that both provoke from others an immediate laundry list of things you must try. This makes both survivors and the chronically ill increasingly reluctant to divulge the realities of their lived experience. Usually, we have already tried most of these modalities. And, most importantly, the experience of being immediately problematized and "solved" amounts to an erasure of the complexity of the human being sharing vulnerable information. We treat illness and trauma like an individual failing that can be solved by cleaning up our behavior, our diets, our spiritual hygiene. But most of us are not polluted with personal shortcoming but rather are caught within webs of systemic oppression and inequities that well preceded our births. Yet once we are sick or traumatized, it becomes our sole responsibility—financially, practically, and emotionally—to solve how our bodies have "kept" the score of a game we never even knew we were playing. This idea of individual responsibility for the aftereffects of systemic dysfunction is called "healthism" and is rampant in everything from new age rhetoric to more standard medical paradigms. Physical and psychological health as atomized within Western ideas of individuality become possessions.

They are objects to be owned, hoarded, stolen, defended. If you lose them, then it must be your fault. If they become tainted by violence or illness, you must strive to purify them.

You can buy back health and purity, though. Just one more supplement. One more somatic experiencing session. One more colon cleanse. One more reiki appointment. One more meeting with an immunologist who is the only person recommended to treat your condition but doesn't take insurance and orders hundreds of dollars of blood tests.

Sitting in my immunologist's office, wondering about purity and health, I was shell-shocked and flayed, skinless from the endless trauma modalities that triggered flashbacks, juggling freelance work, and trying to finish my own book. I was consistently experiencing episodes of severe renal injury for some reason that no one could understand. My feet would swell, my skin would itch, and I'd feel sludged with toxins.

How was this possible? I'd followed the healing path that modern narratives from cancer survivors and celebrity wellness influencers had primed me to expect. Descent into illness, breakdown, diagnosis, and then a victorious ascent back into the kingdom of the fully healed. I had indeed finally received a diagnosis for my illness. I'd been "saved" by my fairy-tale partner. I'd finally broken the silence about my childhood abuse and begun the work to integrate it into a healthier nervous system. I'd spent weeks of time in therapist, nutritionist, specialist, and doctor's offices, taking copious notes. I did breathwork, tapping, EMDR, meditation, intermittent fasting, and boutique probiotics prescribed by a nutritionist who somehow always needed me to buy some expensive new supplement. And that wasn't counting the endless hours spent on the phone negotiating with the Kafkaesque bureaucracy of managed health care for profit. Every doctor needed my records faxed, needed a signed consent form, needed to get approval from my insurance. These phone calls dedicated to paperwork ate up huge portions of my life, with little health care to show for them. Doctor's offices would drop my calls repeatedly. The insurance companies would deny my request yet again. A fasting blood test I'd taken off work to get done was somehow lost in transit. I'd have to drive to my doctor's office to go pick up another script and then steal time to do the test again.

Given how much money and time and energy I was spending on healing and purifying myself, you'd think I'd be feeling better.

Instead, I felt worse. Much worse.

The doctor who was the main expert in my connective tissue disease's connection with autoimmunity interrupted my reverie. "Okay, we need to get you to a surgeon to look at your neck because your skull is essentially collapsing into your spine. Not that the surgeries are very effective. And I'm not loving the blood numbers. Back to the hematologist. With your lung functioning being what it is, we can expect that your heart is feeling the effects. So we need to get you back to the cardiologist . . . check on that aortic valve too. You know you're at a risk of dissection?"

My hands were tingling. I was ascending, mind-balloon on a string, floating on helium up and out of my body. I smiled down at the scene. My partner, Jason, was frowning in the corner, his handsome face disfigured by a scowl I'd come to expect every time I walked in the door a little later than I'd said I would. *Is he mad at me?* For the first time I felt dispassionate about his anger. *Why is he always mad at me?* I wondered, shocked as I finally let the question evolve.

The doctor's voice was glitching, moving up in pitch until it was too high for me to even hear.

"And then from hour to hour we rot and rot . . ." I thought, staring down at the pronounced veins in my hands that the doctor had informed me were a "typical expression of connective tissue disease." My skin was too soft. My bones didn't want to stay in a solid shape. My heart was growing lazy.

I imagined myself amorphous as a compost heap. And instead of talking at me, the doctor was circling me, pouring in water, tossing in a handful of salad greens, pulling out a worm and inspecting it with pleasure, occasionally taking a trowel and flipping some of my moist soil. "You're moving along well," I imagined her congratulating me. "You're past the thermophilic phase and maturing. I'm seeing a lot of earthworms, a lot of millipedes. This is really good news."

Evidence of intentional composting goes back as far as twelve thousand years ago in Scotland, when fields filled with manure and human excrement were used to plant crops. There are examples of recycled organic waste for agricultural purposes in ancient India, China, and across the Middle East.

The first written tract about composting can be found in a set of clay tablets dating back to King Sargon's reign during the Akkadian Empire (2320 BCE). In Egypt, composting was so esteemed that Cleopatra declared the compost heap's hero, the worm, sacred. In 160 BCE, the retired Roman general Cato the Elder wrote instructions on best practices for composting in his agricultural treatise *De Agri Cultura*.

Composting is the process whereby plant and food waste decompose into a rich, nutritious soil filled with fungi, bacteria, and other organisms. The soil produced from composting creates a nutritious and vibrant matrix for agricultural planting, with the added benefit that it also produces compounds that kill off and suppress pathogens that could harm crops. "Greens" and "browns" are the main ingredients of a good compost heap. Greens are rich in nitrogen: moldy leaves, mowed grass, table scraps. Browns are richer in carbon: stalks, woody material, paper. The process is easy enough. Add water. Put outside. Let the heat, the moisture, the spores, and the pollen diffused through the air do their jobs. Of course, you can be more precise about it: shredding matter to increase surface area and "aerating" the pile. But decay is a process that winks playfully at human control. Even the attempt to create an "ingredient" list is a modern innovation, as demonstrated by the anarchic "shit fields" of the ancient Scots. Human and animal excrement combined with discarded food and plant waste provided an alchemical mix that needed little organization. The most important work is done by a decidedly inhuman force—or perhaps it's very human, given that our bodies are composed of more bacterial cells than human cells. Microbes. These decomposers turn a compost heap into a web of appetites, chewing through waste, excreting nutrients and soil, producing heat that further encourages the decay process. A heap of inert matter is soon a pulsing, humming, sweating community of creation.

What, then, is decay? Watching a compost heap transform into fertile soil, it occurs to me that decay is genesis. Decay is the first scene in a comedy of mycelial threads and millipedes and sprouting wildflowers from seeds invisibly deposited by a bird flying overhead. Impurity isn't something to be detoxed with a tea or "completed" with expensive therapy. Impurity, rot, and decay are necessary for new life.

"Shit happens," the saying goes. But if shit happens—if dirt and excrement and rot are necessary stages in the fostering of resilient ecosystems—why are they demonized? Why is shit so easily categorized as dirty or taboo? In a culture that is extremely talented at consuming, we show an equally remarkable inability to understand and honor excretion, death, and decay. Purity culture as articulated through new age spirituality, and biopolitics is keyed toward toxins—both the creation of them through industrial technologies and then the repression of them culturally. While we nitpick over impurities and toxins in our bloodstreams, spiritual circles, and social media communities, we are much more practically abstracted from our actual excrement and the impact it may have on the ecosystem it finally enters. And more macroscopically, we ship our waste products out of cities and homes to pollute and clog less-privileged countries and communities. This doesn't even consider excretion through the lens of pollution. Everything we do creates waste.

It seems interesting to me that all our human attempts to "clean up" ecosystems or landscapes ended up creating the very toxins that are driving climate change. We cut down trees to create sterile fields for glyphosate-frosted monocrops. We blitzed microbes from our surfaces and our bodies and encouraged them to get stronger, wilier, and more resistant to our medicines. Viruses and insects and bacteria and invasive species and molds were dirty. They were waste. But it seemed increasingly obvious to me that when we threw them out, we ended up throwing away the whole Earth.

What is waste, really? What qualifies as waste? Cultural narratives about excrement are inextricably tied to ableism, racism, and ecocide. Professor of sociology and anthropology Alexis Shotwell writes in her book *Against Purity*: "Like most classificatory practices, the aim toward theoretical purity arose from particular practical imperatives. Who can one enlsave? Who has political standing? . . . It is commonplace to understand the idea of natural purity as a racialized concept." Purity is always articulated against its opposite: excrement, waste, impurity. What is waste? Can a human being be waste? If we view ourselves as no longer attached to our waste once it leaves our bodies or cities, are we still ethically implicated in how it acts and participates in the world?

We are good at consuming—peoples, ecosystems, resources. But we are not good at balancing the equation with the necessary creation and expulsion of new matter. What we ingest, we must also pass along once it is transformed by the crucible of our corporality. Excrement is perhaps terrifying not only because it signifies death or interrupts our ideas about liveliness. It also signals that we are not static or complete. We are not a sterile Cartesian mind or eternal Christian spirit. We are matter digesting matter. Matter that stinks and ferments and turns into soil.

Where do we make the cut between excrement and food? Between health and illness? Between purity and impurity? I believe that we must complicate arbitrary cuts between clean and unclean, wasteful and useful. Excrement is less ontologically stable than we might believe. There is a reason the phrase "shit happens" is so ubiquitous. Shit isn't still. It isn't an object. Shit is a relationally constituted "event." To the dung beetle, the dung is life-giving sustenance. The pitcher plant survives on the excrement of the inquiline bacteria and insects that dwell within its curled leaves.

Our aversion to excrement is always entangled with our aversion to the disabled, the incorrect, the dying, and death itself. And when we distance ourselves from death, we are also distancing ourselves from that which feeds life. We are distancing ourselves practically from the very nourishment that would replenish our spiritually anemic culture.

I had confronted my mortality many times since falling ill at sixteen. I was aware that my closeness to death was a type of pollution. It made people uneasy. When I was at my sickest, people had a hard time meeting my eye, as if they might be polluted by my physical liminality.

But death never felt frightening to me. It never felt like any sort of end. Even in the moment when my airways closed and my heart flipped backward, I always felt that whatever came next was closer to the river pouring into the ocean than it was to an ending. What if death was the transition from a solitary aliveness to an anarchic polyphony of aliveness?

The collective deaths of many extinction events have been brief bottlenecks that "clear" ecological niches. After the dust and ash settle, there is usually an explosion of new species and new life. It was only after the asteroid impact that caused the Earth's fifth major extinction that the first mammals diversified, providing the evolutionary ground for humanity's eventual emergence. An asteroid crater becomes a vibrant forest. A grave becomes a womb. The Earth continues experimenting with embodiment. Our meteor-streak lives are too short and small to comprehend the long story of evolution.

Many years before I became ill, a deer, hit by a car, managed to struggle into the woods at the periphery of my parents' property, where it died. It was high summer, frying pan hot, the peeling birch bark almost crisping into cinders under unrelenting sunshine. Day after day, I would visit the carcass and watch as one life melted into a riot of lives. Worms. Ants. Maggots. Beetles. Mushrooms. Death was the moment when life overflowed its cup. Death wasn't an end of life. It was the end of the singular. The deer decayed out of its shape into explosive, generative plurality. One narrative diverged into four hundred narratives.

When we are forced by illness to get close to our own decay, to our own impurities, we can begin to recontextualize mortality, impurity, and decomposition as things integral to the dynamic homeostasis of Earth's complex biosphere. The chronically and incurably sick receive a terrifyingly intimate and accelerated version of this lesson in ecology: a lesson our capitalist throwaway culture has desperately tried to avoid. That lesson far exceeds our simplistic human dualisms of good and bad, safe and dangerous. But it *does* teach us. It forces our bodies to acknowledge that we are never promised stability and wholeness. We are just a doorway through which matter is flowing on its way to becoming something else. A brief shape that atoms and electrons and recycled minerals take on their way to becoming hummingbirds and tomatoes and dragonflies and mountains.

Jason yelled at me the whole week after the appointment with the immunologist. I was exercising too hard. Working too hard. Not going to enough doctors. Not trying hard enough to heal. I was never going to be able to give him children at this rate. I was never going to be able to give him enough. My real crime, now that I can witness these fights from a distance, was that I was potentially going to lose my usefulness. My crime was one of utility. He was terrified that I wouldn't be able to care for *him* or give him children and food and financial support.

I decided not to return to that immunologist, despite her prestige. I had a suspicion that her repeated recitation of my prognosis was going to act on me like a curse—like the opposite of a placebo. It was a tragedy I didn't want to hear and didn't want to tell. I wanted to wake up and tell a different story about what vitality, joy, and miracles were available to me beyond the narrow strictures of wholeness, health, and purity.

I had to admit it. I wasn't healing. Not in the way I'd expected.

I was decaying. But the image of the decomposing deer and the compost heap came back to comfort me. Decay is always a day, a microbe, a rootlet away from sprouting. Maybe I was losing touch with a self and melting into a more-than-human mind. I remembered that in Shakespeare's catalog of plays, every comedy begins with strife and breakdown and every tragedy begins with health and well-being. If you played any narrative out longer, it would tip into its opposite. As Shakespeare's Jaques notes, it is between the ripe and the rot that "thereby hangs a tale."

On my birthday that year, a month after the terrible appointment with the immunologist, I woke up early. I'd planned to work a shift at a friend's vintage store to cover up the fact that my partner wasn't going to make any effort to celebrate me.

Sitting at the counter, watching a light, wet snow fur the street through the frosted windows, I took out my journal. My last entry was from almost a year prior. I'd been too frazzled, too overworked, too sick to write since then.

"I think I've lost the plot," I wrote alongside the date: my birthday.

"If I feel myself, like the compost heap, beginning to melt, maybe it means that I am also melting into another story. A bigger story. A wider cast of characters. Let me dance between ripe and rot," I wrote. "I don't know what act in the play comes next. But I know what my prayer is. Make me bigger than an 'I.' Make me good soil."

CHAPTER 12

Unweaving the Web

YOU CAN FLUSH A TICK DOWN THE TOILET OR SLAP AWAY A MOSQUITO, but you must not harm a spider.

That was the house rule in my family of animist writers who saw their own art form miniaturized in the industrious spinning of those tiny arachnid bards. Spiders were writers too. The only difference between us and them was that they told stories with their whole bodies. Sticky stories. Stories secreted by special glands and expelled sticky like milk, like glaucous tears.

My mother and father gifted me with a reverence for that embodied storyteller, which sewed together a web that was simultaneously a home, an extended brain, and a way of catching and caching food. Stories were not a solely human creation. Stories were sewn in attic rafters, dew-encrusted hammocks slung between dandelion stalks. They were diaphanous silk that could sate your appetite with a captured fly and provide a resting spot for your weary body. Watching a spider stitching together telephone lines one morning, I was curious about the mechanics and found that what the spider is doing involves no actual "spin" or rotation, but rather a full-body warp and weft effort, as it inches silk out of its abdomen by the force of its weight falling under its own thread or extracted by its own legs. The idea of the spinning spider is analogous to textile spinning wheels. By a mechanism of pultrusion, it does not expel the silk so much as it works to remove the silk from its gland manually.

As I confronted my diagnosis of genetic disease and PTSD, I relied on the metaphor of weaving. Wasn't I a storyteller, allied with spiders and cosmic spinners? My working theory was that the more complete my understanding of my unique bodily and psychological failings, the more complete the woven tapestry of my possible health would become. If only I could find the frayed edge of my threadbare spirit. Then I could connect all the loose ends.

Across cultures, storytelling is compared to both weaving and spiders. The spider is repeatedly cast as a bardic deity—the Sumerian spider goddess Uttu and the Ashanti's Ananse. The Moirai of Greece used their dexterous fingers to spin, spool, and splice the thread of a person's fate. And, likewise, in Norse mythology, the three Norns controlled the threads of personal destiny. Ariadne's red thread that Theseus follows through the Cretan labyrinth can be read as a way of weaving the hero into a successful narrative. He follows the thread while we follow him, word by word, through the labyrinth woven within the story. Without a thread, the labyrinth cannot be navigated or "told."

In Homer's *Odyssey*, Penelope—although she is named for the Greek word *pēnē* (πήνη), meaning "weft"— interrupts the simplistic trope of the woven story. Penelope will not simply complete a piece of cloth or tie off the last knot in a narrative episode.

The story is familiar enough. Odysseus, her husband, has been absent for years fighting a war in Troy. Penelope waits patiently for his return, but is soon besieged with suitors and naysayers who assume that Odysseus is dead and that the clever and beautiful Penelope needs a new partner. A simplistic reading of Penelope casts her in the role of the chaste and faithful wife, never losing hope that her husband is alive. But, as an older reader returning to the *Odyssey* with a deeper understanding of historical Homeric tradition, I found that in Penelope's cunning, alternative poetics emerged.

Faced with demanding suitors, Penelope insists that they must wait until she finishes a shroud for Odysseus's father, Laertes. Yet, every night she secretly unweaves her "great web." If we read these fraying threads as representing temporality and narrative progression, leading us on a straight line through the thick tapestry of our lives, then Penelope is unspooling time. She unweaves the Fates/Moirai's threads each night, refusing fate, refusing to complete her shroud, and refusing to end Laertes's life or her marriage to the absent Odysseus. Death is deferred. Widowhood is denied. Time is interrupted.

Penelope instead rejects the smug epiphanic completions of masculine heroic modes. She invokes what poet Lyn Hejinian would characterize as an "open text." As opposed to a text that strives for conclusion and singular interpretation, "the open text is one which both acknowledges the vastness of the world and is formally differentiating. It is form that provides an opening." Hejinian summons Hélène Cixous to explain that "a feminine textual body is recognized by the fact that it is always endless, without ending. There's no closure, it doesn't stop." The opening Penelope seeks not to close is physical—the open spousal space beside her that longs for Odysseus's return. By rejecting the craft of closure, by rejecting the completion of the shroud and its subsequent burial, she is keeping both her marital status and the narrative itself "open." Text and textile are paradoxically kept alive by being repeatedly undermined and undone.

What happens when the spider finishes the web? What happens when the silk dries up? Is that really the point of spinning and weaving? To complete the web? What textile am I weaving when I tell a story about my life with certainty? Is it a bridal veil? A decorative tapestry to be hung up and forgotten? Or is it my own shroud?

Odysseus, like Penelope, survives ordeals not by settling on a single narrative interpretation, but by his cunning instinct to decompose and recompose his narrative to suit the political and social biases of a new audience. I have often imagined Penelope as a stand-in for the Homeric bard himself, weaving and unweaving the shroud and helping her husband to weave and unweave his own story on his meandering trip back to his homeland of Ithaca. To finish the shroud, then, would be to doom her husband to one story that was no longer malleable to shifting circumstances. Penelope calls her craft "a great web," reminding me of the spider in its self-excreted story. Is Odysseus a node of the web, responsive to the tugs and twitches of his arachnid spouse? And what is Penelope as weaver doing when she unweaves the web?

For years, I had subscribed to a narrative of fragmentation and dissociation in my own life. I had been unwoven from health and stability by trauma and chronic illness. I needed a definitive diagnosis, a straightforward healing plot, a devoted partner, a happy heteronormative ending, to weave myself back into the safety of the dominant culture.

As I devoted myself to Western medicine and psychotherapy, I strongly believed that I was weaving a web of healing. But I had forgotten that we are not always the authors of the stories we inhabit and live inside, even when we have a sense of manufactured choice. Just because we are a character does not necessarily mean we are the author writing our fate. To paraphrase Melissa Febos's writing about internalized patriarchy and consent, "We are always unreliable narrators of our own motives." Those motives are often not self-excreted from our silk glands, but instead webs inherited from previous spinners. Spinners devoted to our subjugation and defeat.

It is crucial to understand when we are not the authors of the web. Many of us are the flies stuck within the web's mesh.

Unweaving can be as liberating as weaving. The key is to know when the web does not belong to us. The key is recognizing when the web is not a home but a shroud.

For those of us caught within limiting narratives, *untelling* a story is as important as its initial weaving.

A good story can produce miraculous effects in our bodies. This well-observed phenomenon is known as the placebo effect. Sugar pills or medical interventions without direct physiological effects miraculously produce psychological and physical benefit. They convince our own immune systems to "wake up" and enact self-healing. Placebos often outperform the actual drugs they are being studied against. Our faith in the story about a medicine is often the medicine itself. If the story is told well enough, it can literally save someone's life by activating their own immunological resilience.

When I read accounts of healing in the Mediterranean during the time of Jesus, I understood a contemporaneous cultural belief in miracles and miracle workers set the stage for placebo healing. Spit in the eyes, a hand on your feverish head, and a gathered crowd all praying and rooting for your regeneration created a theater of healing. If you truly believed that God was working through a magician when he performed his rituals, it was enough to wake up your beleaguered immune system. Perhaps these miraculous healings weren't supernatural, but profoundly natural—showcasing the power of good theater and our bodies' ability to respond positively to a well-crafted story.

But equally as powerful as the placebo effect is the *nocebo* effect. A bad story—a story of a degenerative prognosis, expected complications, unpleasant side effects—can manifest these outcomes. This effect, unlike the placebo, is unintentional and rampant within for-profit health care. Doctors who don't make eye contact and give curt answers and forget your patient history do not inspire confidence. Thus, when the doctors give us drugs, we are less likely to believe in their efficacy. The theater of healing becomes the theater of anonymity and mistrust. When a doctor tells us a list of negative side effects for a new drug, we are more likely to experience said side effects. Our expectations have been primed for discomfort and disease. Recent developments within the realm of cognitive science show that predictive processing has huge effects on our internal physical state. Our predictions about our future physical state create our future physical state. Most gravely, when a patient receives a dire prognosis or a list of symptoms attached to a new diagnosis, they are at an increased risk of living out those new stories. Yes, a diagnosis often leads to life-saving intervention. But for those with autoimmunity and complex, incurable conditions, it can also be a thread through a labyrinth you never wanted to enter. Suddenly, you find yourself finishing your own shroud.

Unweaving the web, then, is unweaving the cobwebs that have begun to clog up your mind.

Unweaving the potential surgeries and medical emergencies. Unweaving the predicted decline. Unweaving the belief that miracles don't happen, and healing is hard work.

This unweaving of a story or a diagnosis can feel like madness. It can feel like we are taking apart something that was a home. A web of meaning to grasp onto. But it can also be the necessary decomposing of narratives that ensured our deaths, our defeats, our husbands never coming home to Ithaca, stranded on a distant nymph's island.

Decomposing is the critical word here. Penelope, as a weaver of textiles, had little understanding of physical texts. For her, a narrative was always ephemeral, immaterial, relational, ferried along by boats of breath. In fact, it is interesting to look at the weaving and unweaving of her web in relation to the very storytelling tradition that brings her character into being.

It is well-established now that the *Iliad* and the *Odyssey* are not the product of a singular genius. And they are not even the product of a literate author. The epics predate alphabetic literacy and, although we praise their literary finesse, they defy most modern literary requirements. In the 1920s, American classicist Milman Parry shocked the academic world and revolutionized classical studies and our ideas about orality when he proved that Homer's *Odyssey* and *Iliad* had originally been composed to travel as oral epics. It was only centuries after their initial oral composition that they were committed to writing. Parry showed that the repetitions and structures in Homer are those of an oral text. These stock themes, epithets, plot formulas, and standardized scenes allowed for the epic to be more easily committed to memory and verbally adapted for specific performances. You could "remix" the scenes, characters, and themes to fit a new audience's needs. Parry demonstrated that "every distinctive feature of Homeric poetry is due to the economy enforced on it by oral methods of composition." Professor of English literature and literacy Walter Ong, who carried on Parry's study of orality, noted, "There was no use denying the now known fact that Homeric poems valued and somehow made capital of what later readers had been trained in principle to disvalue, namely, the set phrase, the formula, the expected qualifier—to put it more bluntly, the cliché."

The bardic poets who would eventually be conflated into the singular figure of Homer were originally known as "rhapsodes." The word "rhapsodize" described the performance of oral epic and comes from the Greek *rhapsōidos*, meaning "to stitch the songs together." The weaver and the storyteller were both the stitchers of texts and textiles. To rhapsodize referred to the oral rhapsode's repertoire of stories and myths and epithets he could improvisationally stitch together into an epic particularly tailored to the needs of a specific audience and context. Contrary to general belief, these epics were not memorized word for word. Rather, the traveling bard memorized the general episodes, characters, and an ecology of epithets and standard phrases that, depending on the extratextual inspiration of audience and setting, were stitched together anew with each retelling. It is the reliance on set formulas, on disarticulated stitches of song and cliché, that allows oral poetry to migrate, change, and adapt without ossifying.

Like Odysseus washing up on the shores of strange lands, new places require new ways of telling our stories. If you stick to the old version, you might anger an irrational despot or violate a set of mores. To stay alive, you had to be able to break down an epic to its memorable phrases and episodes and then "stitch" them back together again in such a way that the performance responded accurately to new circumstances. The rhapsode depended just as much on the decomposition of stories as the composition of stories.

In fact, we can think of the traveling bard as being a traveling compost heap: able to alchemize and rot down popular themes and characters so that a new story could sprout for a new audience. Penelope's weaving and unweaving of the shroud mirrors the Homeric tradition. To rhapsodize is to "stitch the songs together." To weave the textile. But to rhapsodize also allows for the unstitching of the songs. The unweaving of the songs that makes room for an opening: a new audience and a new version of a familiar epic.

Like rhapsodes, fungi and bacteria compose and decompose material in order to generate the soil foundation of entire ecosystems. The decomposition process—the unweaving of minerals from stone, nutrients from dead wood—is just as important as the eventual regrowth of new vegetation. The unweaving of the web allows for an ecosystem instead of a shroud. A fresh narrative instead of a dead-end dogma.

When I wrote in my journal "I think I've lost the plot," I felt something liberatory in that uncertainty. To lose the plot, to unweave the web, to open up the story to an alternative ending, is to escape certain defeat and limiting outcomes. My diagnosis, my partnership, and my devotion to healing were no longer widening my life. I thought again of the dead deer melting back into dust and mold and moss, and I thought of the invisible handiwork of microscopic Penelopes, never allowing the text to finish, the ecosystem to halt its regenerative cycling.

Help me, Penelope, I began to pray. *Help me unweave myself from this plot. This prison.*

As my partner and I talked abstractly about how we could afford a wedding without getting help from our parents, buying a house, having children, I imagined an invisible spider opposite me, unweaving the neat tapestry of these shared dreams.

Was this really the story I wanted to live?

Even more urgently, I remembered the catalog of symptoms and break-downs the specialists warned that I should prepare for as someone navigating connective tissue disease and autoimmunity. The web was sticky, and I was caught. But I was realizing that these stories, diagnoses, and expectations were not authored by me. I could potentially begin to untangle myself from their hold. I could unwrite myself from their grasp.

I could undiagnose myself.

I asked myself how I could tell a story without completing my own shroud. How could I unweave a diagnosis?

As I spin narratives about getting sick and pursuing a healing story, I always want to be careful not to finish my story. I want to unstitch. I want to leave space open enough that Odysseus might miraculously arrive home. I want a miracle worker from Galilee to spit in my eyes and wake up my immune system. I need to keep the door open for a miracle that is unheard of in my local tongue, my stock of predictable epithets. One that is able to interrupt the epic of illness I am trying desperately to untell.

The spider builds a temporary home with its silk. But this storytelling thread is not just useful for web-weaving. It is also a practical means of escape from homes and webs and traps within which we find ourselves ensnared. Many spiders practice something called "ballooning" when they need to travel long distances. The spiders climb as high up as they can reach and then expose their abdomens to the sky. They release a gossamer thread into the wind, taking advantage of electrical fields and air currents to force a lift into the air that then carries them aloft, onward. Ships mid-ocean have reported the sight of ballooning spiders, flying through the heavens at an altitude of up to five miles.

In the month leading up to the holidays, I was desperately looking for metaphors that might patch my PTSD-frazzled self back together. And I was also increasingly aware that my stories about partnership and wellness were not webs I had woven. They were webs within which I was perilously stuck.

They were not placebos, waking up my healing potential. They were nocebos—weaving me into a story of decay and struggle and trauma.

Balloon me. If my silk is a story that can be weaved, let it also be a story that can be unwoven. Release me.

Early one morning, on my way to the gym to run before diving into errands and work, I pulled my sweatshirt up to reveal the ghostly surface of my stomach. Above me a slice of moon flickered like a Cheshire grin in the mauve ripples of dawn clouds. The being smiling at me was a storyteller god, a spider of decomposition and frayed thread. A great grinning Penelope telling me to trick the suitors and escape the tragedy.

I didn't know how, but I knew I needed to unweave my shroud.

"Up! Up! Up!" I said and laughed as I imagined a silver string of words, a sticky poem issuing from my belly button and carrying me like a spider up into the wind.

Balloon me. Unweave me from this web. Help me, Fates. Cut this brittle thread.

CHAPTER 13

I Do Not Keep My Heart in My Body

THE LINE WAS FAINT BUT UNDENIABLE. A PINK COMET STREAK ACROSS the sky of my future life. I recognized it because I'd seen it once, years earlier, shivering in a dorm room bathroom.

I'm pregnant.

The key difference between the first and the second time I saw that line was that it was no longer crazy to imagine myself as a mother. It was something Jason and I had discussed frequently in the past year, as we had hobbled together an engagement that was more like a handshake, an approaching union that both our families saw as inevitable given how close we were, how entangled our finances and lives had become. We both wanted children. And we dreamed of buying a country home where we could grow our own food and make tiny miniature fairy villages for toddlers to find with delight. Our friends were beginning to have kids, and I loved the fresh-cut grass smell of their soft heads, the ancient prickle of their unabashed stares, still carrying some cosmic consciousness from whatever existence preceded their new life as a human infant.

It even made sense. I'd just finished the final revisions on my novel about Mary Magdalene and Jesus and I was preparing to shop it around to agents. One creative child had been born—a finished book. Maybe now it was time for another child—this one decidedly corporeal—to be conceived. Didn't years spent writing about a miracle worker merit a miracle for myself? I wished I could summon my own character—my healing storyteller Yeshua—off the page to lay hands on my actual body.

Most of all, as I read the headlines about escalating extinctions and oil spills, I wanted him to lay hands on the Earth. It was always impossible to disentangle my glitchy body from the body of the Earth. As uncapped emissions drove up the temperature, so did my autoimmunity follow suit, smoldering in my kidneys and brain, frying down my bone marrow alongside the melting glaciers.

The ability to conceive a child was a miracle. I was surprised my exhausted body could even manage such a feat. It reminded me of a sterile slab of concrete somehow sprouting an oak seedling.

And yet I did not feel overjoyed. Instead, molten anguish twisted my bowels as I leaned against the bathroom sink, staring at the pregnancy test, willing the line to fade. I was ragged, overworked, and, as always, sick. But even more urgent than those practicalities was the fact that this child had been created by Jason—someone I was having a harder and harder time imagining as my long-term partner, let alone the father of my children.

The child was an ultimatum. A decision bigger than an engagement or a wedding ring.

Did I want to stay in this story?

Over the course of my life, I have grown suspicious of questions that demand a yes or no answer. Life is never binary. It is an ever-shifting kaleidoscope of potential futures—an entangled web of culpability and relationality. Did I want a child? Yes. Did I want *this* child? Maybe. Did I want to be with Jason? I wasn't sure. I couldn't easily imagine a world without his companionship. But was his companionship good for me? No. That was becoming clearer every day. Did I want something bigger and stranger from my life that I couldn't conceptualize or verbalize? Yes.

Luckily, Jason was in the city working. I had that day to wander the house, defer my writing and work, and imagine the sparkle of a cell spinning inside my womb.

All of us began as a cell dreamed into being not by the flesh of our mothers, but by the sunset suction and curvature of our *grandmothers'* wombs. Every woman is born with all the eggs she will release in a lifetime.* We all share a creation story with our mothers. Her own womb bloomed within our grandmother's womb, and within her, the nucleus of our own potential completed the holy trinity of nested life. We are Russian dolls, life nested within life representing how the Earth's biospheric complexity is built out of other smaller lives and ecosystems. We flickered in and out of molecules, planted inside our mothers, who were planted inside their mothers. We and our mothers are both fruit grown in the muscular embrace of our grandmothers' uterine landscapes.

The ovum, or human egg, is one of the largest human cells, visible without the aid of a microscope. Salmon-pink planet. Fuzzed with follicular desire. But like Table Mountain pine cones, the ovum needs fire to open, chemical perturbation to produce life. Life starts as the caduceus of two sets of chromosomes, the twined snakes of genetic information from two different beings. And the billions of beings—bacterial, fungal, viral—that made their reproductive ability chemically possible. The sperm fertilizes the ovum and, slowly, a being emerges into form, and then open air, miniature but, in most cases, delicately molded into a silhouette the parents will recognize: hands, eyes, legs, mouth, nose.

Initially the fertilized egg is totipotent, which means that it is composed of cells that all equally hold the potential to develop into any other type of cell. But as time passes, these cells divide and form a three-layered disc of cells that folds and morphs. This process, called gastrulation, initiates a cellular change from totipotency to a state known as multipotency. As a shape emerges, the relational context of each cell also emerges. One cell knows how to specialize given its location and "neighbor" cells. If we think of human beings as having evolved through a specific environmental embeddedness, we can see the embryo as a microcosm of the same phenomenon. Our bodies evolved to adapt to our environments. In the embryo, each cell begins to "understand" its ultimate role by virtue of where it is placed inside the geometry of the embryo, and by what other cells are touching it. Cell selfhood is composed of a complex network of relational assessments. If we are all constituted by our relationships to one another and to our situated ecologies, then we are also brought into form through a similar process.

* This language is gendered for simplicity but includes anyone born with a uterus. Any gender identity can mother and gestate new life.

I could feel something inside of me authoring itself. I could feel a web being woven. At a moment when I was considering unweaving myself from my partnership and my ideas about healing, it felt strange to feel something tying me firmly back to these structures.

Maybe my future granddaughters were clumping together like microscopic pearls within the tiny shell of my gestating child. I couldn't help but feel profoundly awed by the fact that I could so easily become a complex ecosystem without it appearing immediately visible on my body. In the mirror I was still slender, pale, with dark-circled eyes. But I was no longer just a single self. I was a *world* peopled with dividing cells, seeds, eggs, each with the totipotency to become anything. A kidney. A hand. A child. A grandchild. Each of these cells held the ability to imagine an alternative future. A future that, while I couldn't necessarily see or imagine it, I could host. Each cell had the potential to claim the health and embodiment that I couldn't, on my own, seem to access.

Would this child be healthy? Could something as broken as me produce wellness and vitality?

I kept these questions to myself in the two weeks leading up to the holidays. Life with Jason required emotional tiptoeing. Anything could set him into a rage or jealous tirade. My family lived locally while his lived in the Midwest, and he often used this as an excuse for his temper tantrums.

We'd been planning on an extended holiday stay with his family for months.

When my period was late and I'd voiced my worry to him, he'd yelled at me. "You want to ruin this trip! You hate my dad and you'll come up with any excuse to ruin this for me."

I noted that he didn't say, "I'm so sorry I pressured us into making a risky sexual decision with consequences, but haven't we always dreamed of having kids? Even if my dad and stepmom don't approve, it would be a wonderful Christmas present for my mother. She wants grandchildren so badly!"

I will figure this out when we get back. It's just two weeks. I can decide then. I can tell him then.

And yet when I tried to picture myself pregnant alongside Jason, all I could imagine was a spider shooting its silk into the air, escaping solid ground and floating off into the robin's egg–blue sky.

If months of expensive somatic therapy had yielded anything other than psychic exhaustion and physical defeat, they had shown me that my body was much better at communicating my true emotions than my intellectual acrobatics were.

I had ten thousand excuses for why Jason and I were a good couple. I had stories that kept sticking a thumb in the springing leaks of our sinking ship. I spent the first couple of nights with his family dealing with Jason's constant stream of criticism, in a defensive state that made it impossible to think through whether I could keep this child. Meanwhile, I was putting the final edits on the portions of my novel that involved childbirth.

I want a child. I want to have a family. I knew it with such certainty. But I felt anguish. Physical anguish. I was shaky and unsteady on my feet. It was as if someone had removed several discs of my spine and left me to wobble like a Jenga tower.

The body keeps the score had been my mantra, my koan, my riddle for the past year of deep dives into trauma modalities. But sometimes the body doesn't want to keep the score. It doesn't want to keep anything at all.

It unweaves the web of a possible future.

The child landed in my womb. And then it shot silk into the air. It ballooned.

On Christmas Eve, in the middle of a huge party thrown by Jason's mother, I began to miscarry. The cramps were violent—bad even for someone familiar with endometriosis and blinding menstrual pain. I hobbled to the guest bathroom amid the revelry and turned on the shower, crouching while carnation-red blood and clumps of tissue circled the drain. My consciousness desaturated. I was going to pass out.

Eventually Jason found me in the bathroom, his face in the typical leonine scowl that I had once found handsome and now found terrifying.

"What are you doing? You've missed the entire party!" he hissed even as he saw me sitting in a pool of my own blood in the painfully chic glass shower that was placed in the middle of the room, like a zoo display cage.

"I think I am miscarrying our child," I whispered through tears. "I might need to go to the hospital."

Ehlers-Danlos comes with an increased risk of hemorrhaging. Years before, following my abortion, I had serious bleeding issues that brought me back to the ER. I should have been evaluated medically.

"Stop it. Stop making shit up. We have already talked about this. You get so anxious it ruins everything. You have your fucking period. We are not ruining Christmas with my family."

In that moment I was suddenly glad that all the somatic therapy hadn't "cured" me. I was glad I could still intuitively dissociate.

As I watched my blood pinken the puddle of water around me, circling me and circling the drain, I saw myself as the center stamen of a blooming flower. I imagined my mind dropping out of me, following that child out of my body and into the drains and piping of a city that was not my home.

Jason looked at me coldly, his arms crossed as if waiting for me to admit I was kidding.

In that moment, I was glad that I did not have a heart on hand to break or to lose.

I was glad that my heart was not in my body.

From the farm field I can see the Catskill Mountains where I was raised, their irregular stone scrawl a signature I would recognize even if it was signed in sand on the shores of a land far from here. Here is a field outside of Tivoli that I walked every dawn in the months following quitting smoking. Quit starving myself to death. The field is a patchwork of smaller fields, the faded grid resurfacing again when the snow falls. Hung in the right-hand corner of the farthest quadrant is a pond. Every morning, I would sit at its shore with the geese and watch the sun break free from the mountains, staining umber the river just visible through the leafless trees, before continuing my perambulations. Eventually, one morning the geese departed, cleaning the sky with their determined Vs, stealing the last pollen, the last sweetbitter smells of autumn mildew away on the downy barbs of their retreating wings.

I went to the field in blizzards. In starlight. In prayer. In grief. In solitude. I went there every season, and once, in early May, I felt a pinprick of heat in the center of my chest before turning to spot, watching me from the distant tree line, the blush of a fox, his fur like blood surfacing from the internal pulse of the forest.

In a journal from the end of college I scribbled, "How could I ever have an intimacy with a lover like I do with the field?"

When I met Jason, I briefly thought he was such a field. He was a landscape of geese and foxes and forget-me-nots. He was stone carved by glacial heft. Mountains built from ancient seashells.

When we finally disarticulated that Christmas—coming apart like words from languages with different conceptions of time—there was nothing left of that original fiction. He was no field, no ruffle of wind through a stand of aspens. He was a person not a place.

When Jason sat across from me, days after the miscarriage and our return home, and told me he did not love me and did not want to be with a woman too sick to bear his children—that he wasn't interested in caring for me as I got sicker and that he no longer wanted to marry me—my heart did not break. My heart did not break because I do not keep my heart in my body.

I keep my heart in bigger bodies than my own. My heart is in that field outside Tivoli, stippled with clover stars and Queen Anne's lace cosmos. My heart is in the fox watching his sleek reflection in the pond surface. My heart is in the migrating geese. My heart is in the shed molecules of totipotent blood that once held together the egg of a potential future.

Growing up, as I read *Harry Potter*, I was always upset by the idea of the horcrux: an object or being that carries a splinter of your soul. It is created by an act of violence. I didn't believe that putting your soul or your heart in objects was the ultimate sign of evil. It was a profound act of safekeeping.

Now I understand that this need to keep our souls whole, our hearts stable in our singular selves, is a simple disguise for a Christian aversion to matter. The soul must be whole. Individual. Immaculate. The heart must stay inside the chest. But as a survivor of violence, a navigator of incurable physical illness, I was becoming more and more certain that it was important to stow your love somewhere else sometimes.

Your soul and your heart are not weakened or corrupted when they are split and offloaded into other beings and places. Sometimes they are spared the harm. And sometimes they are actually strengthened.

In the years following the onset of my illness, in emergency rooms and ambulances, I would dive through my own heart as though it were a portal to the lands where it had been planted.

When doctors told me how my body would decay, I was glad my heart was not in the office with me. Years earlier, I had placed a part of her on the shores of the Battenkill River. I placed her in the bodies of friends who have since passed away. And those friends have been fed back to the Earth. What happens to a heart when it is translated through bodies, through materials, through different lifetimes?

When I sat in a cold shower miscarrying, my partner watching me with contempt, I was glad my heart was twined with willow roots, hung as a lace of frost across the stone fontanel of Overlook Mountain.

Perhaps, grown from the soil of my friends, the seasons of my far-off fields, my heart sprouts again as a sunflower. A spear of witchgrass shivering under the velvet tongue of a deer.

The heart was not made to be kept or protected. It was made to be split open and scattered like the milkweed pod. It was made to be flung on the winds to distant soil. It was made to be planted.

And when Jason finally left after a month of waffling and deception, I learned something that made me glow.

When we conceive and an embryo grows, its placenta fusing with our wombs, cells from the fetus pass through the placental barrier and establish a new cell lineage in our bodies. The mother's cells also pass in the opposite direction, entering the fetus. This bodily cross-pollination is called fetomaternal microchimerism. These chimerical cells live on for decades, and science has yet to understand their exact function.

But I cared little for the science that winter. I felt thankful that although I had an abortion and a miscarriage, those experiences had unwoven and rewoven my physical body, seeding me with secret cells. Ancestor altars to beings that had arrived at critical moments to save me from the wrong story.

My miscarriage ruptured my relationship. It also saved my life.

And my heart, threaded through with the chimerical cells of my secret children, was kept safe by a strange paradox.

My inability to heal had kept my heart from breaking. My dissociation had revealed a precious secret just in time.

Our single bodies and single selves are too small to hold the big weather of heartbreak and grief. Our symptoms and neuroses are sometimes the deepest expressions of our innate bodily creativity and our desire to survive.

I had spent thousands of dollars trying to heal my dissociation and my trauma responses. And yet those very symptoms came to my aid in a moment of desperation.

What if the parts of me I desperately wanted to fix were actually the parts that *kept* me alive?

CHAPTER 14

Living Between Stories: Hermit Crabs and Cocoons

WHAT DOES IT FEEL LIKE TO LOSE THE PLOT? WHAT DOES IT FEEL LIKE to wake up one morning, smoke flattening the sun into a clementine penny, and realize you do not recognize the shape of your narrative? Everything is gelatinized. Formless.

For those with illness, for those experiencing dramatic loss and grief, for refugees, for those exiting marriages, for survivors of assault, the experience is not fluid. One story does not neatly pour itself into the shape of another. The next chapter doesn't arrive.

In March 2020, I was between webs—between stories. I was unwoven. A spider floating on threads of electricity over the ocean of uncertainty. All my ideas about healing and wholeness felt like a sweater grown too small. It was time to take it off and exchange it for a better fit. A new story. A new shell.

The miscarriage had revealed the rotten foundations of my relationship, and within a month Jason and I had split up. He left gracelessly, angry that he couldn't continue relying on me for sex or emotional support even though he no longer wanted to be my long-term partner. Meanwhile, I was glad that a year earlier the black mold had foreshadowed the metaphorical rot in my partnership and destroyed most of our shared belongings. When he left, though, I was stuck floating a rent that was too big for my cobbled-together freelance lifestyle and my massive medical and therapeutic costs.

True, the breakup felt liberatory—like shrugging off a heavy pack at the end of a strenuous hike. I was suddenly weightless. Energy I hadn't realized I was siphoning off to emotionally care for my combative and jealous partner was suddenly made available to me.

I could sleep deeply again. I went on longer runs. I stayed up late reading by candlelight. I made my own schedule without worrying about cooking some- one else dinner or reminding them to call their dad. Initially, I was assured that something better would come my way. I'd find a way to pay rent. I'd find a better partner. Someone who wanted all of me enthusiastically, someone who sup- ported and enjoyed my outspoken feminism, someone who was passionate, driven, and self-sufficient.

I'd just finished my novel and was lucky to sign with an agent almost imme- diately. I felt certain that I'd soon begin my life as a published author. My story about a miracle worker would finally enact miracles in my physical life.

And then people started to sniffle in the coffee shops where I was exper- imenting with casual dating. A woman at my gym mentioned a weird virus in China. I immediately found the news article and texted it to my friend Hannah: "Is this it? Is this the big one?" We'd both shared a suspicion that we were on the brink of a pandemic since college and made a habit of sending bird flu and Ebola headlines to each other.

Turns out, after years of false alarms, we were finally right. This was indeed "the big one."

The Covid-19 pandemic was terrifying for all of us. It was lethal for a large part of the population—a fact our country still refuses to honor or properly acknowledge. People immediately started to die. As a chronically ill person with a history of asthma and pulmonary dysfunction, I sat up those first nights trying to decide what precautions I needed to take. It might not be safe to see anyone, let alone touch a gas pump or go to buy groceries. Two weeks of com- plete isolation stretched into three. Then four. Then a whole month accumu- lated with no end to quarantine in sight.

I dove from a marriage plot into an abyss misted with solitude and global paralysis.

In Tibetan Buddhism, the term *bardo* refers to the liminal realm between death and rebirth. A soul confronts and works through its karma—the accumulated consequences of its previous behavior—before entering a new body and a new life. The experience of narrative bardo, though, happens firmly and uncomfortably within the same life. You don't get a new body. Or if you do, it is often the body you accidentally arrive at through unexpected illness or accident. The people around you don't necessarily understand that, while you might seem normal, while you might wake and eat and participate in daily tasks, you are not moving in any direction. No plot shows you where to step. Your feet dangle off the cliff's edge. You are between stories.

A month into quarantine, I sat in my living room. I sat between stories. A potato bug on my windowsill crackled and jumped like a spark loosed from a campfire. I pulled a card from my Tarot deck. I'd given amateur readings to friends and family for years, but in the aftermath of my breakup and miscarriage, I kept grasping for a foothold, a cosmic answer. *Please, tell me what to do.*

The Fool. The Fool card is the zero of the Tarot, standing outside of linearity and organization. The Fool is both the first and the last card, living interstitially as a nonparticipant in the dramatic narrative of the Tarot. I closed my eyes and imagined my foot hanging in void air like the figure on the card.

"As if there were a story. As if it could be told," reads one of the final lines in my mentor Ann Lauterbach's poem "Company."

As if. As if. When I looked at the past ten years, I *did* feel like a fool.

As if I was going to get better.

As if there was going to be a miracle drug.

As if anyone would love me enough to be my partner.

What a fool I was to think that there would always be another chapter.

The Fool card insisted that I jump, but I laughed at the pointlessness of the gesture. Hadn't I been jumping for years? Disease, heartache, and ecological collapse had already pushed me off the cliff before I ever had the chance to *choose* to jump.

So many other species had been forced to jump, trying to salvage life on islands of plastic trash, sending out love songs to mates that would never arrive. I listened to the mating song of the last Kaua'i 'ō'ō bird again and again, tearing up during the pauses, knowing they represented the lover that would never arrive. The last of a species is called an endling. Our world is filled with endlings.

What if I wasn't between stories? What if, with my crooked body, I was actually the Kaua'i 'ō'ō bird, writing love poems for a lover who would never arrive? What if I was an endling?

I stared at my disinfectant-blistered hands, sterilized for safety, kept safe from the tenderness of touch. Who could possibly help me navigate the bardo realm between different lives that, paradoxically, exists within a single life? I'd been to countless doctors, bodyworkers, acupuncturists, healers, therapists, nutritionists, psychics, and physical therapists, and no one seemed to have good advice on how to navigate the uncertain and the incurable—the questions that opened up like badly healed wounds, rejecting the scabs of flimsy answers. What is the plan for when there is *no plan*?

When we receive a diagnosis, when we fall ill, when a partner leaves, we feel the cards fall out of our hands. We are not holding a book or a story. We are holding the zero, the empty air past the cliff's edge of the Fool card.

During those first weeks of quarantine, I kept thinking of the hermit crab with a fleshy stomach, a delicate structure, and the dire need for a shell that its body cannot independently produce. These little crustaceans make do with snail shells that they eventually outgrow. The curious moment occurs when a hermit crab, spilling out of its shell, exceeding its narrative, finds another shell that is a little too big. Instead of trying to enter this spacious shell, it waits patiently, sometimes for up to eight hours, for another, slightly bigger hermit crab to arrive and take the big shell, discarding a protective home more suited to the original hermit crab. Sometimes as many as twenty crabs will congregate and perform a truly amazing ritual called a vacancy chain. When they have finally assembled, the crabs will quickly evacuate and exchange shells, each claiming the new one that best suits their size.

What does it feel like to be that first hermit crab, overflowing its shell, waiting beside another shell that it also cannot properly inhabit? What does it feel like to be so soft, unprotected, and incapable of immediately producing a new story? The hermit crab says wait. And he also says that we never reach the next story on our own. We need a group. A group of people all willing to vacate and exchange their stories. Even more wildly, these stories do not belong to any single one of us. They were produced by something outside of our species. A snail. The story that will fit your new body, your new desires, your new needs, will be intimately excreted by a being living well outside the bounds of the human.

Perhaps when we are jellylike, formless, and without a guide, we should look outside the bounds of human culture and narrative for our new shape, our new shell.

When I woke up and found the bed empty, myself still surprised by the lack of a partner. When I went through a quarantine day without seeing or speaking to a single person. When I felt myself in my own private version of the movie *Groundhog Day*, increasingly unmoored from a sense of linear time, I began to wonder, "What beings have left behind their shells for me? Shall I wear the skin of the mountain, the creek, the blue heron for a while? What feral, furred, horned, lichenized stories can I live inside briefly while I navigate this narrative bardo?"

Hermit crabs, when at a loss for snail shells, have been known to live inside pieces of wood and stone. Shall I be a tree today? A moonlight streak of quartzite in the cliff face?

Maybe I was an endling. But that didn't mean I couldn't break the rules. Maybe my love poems were made to stretch symbiotically across the chasms of extinction into the yearning of songbirds and bumblebees and seaweed.

I kept the Fool card face up on my altar, decorated with pictures of ancestors, hawk feathers, and splinters of mica. Often, I would pause and stare down into the zero hovering above his handsome head. I thought of the electron swooping around a nucleus, denying a single story, living between classifications as a particle and a wave. One of the most intriguing aspects of the electron, the study of which led to quantum physics, is its ability to "hop" orbits around a nucleus without being traced. The only way we can locate where the electron has gone is by the photon it emits when it jumps orbits.

I imagined the Fool card jumping off the cliff and then thought of the electrons jumping between orbits, between the solidity of the particle and the oscillation of the wave. The story and the uncertainty. What if something beautiful happened when we jumped between stories? What if we, too, emitted a photon of light as we navigated the gray realm between narratives?

While I hovered between particle and wave, between stories, it was not lost on me that while I didn't have a narrative, I was not completely without a shell. I had a definite container.

My larger shell was the Rondout, my neighborhood nestled alongside the confluence of the Rondout Creek and the Hudson River. It was within this radius of about five miles that I ran back and forth, walked obsessively, and began to know each curl of vine, each twisted sycamore trunk stitching the land to the river with its probing, water-hungry rootlets.

And within that small patch of land was my even smaller apartment—now completely mine. A space that no one entered or left but me. Where I sweated and cried and sang and exhaled and inhaled and bled, churning a delicate metabolic stew of my own materials. It began to feel like an extension of my own body: hard keratin excreted from my forehead, webbing pulled out of my abdomen and spun around me, a cocoon tailored to my physical and psychic dimensions.

I remembered my discomfort in the months leading up to quarantine. My flesh felt too tight. My relationship felt too tight. My stories were skin I needed to shed. And I was reminded of those green and black striped caterpillars weighing down milkweed blossoms in my parents' backyard. What did it feel like to occupy that liminal state just before the cocoon? Did the caterpillar know what was coming? As I researched, I took notes that soon softened into something like a poem.

> The oak leaf tastes like destination. And origin. Briny and dense
> as the biotic oceans of the Precambrian period. Then, the hairs on
> your face bristling with appetite, grasping another textured expanse
> of leaf with your jaw, you bite, and the flood of taste is freshly wet,
> each nourishing molecule of xylem edging you closer to the place
> where all senses, all time, condense and melt. That nacreous nest,

spun of moonlight shaved from the lake's face. The cocoon where, you
will no longer eat leaves; you will eat yourself.

It struck me that a chrysalis flickers symbolically. While we typically view it as
a symbol of birth and transformation, it could just as easily be interpreted as a
self-excreted coffin or tomb. A caterpillar doesn't decide to make a chrysalis.
The chrysalis starts to form when they begin to outgrow their skin. When, leaf-
fattened, the discomfort of one state of being begins to chemically crescendo,
this signals the release of the hormone ecdysone and the suppression of the
caterpillar's "juvenile" hormone. Transformation is precipitated by deep, somatic
discomfort. The caterpillar's appetite, its thirst for green—the color, the taste,
the texture—stretches its silhouette to the point of destruction. This moment of
reaching the agonizing limit of one story and one form of embodiment without
having any sure sense of the next stage was familiar to me.

But as quarantine lengthened into a year, I had to struggle with the difference between the ritual of initiation and the unexpected somatic initiation.
The ritual is a cultural event—honed for maximum effect as it was passed
down generation to generation. It is anticipated, prepared for, performed, and
assisted by a community of elders. The other type of initiation is decidedly
nonconsensual and lonely. Sick people and bereaved people are often told they
are going through an initiation. But I always want to counter with, "It's only
initiation if you survive." Too many of my friends have died during a struggle
that could easily be fetishized as a mystical ordeal. These ordeals are only
meaningful if you safely get to the other side. Many do not make it to the distant shore or the next shell. Many do not grow wings. While our skin is busting
open, our body cascading into waves of chrysalis-building chemicals, it may be
impossible to classify our experience as either terminal or germinal.

Inside the cocoon, the caterpillar digests itself. It deliquesces its nervous
system, guts, mouth, eyes, muscles, and legs. What does it feel like to melt? I
would hesitate to say it feels like "becoming yourself." What if one day, after
a big salad, you suddenly started to feel very sick. You went to lie down, rub-
bing your temples. Maybe a migraine was blooming behind your eyes. Then,
suddenly, you realized your skin was sloughing off. There was a tidal pool

where your chest should be. There is every reason to believe that the caterpillar's metamorphosis feels terrifying. Or that it feels like death. I wonder if the radical inability to classify the experience is a necessary ingredient in transformation. Each one of the caterpillar's cells has held this secret ability to self-destruct since birth. This, to me, seems the most comforting thing. Even if the mind is destabilized, literally liquefied, by the transformation, even if the body puddles, you are being "authored" at a deeper level than mind or skin silhouette. You are being distilled by the intuition of your own cells. A few "imaginal disc cells" remain constant that then "use" the slush of protein and matter to compose a butterfly.

Whether tomb or womb, the cocoon is a vessel. An autopoietic boat through the meltwater of your own transformation. It both creates and shapes disorder. An interesting fact is that the caterpillar and the butterfly both "fit" inside of the cocoon. When we digest ourselves, we create ourselves. Not a single cell is expendable. Nothing is discarded. The butterfly, then, is a remarkable act of inclusion. No part of the caterpillar will be exiled from the ecstasy of flight. Yet no part of the caterpillar will remain unchanged.

Does the butterfly share a common self with the caterpillar? They are composed of the same material, but the phase change is so dramatic that it is hard to believe the flavor of consciousness remains constant. What type of an "I" gets translated through the cocoon? There is no way of knowing for sure, but studies have arrived at an astonishing fact. Although the nervous system of the caterpillar and the brain are thoroughly disintegrated, the butterfly retains specific memories from its time as a caterpillar. This fact destabilizes modern neurobiology's insistence that, despite a lack of proof, memories are stored in the brain. A study completed by Georgetown University biologists showed that tobacco hornworm caterpillars given mild shocks when exposed to certain smells retained the aversion and fear of the smells post-metamorphosis. One of the members of the study, Martha Weiss, has mused that this could explain how certain female butterflies remember which plants are safe to lay their eggs on. These were the same plants they feasted on as caterpillars.

Maybe it was the lessened air traffic, the air unburdened of exhaust, but the spring that bloomed out of those first months of quarantine was particularly ecstatic. Each wave of flowers and color exceeded the last, reminding me of the last ejaculatory madness of a small-town fireworks display. It was more obvious than ever before that these plants, with their fleshy petals and cloying scents, were reproducing. And the butterflies, when they arrived, seemed like love messengers, churning the air thick with biosemiotic odes: pheromones, spores, and seedpods. I watched their blue, umber, and lemony-yellow wings aerate the space between leaves and found that I was less and less interested in concretely solving the mystery of butterfly memories.

What does it mean that certain memories make it through the cocoon? What do we hold on to when we feel like we are dying, melting inside the very structures—bodily and culturally—we thought constituted a self? At what point in reconstitution, at what level of cellular complexity, does the butterfly stop dying and start becoming? What does it feel like to break through the green skin of the cocoon?

When we feel our skin start tightening, our cells thawing into fluidity, what memories, what tastes and plants and ideas and loves, do we decide to take with us through the cocoon?

Yes, shells protect and guide us through the oceans. Stories deliver us into events and relationships that generate personalized meaning and movement. But sometimes, we must expose our soft bodies. We must sit outside the shells. We must electron jump between orbits to produce light.

I stood on the moss-furred hill that overlooked the Hudson River and watched butterfly wings, bird wings, and invisible waves of pollen wash clean the world of its previous season. I knew that while I felt unmoored, exposed, and without a next chapter, I was potentially being offered a moment to wait for a better story than I could possibly author for myself. My only job was to stay very still and not try to accelerate through the uncertainty.

I opened my arms up to a season of unknowability and asked, "Okay. I'm in the cocoon. What love will I choose to remember? What love will I recycle and embroider into the pattern of my new wings?"

CHAPTER 15

Catching Feathers, Comets, and Coincidences

WE IDENTIFY TIME WITH OUR BODIES—OUR SOMATIC REACTIONS TO certain scenarios. The feeling of being "on time" is coupled with a sigh of relief and a steady heartbeat. Being "out of time" is a hitch in our breath, a citrus flush of adrenaline buzzing below our tongues. If we "have time" it is almost a physical space, languid as sunshine-warmed ocean water, that we can move through at our own whim. Our bodies feel loose in the joints, our bellies are soft, our spines remain fluid and aligned when we "have" time.

But what does it feel like when we exit time entirely? What does it feel like when we step out of the cultural metronome into the no-man's-land beyond sundials and schedules?

Quarantine paired with the dissolution of my partnership had the effect of completely erasing my sense of routine and progress. The groove of shared coffee and grocery runs and morning gym visits was suddenly gone. So was my ability to take my work to a local café for an hour, using the presence of strangers to motivate me into performative productivity. Doctor's appointments were canceled. Family gatherings and holidays were canceled. All external markers of forward movement flaked away like salt from dried tears. Goals were desaturated. Life was one long, unpunctuated sentence without discernible syntax or shape. I stumbled between nouns, searching for the compass of a verb. Where should I *go*? I had thought I was headed toward marriage, partnership, selling a book, healing my trauma, and regaining my physical health. But suddenly, those normal signposts of achievement weren't just distant. They were utterly erased.

I thought of the Earth with its stuttering seasons, struggling to create its own biospheric syntax as we continually damage its ability to keep time.

No wonder I was out of time. The Earth was struggling with temporality too, desperately attempting to create a new rhythm that allowed species to flourish while we actively interrupted its efforts.

As my dreams unstitched from my brain and frayed into pollen and eiderdown, I started to take long ouroboric walks through my neighborhood to keep up the pretense of velocity. Yes, I had no destination in sight, no goalposts that felt attainable, no way to mark the passing days. But I was still *moving*, right?

It was on these walks that I started to catch feathers.

At first, the more I walked, the more I encountered feathers on the ground: hawk and owl and bluebird tokens. I kept them in a glass flower vase as though they were a bouquet of different types of flight. But then the feathers were no longer below me, but above me, in motion, falling from the sky and from the birds themselves. Little did I know that in March 2020, behind the Pacific blue of a noon sky, behind the birds and their feather-fraying migrations, something else in the heavens mirrored their flight. Something else was falling upward, downward, curving, moving through our world, queering time with its cosmic stitch.

C/2020 F3 or Comet NEOWISE was first spotted by astronomers on March 27, 2020, concurrent with the first lockdown. But unlike the spiked star of the novel virus, the comet was ancient, returning to us after an orbital period of 6,700 years, with its last sighting in the fifth millennium BCE when both the Assyrian and Egyptian calendars are calculated to have begun. From a certain perspective, NEOWISE last arrived at the beginning of linear time, the beginning of imperial civilizations. What did NEOWISE's return herald? The end of time? The end of civilizations?

Timelines collided, condensed, turned backward. I've always liked to think of comets as sewing needles, stitching together time periods at great temporal distances. When I was younger, and the news arrived that a comet was passing overhead, I would ask my parents how "long" it had been since it had said hello to Earth. Four thousand years, 6,700 years, 50,000 years—the durations, the stitches, were difficult to conceptualize. Could you fit that much time in a graph, in a clock, in an open hand, an open eye?

Would a comet returning to us notice how many species had been erased, how much green had faded into concrete gray, how much human clamor covered up lost frog song since it had last paid a visit? Could it notice a breadth of loss our brief lives would never be able to encompass? What vitality—what lost ecosystems—might it remember from its last pass by Earth?

I would lie on a beach towel in the backyard and look up at a malachite-bright streak in the heavens—a green slit in the night sky like a cat's eye. A comet could include a lost age in its arcing embrace over Earth. Perhaps the Upper Paleolithic. I dreamed of an ancestor chipping at an ivory tooth, creating a theriomorphic lion statuette in Germany. I pictured glaciers translating their alabaster heft into rain clouds, initiating the humid Mousterian Pluvial period in Africa, steaming plains into plush viridity, coaxing birdsong out of the ecotones that slip like skin along the serpentine shores of new rivers. Inside the comet's stitch forward in time's tapestry, most of the megafauna will go extinct. But I could still feel the drumbeat of mammoth hooves through the moss. I could still pretend to scent the electric sting of saber-toothed cats slipping through dense undergrowth.

Fifty thousand years ago, when a comet passed, it saw me. But it saw me as a dispersed version of myself: carbon laced into a fern, an electron unzipping the solidity of an ancient shell, a vasculature of iron still threaded like secret blood inside Earth's crust. Each comet remembers when I was numerous, still a pantheon of different beings and materials.

What does time feel like to a comet? Is the comet, taking thousands of years to complete its path, on schedule? Does a comet ever appear early or late?

The instant of the bee is much shorter and sharper than the instant of a human being. The instant of a comet may stitch together millennia. Modern physics tells us that space and time are one and the same. Quantum physics tells us that many different times may exist contiguously, in different universes. In fact, Heisenberg's uncertainty principle shows us that, like the electrons that constitute our molecular bodies, we are less like static matter and more like streaming waves of energy. We are vibratory songs, plucking the string of a duration that may not be as linear as we think it is.

Does time only move forward? The asymmetry of time, also known as the "arrow of time," only exists in closed systems, those characterized by a move into entropic disorder. But Earth is not a closed system. Evolutionary biology provides us with another "narrative." Time does not move downhill toward disorder but, instead, travels uphill toward increasing complexity and creativity. Philosopher and scientist Alfred North Whitehead drew on the work of Henri Bergson when he posited an idea of a subject that is defined physically by its causal relationship to the future, but, conversely, is retroactively and mentally oriented toward and into the past. The string vibrates. The wave of a sound reverberates back and forth, from the long ago to the distant future. Where is the original cause? The original song?

In the seventies, American neuroscientist Benjamin Libet demonstrated that subjects, when shocked for varying amounts of time, would create an automatic subjective referral back to the start of the shock, even before they had mentally perceived it. Material reductionists have used this as an argument against free will. But perhaps it is more interesting to think of "Libet's Delay" as a moment when time spills both ways. The idea of a brain sending back "readiness potential" for perception and physical response troubles our idea of sequential events and causality.

The strange thing about catching feathers was that it depended on no modulation in my speed. If I saw the feather I would continue forward at the same speed, my hand outstretched, always connecting with the feather at exactly the right moment. The first time it happened, with a raven, I was stunned that I didn't have to run or change my pace at all. But this continued with starlings, bluebirds, goldfinches, and doves that live under my favorite abandoned bridge. The most alarming catch was the eagle feathers released from a tussle high up in the sky, streaking downward like a shard of lightning. After catching them, I laid them down on the ground, afraid they might light the dry grass aflame. The catching of the feather always depended on complete trust in my speed and pace. I just had to hold out my hand.

Yes, I felt "out of time." I felt exiled from the scheduled programming of health and happiness.

I had tried for years to keep up. Maybe this medicine, this supplement, this trauma model, would bring me up to speed.

But maybe, although I wasn't living inside human time, I was on time for *something*. The feathers interrupted my ideas of timeliness.

What if progress, that rallying cry of capitalism and patriarchy, wasn't my friend? It certainly wasn't my body's friend. That I already knew. I was constantly struggling to fit my disabled body into a workday. I held a conch shell a friend had gifted me years earlier and peered into the flesh-pink spiral. What if I needed to live more recursively? More deeply? What if I needed to return to certain places and events again and again? What if time spilled backward, not forward?

Human time didn't suit me, and it also seemed poorly matched with the temporality of the biosphere. The one thing it seemed good at was creating damage fast. We could eradicate whole species of plants in a millisecond for the sake of "progress." And yet, what were we as humans hurrying toward? Every species eventually becomes something else or goes extinct. Were we really in such a hurry to reach the final act? And how could one of the youngest species on the planet possibly think it was solely capable of geoengineering a complex tapestry of ecosystems, woven and rewoven over the course of millions of years?

My body was sick, yes. But maybe not in the way I had thought it was. Maybe it was sick of human time. It needed glacial time. Microbial time. Mineral time.

I was playing with these ideas of time later in July 2020, running down my favorite Catskill mountain, high on adrenaline and summit worship. Weeks of quiet time spent outdoors and outside the metronome of collective productivity had given me a slight boost in physical energy. I imagined my immune system exhaling. I felt looser and more relaxed, more able to access the activities that gave me joy. Streaking down the mountain, I felt a kinetic electricity flicker up from the bluestone beneath my sneakers. I breathed deep the peppery scent of mustard greens, flexed into the sunlight licking my shoulder blades. I glanced backward, for no particular reason, and stopped my movement for one second.

Was it a sound? Another hiker?

And then I heard it. A rattle that was more energy than it was a sound. It surged from my tailbone up to the crown of my head.

An eight-foot rattlesnake had been crossing the path. I had heard local folklore that one that big lived on the summit but had never truly believed in her existence. But here she was, rattling through my disbelief. She lay one inch from my paused foot, the step that I had balanced on when I'd decided to look back.

I froze as she continued to rattle and flowed back into movement, cutting a circle not once but three times around me, before pouring herself back into the undergrowth.

I've used an epinephrine pen many times for allergic reactions. But nothing has ever amounted to the surge of adrenaline that flooded my body at that moment. I felt blessed. Every cell of my body felt citrus-bright and electrified. As she circled me, I did mental calculations about how long it would take to get down the mountain and back into cell service if I was bitten. Two hours at least . . . and that was two hours too late.

But the rattler didn't care about lateness. The rattler did not come to bite me. She came to circle me. To show me that time was not a straight line. Time was an embrace, not a taskmaster grinding me into a concluding exhaustion. The narrative did not need to end with tragic finality and a poisonous bite. The narrative could end where it began, in the instant that flowed both ways.

It was around this time that I first heard about NEOWISE. But when I looked into how to view the comet, I was discouraged by how difficult it would be. You needed to drive to a specific hill or lookout and then scan the sky at a specific time of night on a specific day. I was bone-weary by that point, trying to figure out how to support and protect myself financially and medically during a pandemic. I resigned myself to "noting" the comet's passage without actually seeing its flight.

But in late July, when the air was jelly-thick, the mood moribund and waterlogged, my friend Hannah invited me to her home several towns over.

Hannah, one of my closest friends, had been through the breakup of a long-term relationship alongside me, and we had chosen to include each other in our quarantine bubbles early on. During the visit, I stayed out later than I expected, walking down to the river with her, spelling out dreams with such care that I wouldn't have been surprised if they had tattooed themselves into the water, slowly elongating into illegibility as the river current carried them into the sunset.

When I finally headed home, it was close to midnight. I was driving slowly along the old road that wove in and out of valleys and forests, keeping my eyes peeled for the gemlike prickle of raccoon eyes at the edge of the road, when something very strange happened. I came around a curve and my headlights illuminated a snaking traffic jam leading all the way up the slender country road. I waited patiently, watching moths flit in and out of my headlights. Finally, I'd waited so long that I got out of the car and peered ahead. The jam was almost ten cars long, and blocking the way was a huge cargo truck that had crashed horizontally across the road. It was an absurd sight. I had no idea where the truck had come from. Another road? If so, where? I didn't see one. It reminded me of the movie *Donnie Darko*, in which a plane crashes out of thin air, ejected from another timeline.

Someone was calling the police. But I didn't see how this mess was going to be cleared up anytime soon. Resolving to be in bed within the hour, I pulled my car out of the lineup and programmed my GPS to another route—one I'd never taken before.

At first the drive was pleasant. I blasted Fleetwood Mac. I rolled down the windows. I unleashed my full show tune voice to the crickets and frog song, putting a Bette Midler spin on "The Chain." But then forty minutes passed. Fifty minutes. The GPS kept steering me along, but I realized with a jolt that I was in deep country. Somewhere I did not recognize.

There was not a light on in a house for miles. And I had no cell service. As a country mouse, I am used to GPS dead zones, and I know that if you set a GPS while you are in range of service it will continue to direct you through patchy coverage. But if you try to reroute, the system will glitch. I glanced down at the blinking blue dot of my car in a yellow splash of virtual landscape. I didn't want to stop the car or pull over. "Keep driving," said a part of me—still small, at that point—that I'd been listening to more and more, toning it like a secret muscle. And then the voice said, "Stop."

I was on the edge of a vast field, which was stubbled with silver grass. The light came not from the waxing moon but from a bright streak, hung like a zipper at a slant across the sky. NEOWISE, I realized, dumbfounded. I pulled over, leaving the car and the GPS running, and got out, walking to the edge of the field. I would learn later that the comet was at its perihelion, closest to the sun and thus brightest, on that night. For a long time, I stood there gazing at the comet: it was static, but its double-tailed form and its incisive diagonal cut implied movement and great speed. Particle and wave. Oscillating. I wondered if this was what an atom felt like, surrounded by leaping electrons.

"Wahooom," something exhaled. I jumped backward to see that a giant stag was sitting at the edge of the field, directly in front of me. If I had reached out my hand a second before, I would have been able to grasp his antlers.

"Oh. You!" I cried out, feeling a great wash of recognition. A feeling of right-ness that overflowed any narrative of self washed straight into the star-polished eyes of the stag. Carefully, he stood and harrumphed again. And then he turned, dashing off into the field as if chasing the comet to where it must, from my van-tage point, eventually enter the atmosphere and imbed in the landscape.

When I got back into the car, shaken, I took out the GPS. Somehow, with-out service, it had redirected me. I was now twenty minutes from home. I drove slowly, thinking about that time-old phrase "Nothing that is meant for you will miss you." If I didn't go out to find the comet, it would come to find me.

Was it coincidence that the truck blocked the road? That my GPS glitched so perfectly? That the stag was waiting for me? Coincidences flood my life, flowing to the lowest valleys, the moments of desperation and need.

The feathers floated into my hands from above. They felt like a reassuring sign that even though my narrative had melted, I was still, in a more cosmic sense, on time. Years earlier, in September 2018, I went to visit a friend in Kingston at night and the GPS malfunctioned, routing me to the wrong spot—a wine shop near the river. I stood there, gazing at the old building and wonder-ing why I was flooded with déjà vu, before getting back in the car. Months later, when Jason and I were forced to flee our black mold–infested farmhouse, the only affordable apartment in a nearby town was above that wine shop.

What is coincidence?

To coincide comes from the Latin words *com*, meaning "together," and *incidere*, meaning "to fall upon." A coincidence is a falling star. A double-tailed comet that appears as if, like the two rivers that make their confluence outside my home, two streams of cosmic dust have finally joined together as one. A coincidence is like NEOWISE—a stitch in the sky, pulling together the fabric of this moment and another moment thousands of years before.

I think coincidences stitch us into deep time. They draw us into the fabric of a story that is longer than a human lifetime. Longer even than the rise and fall of a civilization. And I have a hunch that coincidences are also the "falling together" of stories. When two people are meant to meet, when someone is supposed to live in a certain ecosystem with specific beings, those narratives will begin to signal to each other. The clue is to follow the cosmic GPS even when the night is dark. Even when you feel certain you may be lost. Even when you are sure you are out of sync with the culture's idea of time.

In the moment when the rattlesnake left me circled, adrenaline-electrified, I knew I wasn't late. I was in a bigger temporality than human time. I was on the mountain's time. More-than-human time. If I hadn't looked back and paused, I would have stepped on the rattler and probably been bitten, hours away from medical help.

I still don't have any answers about time. But I don't try to hold it or catch up with it anymore. I trust time. I trust its circle. Its physicality and embrace. Its intimate overlap with the landscape. And I trust that when the time is right, I'll hold out my hand and catch the feather.

CHAPTER 16

Mentorship with the More than Human

FOR A LONG TIME, I HAD LOOKED TO DOCTORS AND THERAPISTS FOR advice. I had prayed at the altar of healing and medicine and human experts.

Make me whole and make me healthy.

But what I was really saying was close to: *make me normal. Make me fit in. Make me human.*

Ejected from a belief in wellness and happy endings, I trembled like aspen leaves in a thunderstorm—flummoxed, kinetic, fresh. I desperately needed a new paradigm and a new teacher. But I didn't think another book or podcast was the answer.

It was time to call in an animal guide.

The shape and flavor of my life have been fermented, sculpted, and guided by the seasons of the Earth and the seasons of the spirit. I have known winter years and summer years. I have lived inside spring moods and autumnal dreams. The moon's mutability has taught me to change daily, nightly, honoring that my identity is a verb flowing between my body and the entire wild world. My life has been illuminated by the profligate warmth of midsummer sun and by the thin, steely light of January stars wheeling across the cosmos. My life has been saved by rare comets cutting through a dark night of the psyche to provide light enough to keep me moving, keep me living into the possibility of more life, more roads to joy.

But most of all, my life has been repeatedly transformed by unusual encounters with wild animals. True, I was lucky to grow up on an "accidental" farm, otherwise known as my parents' unofficial wildlife rehabilitation center. We fostered injured swans, fed nine baby possums with an eye dropper, and adopted every stray cat or dog that arrived at our door. These animals were my family and my teachers. My parents were clear they had personhood and wisdom on par with any human adults I admired. A Chinese goose called Samantha taught me about self-respect and loyalty. My irascible old tabby Teacake taught me about breaking the right rules, giving no shits, and confronting demons. My long-lived goldfish taught me that the spiritual magnitude of a being has little to do with the size of its brain or body. When I "buried" my two goldfish, Buzz and Glory, in our pond, a giant wind raged off the mountain, fleecing all the neighboring oaks of their leaves and ruffling the tea-colored surface of the water. In death, we reveal the breadth of our exhale.

It was the encounters with wild animals that I came to associate with an extended mentorship or lesson. Often this bird or snake or wildcat would appear to me for a moon cycle, a month, or a year, repeatedly inserting itself into my life until I gave it my full embodied attention. I tended to attract the "big guys." Black bears. Mountain lions. Black widows. Rattlesnakes. Wolves. Rabid bats. Bald eagles. Albino stags.

I stood on the hillock overlooking the Hudson River and looked at the quarantine-muffled world. Less smoke, less boats, less people. More birds. More green. More space for frog song.

Who would show up this time?

I think I was expecting something sexy. A red-tailed hawk. Or a randy coyote. But the animal that *actually* showed up was decidedly unsexy. She was plump, furry, and looked at me with suspicious eyes. And despite her near-spherical shape, she was capable of great, if ungraceful, sprints across uneven terrain. Her habit of streaking down a hill and diving into an invisible hole soon had me calling her Land Seal.

Woodchuck, or Groundhog as she is also called, had come to teach me.

At sixteen years old, waiting for the bus in the winter dawn, I felt each breath dense and vibratory with an incoming blizzard. That anticipatory feeling was not just the product of the storm. It had been building for months, like a migraine's pressure on your optic nerve. It had been curving photon paths into my eyes, flashing phosphines in their corners.

When someone—some elemental or animal being—wants to meet us, they put a hoof, a paw, a claw into the territory of our lives and push down, generating a sink in the landscape so that we cannot escape the gravitational pull of inevitable contact. Everything rolls downhill.

Take a piece of paper. A pen. And draw your life. In most instances, we draw a line, slicing the paper with a linear horizon, a thrust of causality, segmented by birthdays, achievements, graduations, marriages, illnesses. There's a lot of talk about how, in Western culture, we've discarded the rites of initiation that provide true transformation, instead enshrining capitalism's weak substitutions like the buying of a car or a house. But our desire for real initiations remains, and it still often depends on a clear demarcation of before and after. A syntactical structure in which one word leads naturally to the next, and punctuation cleaves breath pinned to paper, leaving accumulated meaning in its wake.

My life has not been straight. It does not make sense read left to right. It is reticulated, queered by encounters and events that I could not plan for or understand with any human frame of reference. I like to think of my life as a territory that is being continually redrawn—where one event, no matter its location on a linear timeline, pulls all the others into different topographical formations and physical elevations.

Let me ask you again to draw your life, but now with a slight shift in perspective. Do not draw a line. Draw a map of the encounters you have had with animals, insects, birds, weather systems, and microbes that have metamorphically rearranged your matter. Draw a constellation of these encounters. What shape does your life take on when it is no longer articulated by the grammar of human progress?

I am not built by birthdays or promotions. I am made by moments of interspecies impact.

The mountain lion had been rearranging my territory for months. There was no way I was going to miss my appointment.

Early in those morning hours, I looked up the pine tree–lined mountain road. Everything was aluminum-bright, polished and blanched of color by the snow-heavy sky. But slinking toward me was the one deviation, the one point in color: something blond and muscled as starlight.

The mountain lion was long and low to the ground. Its tail seemed like an umbilical cord, connecting it to the stone womb of the mountain from which it had just emerged. And it fixed me with its eyes, stitching me to that moment and shifting every moment that would come before and after.

The mountain lion's gaze changed the altitude of my birth and the shoreline of my death. It shifted the magnetic poles on my life's axis so that the violence that had happened in my childhood was no longer behind me; it was ahead of me, ready for me to reenter its barren terrain and find a way to garden in rock clefts, tuck seeds into small patches of moss.

I had grown up with cats, and I knew instinctually that to turn around and run was to invite a chase. Instead, I let the mountain lion's eyes move through mine, through the back of my head, like they were threading a needle. And we were both embroidered as a single seam into those first snowflakes, the fraying moisture of the blizzard's beginning. The lion stopped just six feet from me, watching.

Slowly, slowly, I backed up, keeping the thread between me and the big cat taut and alive all the way down to the driveway until, curving back behind trees, I sprinted to the front door of my parents' home. I was citrus-stung with adrenaline. Bright and tangy with the infusion of the mountain lion's otherness.

Since then, I have become more sensitive to the shifting topology of my life. I notice when the gradient shifts and my feet point downhill. Suddenly, I'm snowballing toward some inevitable encounter. Everything in my life, from flat tires to late appointments, is conspiring to make sure I am perfectly on time for another moment of contact. Not on time for human events, but for those truly important convergences between species. You cannot plan for those events; you cannot go seeking them artificially. But you can also learn how *not* to fight uphill when you feel the gravitational pull of these transformative encounters, when you feel the map of your life begin to rearrange itself.

My life is not a line. It is a shifting topology of encounters. The map of my life is redrawn daily by microbes and daylilies and corpulent clouds. Every being has been a geological shift in my landscape, carving different mountain ranges through what I had previously deemed important. I am rendered malleable, livable, an ecology of shifting summits and fertile valleys by the ways I make myself available to the irreversible impact of these encounters.

At first her approaches were tentative. She appeared next to me at my sit spot on a hill overlooking the river, in the place that had been special to the Munsee Lenape for thousands of years prior to colonization. But then she became more audacious. She tweeted and clicked her yellow teeth as she sat next to me. She dove between my legs while I was on a run. I would feel a prickle of scrutiny and catch her watching me from a distant neighbor's lawn.

Woodchuck.

By Woodchuck's tenth approach, I knew I could not ignore her entreaties. I admit, at first, I felt judged by her. Woodchuck seemed to be asking why I was meditating so much. Why was I walking and running so obsessively? Woodchuck munched grass several feet away, eyeing me derisively. She made me look at myself through her rain-glossy black eyes. What *was* I doing? I was exercising obsessively. Rigorously maintaining rituals of "self-care," although they never delivered me the healthy body they were supposed to summon. I was doing all this human busy work, but I was not maintaining a complex network of tunnels, complete with bedchambers and an actual bathroom. I was not mating with others of my kind, gestating handfuls of warm fur. I was not eating clover and grass. I was not sliding through the grass for the pure thrill of its dew-slickness against my fur.

Okay. I'd really like a different animal teacher, I pleaded with the universe.

I read and reread my novel about Jesus and Mary Magdalene as it started to receive its first rejections. Jesus depended on nature metaphors for his most important spiritual teachings. But he never summoned beautiful animals and benevolent plants. Instead, he would insist that a pernicious mustard-green weed was equivalent to the kingdom of God. To his first-century farmer audience, this was the very same weed that was capable of destroying crops overnight, leaving a family vulnerable to starvation and penalties for their subsequent inability to pay taxes.

Maybe the biggest spiritual lessons came from the unlikeliest allies. The compost heap. The weeds. The weird animals.

Woodchuck was initially coy, but then she started to come closer. I'd be deep in reverie, trying to understand what to do with dreams that melted away with more speed every hour. And then, hearing a snuffle, I'd jerk awake. Woodchuck would be sitting so close I could feel her breath, see her goofy feet splayed, her paws held up like a rodent hierophant, proclaiming some good news I couldn't understand.

"What?" I'd scream. And then she would streak away, dropping into her secret passageway through the hillside.

Different woodchucks appeared in different locations. There was a version of her that lived closer to the river. A rare, near-impossible mountain woodchuck appeared on one of my many solo hikes. She shadowed me everywhere. I tried to dig into ancient Indigenous lore from the Hudson Valley area to learn more about her, but came up only with the fact that there had been a figure called Grandmother Woodchuck.

She did not seem like a benevolent grandmother. I couldn't decide what she reminded me of as she stuck her head up from one of her many entrances into the hillside, chuckling and snorting. It took me several months to realize who it was that reminded me of Woodchuck.

Woodchuck—ungraceful, unpredictable, athletic, desirous of good food and underworld coziness, tricky, discerning, and always up for being the funniest one in the forest—was a reflection of me. Or the me I had lost and needed to reclaim. The me who was hidden in the grass-plush, well-swept underground vaults of my groundhog guardian.

Soon I was feeding her carrots, cherries, and handfuls of clover I picked from behind my apartment. And soon she was brazen, approaching me when I was with other people, making our relationship public knowledge. Once she charged me, erupting from behind, sliding between my legs while my friend

Hannah yelped and jumped away. "Okay. You are not making this woodchuck stuff up," she laughed afterward.

While I was enchanted, the trick was alarming enough that it shocked the people I was with. *Okay*, I thought. Noted. *Be alarmingly quick. Acrobatic. Entrance lovers with physical feats that frighten everyone else who is present. Sit very still in the sun until your fur sparkles like mica embedded in a cliff face.*

Woodchuck wisdom invited me to regrow my childlike confidence, my love of play and dirt, but she certainly did not help me get any dates.

It wasn't until May, driving home on the highway through a freak hailstorm, that I finally understood her appearance. Cars streamed by at seventy miles per hour, sending sheets of rain in their wake. My windshield wiper could hardly keep the road visible through pellets of ice and water. And yet I saw her. Rain-soaked, caught against the dividing guardrails with nowhere to safely run, was Woodchuck.

I didn't think. I threw the car into park in the middle of the highway and jumped out. I held my arms out to Woodchuck and Woodchuck leapt into my arms. I ran through cars to the forest with Woodchuck in my arms. She was surprisingly light. A soggy loaf of bread. But the energy within her was almost nuclear. She smelled like cut pine, like a lightning strike, sharp and inhuman. As I put her down, she turned back and lightly nibbled my hand. It was not even a bite. A parting kiss. Her eyes were liquid cosmos. She dove in between wet barberry bushes and was gone.

"LADY. THAT WAS THE CRAZIEST THING I HAVE EVER SEEN. YOU MUST BE INSANE," a woman screamed at me as I ran back to my car.

"I AM! I AM VERY STUPID," I screamed back, already cursing myself internally. I'd had rabies shots years before. But could woodchucks get rabies? *Shit.* My autoimmune condition meant I had terrible reactions to vaccines. And I was also nearly phobic about rabies. Why had I done such a stupid thing? She hadn't broken my skin, but her kiss had landed next to an open cut on my hand.

The New York State Department of Environmental Conservation was firm when I called for advice. I needed the full rabies vaccine protocol. Five different shots over the course of two months. Hyperventilating, I sat with my Tarot deck and pulled a card. *What is this about?*

Strength. The card depicts a graceful woman taming a lion. Courage. The ability to touch and relate to animals.

A neat conclusion to my encounters with Woodchuck is that the series of rabies vaccinations was a helpful exposure therapy to the hospitals, shots, and medical care I had been avoiding since my disillusionment with my quest for healing set in. Woodchuck forced me to reflect on the fact that there was no purity when it came to surviving in a body. Even though I was cynical about the medical system's ability to *fix* me, I still needed life-saving medicine occasionally. The woodchuck kiss and subsequent vaccinations necessitated a cardiac evaluation I had delayed due to quarantine. And, most importantly, the shots enabled me to freely, and safely, touch and interact with wild animals, something that started to happen with increasing frequency after that wild rescue on the highway.

But Woodchuck taught me something much more important than that too. She taught me that sometimes we don't understand our purpose. As we sit, high on human supremacy, we always assume that we are the main character, the main species. After my season of woodchuck mentorship, I was not entirely unconvinced that my whole life wasn't just about that moment on the highway. My whole life had primed me for that unthinking second when I leaped out of my mind and into action. Maybe I was born to save Woodchuck. And Woodchuck, reflecting my spunk, my ungraceful physical agility, my brand of weird humor, saved me.

Seemingly every day a new guru, spiritual teacher, or self-help sovereign gets outed for sexual misconduct and harmful behavior. The followers of these people float off, betrayed and ungrounded, tugged between a desire for instruction and an increasing suspicion of all institutions. As much as I am an advocate of tapping into our own intuitions, I think the need for external guidance and mentorship is real. I just think we've been looking for it in the wrong places. We don't need any more human teachers. We need to engage in an active, humble mentorship with the more-than-human world. We need more woodchucks and mountain lions. More mustard greens and microbes.

We need other species to teach us how to enter into an ecosystem of knowledge, rather than a single species soliloquy.

Months after my woodchuck encounters, I was walking by a familiar field when I saw a woodchuck I knew well, lying dead. But she wasn't alone. Thirteen huge vultures had descended. They were gracious and coordinated in their feast, letting two dine and then floating away, so two more could approach Woodchuck's feast. My horror dissolved into wonder. Woodchuck was becoming wings. Becoming beaks. Becoming many, many different beings. I realized, dead or bumptiously alive, that her lessons would never stop arriving.

I knelt in front of that interspecies altar of appetites and whispered the words of one of my favorite poets, Linda Hogan.

"To enter life, be food."

CHAPTER 17

Landscape as Lover: Ecosexuality and Queer Ecology

I ALWAYS KNEW THAT MY SEXUALITY WAS WEIRDER AND QUEERER THAN the heterosexual romance. As a survivor of early sexual abuse, it was very hard for me to view human sexuality apart from cynicism and wariness. This was difficult, as I was also a profoundly sensual, romantic person. I felt as if I had been robbed of my own sexuality by my fellow human beings. It was always contaminated by other people's desires. My sexuality felt truest, safest, wildest when I reframed it as ecological: a tentacular web of wants and needs that exceeded my ability to perform sexual viability and to reproduce.

I felt most sensual—most in touch with my eroticism—inside of the forest, where it was densely particulate—with mildew, with spores, with moth-dust from wing beats, with water molecules, with slow ropes of sunlight strained and frayed through the pine needles. The ghost pipe glistened against the shadows, still in curled supplication to the Russula mycelia that fed her spectral body. Nearby, the underground fungi of the Russula fruits: the waxy red mushroom wearing a hat of bleached leaves it had pushed up from beneath. I could imagine all the strands of mycelium pooling and loop-ing below my feet. Kissing into elm trees. Sucking in sugar and dispensing minerals. Always hand-holding. Always interrogative, interspecies, engaging in a lovemaking that doesn't strictly belong to the fungi or plants or trees or bacteria involved.

Surrounded by air sparkling with pollen and dust seeds, I imagined two skin-silhouetted swarms of fireflies and bacteria dancing across soil pulsing with rootlets and mycorrhizae. Two human ecosystems. Each of their footsteps presses the ground, sending signals through miles of mycelium. Each breath passed between the lovers is chock-full of smell and the ecosystem's particular biome.

How many beings constitute a romance? This isn't so much a question of polyamory. It is more a question of self. How many "I"s am I? How many nested beings live within my gut, my breath, my eyelashes? Can I love you with all of them?

When a being that is constituted by a mutualism mates with another being constituted by a mutualism, it is difficult to quantify how many beings are involved. How many species create a reproductive event? How many "I"s does it take to have an erotic experience? The feminist in me wants to say one. But the erotic, dumbfounded animist in me knows it takes almost one hundred trillion bacterial cells. It takes the anarchic fusion that generated my very cells: the endosymbiotic theory demonstrates that originally separate prokaryotic organelles fused to create our building-block eukaryotic cells. And if my lust, my corporeal compulsion to touch and fuse and kiss, is, in part, catalyzed by a hormonal impulse to reproduce, then I must also include the virus that taught my body how to reproduce with a placenta. Over two hundred million years ago, an ancient retrovirus taught us how to create the proteins that develop wombs. Wombs may be human. But they are also plural. They are also viral.

The world is plush with love. Anarchic love that wears no face. Love that bites and pricks and explodes morphologies. Love that turns our own bodies into a meshwork of molecular eroticisms. Love that needs no nuclear couple.

I will never forget, at eleven years old, sitting in the window seat on a plane ride home from seeing family in the Deep South. It was late in the day, and we were passing over a series of mountain ranges. I grew up in the shadow of a mountain. I know their smell, their weather, their moods. But in that moment, I realized I'd never seen them from this vantage point. They swelled like flesh, they rolled like low-tide waves relaxing from the shoreline, they were electric blue in the dusk. Clouds crowned a few summits, forming a milkweed fluff of liquidity. I felt my breath hitch and my senses prickle. A flush of honey warmth bloomed from my belly. I came back to life.

It was the first time I had a sexual experience that felt like it belonged to me. And it belonged to me because it belonged to the Earth, the biosphere itself. I leaned into these experiences as I grew into my sexuality. Standing in a field during a thunderstorm. Piercing cold lake water with the sword of my body. The soles of my bare feet tattooed with river stones. When I read the exquisite eco-memoir *The Living Mountain* by Nan Shepherd, I recognized myself in her voice:

> **Walking thus, hour after hour, the senses keyed, one walks the flesh transparent. But no metaphor, transparent, or light as air, is adequate. The body is not made negligible, but paramount. Flesh is not annihilated but fulfilled. One is not bodiless, but essential body.**

Sex with human beings felt fraught and dangerous for me. Feelings of desire for the same gender that had done me harm were often hard to understand. But I felt myself fulfilled—as "essential body"—when I let myself slip into and merge with a landscape. As someone who felt their senses, and their sensuality, had been hijacked early on, I found a way to reclaim these parts of myself through a slow courtship with the natural world. I was delighted to find that my ecosystem was even queerer, even stranger, than I was; and as my relationship with plants, fungi, animals, and place healed me, I was able to lean into and accept my own queerness. My off-center desires and ways of loving.

Many years later, when I learned about the idea of queer ecology, I recognized myself.

What is queer ecology?

Queer ecology as an interpretive framework seeks to disrupt how heteronormative projections onto nature produce bad science. Queerness, it turns out, isn't a rarity inside ecosystems. It is ubiquitous, from flowers to insects to fungi. Queer ecology seeks to trouble how cultural dualisms get grafted onto

entangled, complex ecosystems. It "interrupts" the tired monologue of hege-
monic heterosexuality and the sterile fiction that we as humans are, in fact,
differentiated from the natural world. It encourages thinking erotically outside
of extractive eroticisms. It melts power dynamics and pulls the rug of linearity
out from underneath the "narrative" of sex. What does nature have to teach us
about queerness? If we are fruiting bodies of our larger ecosystems, densities
of mushroom and mineral and meaning erupting from the forest floor, how is
our individual queerness an echo of larger tentacular sexualities?

This is an attempt to answer a question that I think should have a different
answer every day.

What is queer ecology, I ask again? You should get a different answer from
anyone you ask. Heteronormativity, as wedded to patriarchal capitalism, wants
singular answers. Or binary couples that can produce nuclear families and
nuclear ideologies. It wants to locate and commodify disciplines, to banish radical paradigms to academia where they wither inside tautological arguments
between like-minded, similarly privileged people.

Yes, nature is profoundly, rambunctiously queer. Bdelloid rotifers are par-
thenogenetic, reproducing asexually. Bluehead wrasse fish practice sequential
hermaphroditism, changing genders to suit different ecological pressures. In
some fox populations, 95 percent of females do not reproduce and, instead,
form monogamous, homosexual pairs. Red squirrels alternate sexualities
seasonally and rotate between multiple partners. Bonobo monkeys are typically bisexual, and studies of them have shown that homosexual encounters
between females establish social connections between different populations.

Queer botany gets even weirder. Orchids imitate the shape of female bee
sex organs, and sometimes male bees preferentially pick mating with orchid
flowers over mating with real female bees. Parasitic plants, myco-heterotrophs,
and mutualistic arrangements between fungi and plants blur the boundaries
between pairs. When a being constituted by other beings mates, where does
the sexual act end and begin? Does it flow over the species line? Do sexual
partnerships bloom into and involve the mutualistic and parasitic components?

Queerness, in its oldest etymology, means off-center, strange, or oblique.
And the root of ecology is *oikos*, or "home." For me, queer ecology was

beyond a definite definition. It was my off-center, strange reclaiming of sexuality after violence.

It was to that off-center home that I returned after Jason left me. I needed a partner who didn't require me to define my gender or my reproductive viability. I needed a partner big enough to hold all my sorrow and love and uncertainty. A partner who understood what it was like to sustain damage and feel betrayed by your intimate collaborator.

The Earth, attempting with her climate to soothe and deescalate the human species' destructive bent, seemed to understand this experience intimately. The Earth knew what it was like to be violated and betrayed and then to transform into something wilder and more vital. The Earth knew how to absorb asteroid impacts, create new species of butterflies, shift her green skin around sunlight and sorrow, extinction and extraction.

At first, I thought I *was* heading toward another human lover. Someone who, unlike Jason, could hold all the paradox with me—the illness and the joy, the frighteningly uncertain future, and the mundane pleasures of homemaking.

For months I could feel something anticipatory sparking in my body. A tachycardic hitch. My inhale was misdirected, not to my lungs, but instead to inflate some unspecified organ. A balloon halfway between my ribs and my heart.

The feeling was familiar. In the week leading up to meeting Jason, I'd experienced a similar bodily premonition. It was as if I could feel the future refluxing into the present. Like bird tracks glyphed across fresh snow. Like frost strung across the juniper in a scrawl that seemed to be communicating something of great importance. My near future was so wildly changed that it was trying to prepare me for an arrival: sending notes back in an alphabet that was as of yet illegible.

A person, I decided. *There's a person coming for me*. Although they weren't visible on the horizon, it was as if my body could already smell their approach and was preparing me with minute adjustments, molecule by molecule.

Months into this feeling, a visiting friend had to return to the city unexpectedly. She gifted me her leftover time at her Airbnb. "Think of it as a staycation," she said.

While it felt odd to pretend to be a tourist in my own landscape, I welcomed any punctuation that might add syntax to the meaningless stream of quarantine days spent in the same place, in the same way.

The house was perched above a stream that abuts my favorite forest preserve. But I'd never been on this side of the stream before. That first morning, only ten feet across the current's width, I rocked back and forth on the shore's pebbled banks, feeling as if I'd been transported to a different country. An ivy-illuminated break in the trees revealed an unfamiliar length of the stream. Slabs of bluestone stepped down to create an uneven staircase, dragged into place by glaciers, sanded into silken curves by a liquid song that has been sounding, unstopped, since before humans made music.

It stung me awake, no need for coffee. I followed the thread of adrenaline down to the stream and slipped off my clothes, standing ready for baptism. Dawn pinkened the stream water like blood rushing up to the skin under the pressure of a lover's touch. Japanese primroses blinked through blue shadows on the opposite shore. I could smell the overlap of stone and water, the sunlight inhaled by beech leaves, translated through miles of mycorrhizal fungi, and now exhaled as the thin scent of violets. I could almost spot the golden web of exchanged sunlight and minerals and sugar hanging on dew, a holograph of the underworld.

After I swam, I lay back on a stone step, amazed at how my body fit like a key into the stone's lock. When the door of the stream swung open, unbolted by my body, there was no sound, but something, long clenched, finally melted in my chest.

Yes, I had been right to suspect that someone was approaching me. But that someone was not a person. It was a place. I sensed my lover. And here they were. Bigger, wider, older than I had ever expected. And yet the recognition was instantaneous, mutual. Our bodies clicked. I was made for stream and stone. For this ancient monument to glacial footsteps. I was coming home to darning needles and hummingbirds and wet-eyed does.

"Hello," I whispered. And the answer I received needed no human voice. It used my own body as its instrument, a chord of chill air curving up from the water across my collarbones and causing me to cry out in response to myself.

"Oh!"

Homophrosyne is the ancient Greek word used to describe the union of two people who are alike in how they think and feel. The term is most often associated with the intellectual and emotional resonance between Penelope and Odysseus in the *Odyssey*. When I first heard the word, I felt it encapsulated the type of romance I wanted. Two intellectual peers, united by a shared creative view of the world.

But although they are said to share a mind, Penelope does not recognize her husband immediately upon his return. Rather, it's his secret knowledge that their marriage bed is a tree that finally alerts her to his true identity.

> **Who has set my bed elsewhere? Hard would it be for one, though never so skilled, unless a god himself should come and easily by his will set it in another place. But of men there is no mortal that lives, be he never so young and strong, who could easily pry it from its place, for a great token is wrought in the fashioned bed, and it was I that built it and none other. A bush of long-leafed olive was growing within the court, strong and vigorous, and girth it was like a pillar. Round about this I built my chamber, till I had finished it, with close-set stones, and I roofed it over well, and added to it jointed doors, close-fitting. Thereafter I cut away the leafy branches of the long-leafed olive, and, trimming the trunk from the root, I smoothed it around with the adze well and cunningly, and made it straight to the line, thus fashioning the bed-post; and I bored it all with the augur.**

The place of recognition does not exist in the physicality of either lover, but in the overlap between them. They do not see each other and immediately reunite. There is distrust. Disguise. Trickery. For people who are said to share a common way of thinking, their minds do not immediately lock into each other. Instead, the recognition is displaced from the lovers to an actual "place." The olive tree's rooted endurance is both their marriage chamber and their shared sense of self. Their shared mind, implied by the term *homophrosyne*, is not so much a mind as it is a tree. An ecosystem.

Odysseus is not exactly coming home to Penelope. Penelope is not exactly coming home to Odysseus. They are both coming home to the tree. The root system. The central pith of Ithaca.

Homophrosyne, for me, is an ecological term, too large for heteronormative pairings. It is a homecoming between a person and a place. The shared mind of this recognition has little to do with human intellect. This is a multispecies mind with no central node of cognition. It is slipping our uprooted body back into a root system that knows how to feed us sunlight and hold our trunks steady. The wits of both Odysseus and Penelope do little to bring them back into resonance. How, then, can I reclaim my own *homophrosyne*, not as being denied or dislocated in some person I have yet to meet, but as fully arrived in locations?

If I think of my own body as an assemblage of recycled minerals and molecules, what reunions is my shape facilitating that I do not even note? My body is an unknowing ship, carrying carbon to the valleys and mountains it loved millions of years before it coalesced into the shape and flavor of my personhood. When I slipped into that stream, I was returning matter to matter, from which it had been separated for eons. The love I feel for landscape might be the quorum sensing of my microbiome, all the different ingredients in me detecting and longing for microscopic reunions. In the act of slipping into the stream, I became like the tree that united Penelope and Odysseus.

I did not come home to my lover. I became the place where lovers come home to each other.

Sometimes the love story gets told by chemicals and archaea and fungal hyphae and trophic waves of decay and rainstorms. Mostly it happens on scales both too microscopic and too macroscopic for a single human to observe its erotic sweep.

The important thing to remember is that there is no main character in a love story. Like the fungi that connect different species of trees and endophytes and grasses and myco-heterotrophs, it is hard to tell where the love "lives." It doesn't dwell in one body. It moves. It flows.

After Jason left, I slowly retreated from dating. I was too raw from trauma therapy and confronting my early sexual abuse. I wasn't ready to be vulnerable again, and after Jason I doubted whether there was a human partner I could trust not to hurt me.

I shut down. I closed myself off.

But let me unweave and reweave that human story. Let me write myself into a bigger story.

When I relaxed my need for a human partner, the whole world showed up.

I have been touched by woodchucks and rattlesnakes. I have breathed in phlox pollen and exhaled carbon that was sucked into a black bear's moist nose. I have mellowed inside river water. Photons directly from the sun have inscribed my eyes with luminous, wordless sonnets. My eardrums have been pressed by the high, clean scream of the hawk.

I have not been inside a love story. I have been a love story: my very body a clamorous, complicated interplay of beings disagreeing, singing, swooning, and melting together.

As a year, then two years, passed during which I did not take human lovers, I realized that I was not really "single." I was deeply plural: my whole life was erotic, flush with sensual, multispecies love.

I didn't know if I would ever find a human partner again. But the second spring after my miscarriage, I leaned my head under a blossom-beleaguered lilac branch and inhaled deeply. I could feel the perfume riding molecules into my blood, pressing delicate nodes of pleasure all along my spine, under my tongue, in the stamen-straight center of my own flowering brain.

I inhaled again, thinking, feeling, exalting.

I don't know where all this love comes from, where it goes, what to name it. But I know that every time I breathe out, it overflows.

CHAPTER 18

The Birth of
The Flowering Wand

"WRITING, WRITING, WRITING," THE PSYCHIC REPEATED. "WRITING IS ALL you're doing."

"Are you sure?" I was confused.

"Yeah, I see you at a . . . dining room table with your computer. Writing. Three more books. It's all going to happen very fast. Really fast. And then love will come."

I hadn't gone to the psychic to ask about work. I'd come to ask about love. And healing. I knew I wasn't going to get better in any sort of traditional way, and I had my doubts about heteronormative romance. But was there something else to dream toward?

I do not make a practice of regularly going to psychics. I don't like to outsource my intuition, preferring instead to trust the birds and animals and dreams that find me where I am planted. But as the pandemic lengthened and Jason posted pictures of his new girlfriend on social media, I felt desperate for some validation that it was still possible to find someone wild and kind with whom I could share my life. That there was some way to occupy my sick body with more joy. Could someone love all the impure and shadowy parts of me? Could *I* love all the darkness in me? Did I have to do more work before I was healed and healthy enough for love? Could I still, someday, have the family I had initially dreamed would include Jason?

"Well, I just got an agent for my Mary Magdalene novel. And my agent encouraged me that it should sell relatively fast," I offered. "I'm not sure I have the energy to write another book before I sell that one!"

"Don't let anything get in the way of the books when they come through. Just write, write, write. And no more chicken and turkey. You're allergic."

I filed away this information with a wry smile. Chicken and turkey were some of the *only* foods I could safely eat at that point. And there was no way I was writing another book before selling my Magdalene novel. I was beyond exhausted.

But then quarantine didn't end. Winter tightened my isolation into a crystallized prison. A freak accident ripped off part of my knee, which then refused to heal correctly. I was not only apartment-bound, but I was also bound within my home, unable to even walk to the kitchen.

A friend I hadn't seen since before the lockdown committed suicide. Then another. Love didn't arrive. And my novel was rejected dozens of times. I came to expect the nauseating compliments that accompanied the rejection: "A little too long and literary for a popular audience. But excellent writing," and "Incredible prose and research, but I just don't think there's a market."

Cancer claimed a friend so quickly that, restricted by my own illness and the threat of Covid, I was unable to visit him to say farewell. While other able-bodied friends played with pandemic regulations, I knew that my health conditions necessitated extreme precaution. I barely saw anyone at all. And no one came into my apartment.

By March 2021, my novel had been rejected more than twenty times.

No love. No books. No hope. No health. No plot.

I am not someone prone to depression. I have known soul-shredding sorrow. I was familiar with defeat and anxiety and emotional pain. But, despite the daily companion of physical anguish, I had always tried to sprint through periods of emotional blueness.

Finally, there would be no more running. I was knee-capped, literally. The wound on my knee took months to heal, requiring a specialist to remove the superficial scab and scrape it out every week so it could heal from the bottom up.

I was swaddled with gray mist, hung upside down in the underworld, run through with rot. I had reached something that felt much deeper and darker than that ten-letter word: *depression*.

Enforced presentism is a term coined by anthropologist Jane Guyer during the pandemic to discuss the experience of being dislocated from linear time, yet stuck in the present moment without recourse to imagine a future or romanticize the past. Events that disrupt our sense of justice, fairness, and hope rupture us from time. While many people identified with this type of rupture for the first time during the uncertainty of quarantine, those with chronic pain and incurable conditions were already intimate with this flavor of agonizing temporality.

In moments of extreme pain, physical or psychological, we become stitched to the present moment. It becomes impossible not to be radically present. We can no longer count on a future. And our bright-minded, able-bodied pasts don't feel like they belong to us anymore. Often the pain is so intense that there is no escape in any direction.

Forced to confront how those years of therapy and medicine had made me sicker and sadder, I realized my imaginary healthy future no longer existed. Where was the goal I could orient myself toward? And my past— tangled up with Jason and my previously healthy selves—felt utterly disconnected from me.

Most quarantine days I was so physically ill I would end up at 4:00 p.m. lying on the floor of my apartment, trying to follow my breath through a moment with no punctuation. I was stitched to the present with radical intensity. There was no nostalgia for the past and no ability to envision the future. My breath was a needle, piercing the cloth of me with each inhale, embroidering an embodied instant. The inhale was white-hot anguish for one-eighteenth of a second, the exhale a nonconsensual witness to a complete meltdown of every one of my dreams and imagined lives.

I logged on to social media and saw that a woman I knew with Ehlers-Danlos had just died. She was younger than me. She had seemed healthier than me.

What if I only had a year left? Less? What if I didn't get to publish my novel in my lifetime? What if I wasn't going to live long enough to write all the stories

I so desperately loved? What if I never got to experience love and partnership again? Never got to grow a family? What if all my beliefs were wrong? What if I was wrong about . . . everything?

In my childhood favorite, *The Once and Future King* by T. H. White, the wizard Merlin instructs the young King Arthur:

> **The best thing for being sad . . . is to learn something. That's the only thing that never fails. You may grow old and trembling in your anatomies, you may lie awake at night listening to the disorder of your veins, you may miss your only love, you may see the world about you devastated by evil lunatics, or know your honour trampled in the sewers of baser minds. There is only one thing for it then—to learn. Learn why the world wags and what wags it. That is the only thing which the mind can never exhaust, never alienate, never be tortured by, never fear or distrust, and never dream of regretting. Learning is the only thing for you. Look what a lot of things there are to learn.**

The boy Arthur, like the sixth-century bard Taliesin, learns not by book, but by becoming. In a sixth-century poem attributed to Taliesin, we read, "I have been a blue salmon, I have been a dog, a stag, a roebuck on the mountain . . . A stallion, a bull, a buck, I was reaped and placed in an oven." To become a storyteller, Taliesin has to live other lives, other stories. But the most important overlap between the young Arthur and Taliesin is that they learn not by becoming other human beings. They learn by entering into badgers and fish and insects: the minds of the more-than-human world.

The only distraction from endless days in isolation was my maniacal research into other species and mythology. These two seemingly opposed passions had been the guiding stars of my life, but that second quarantine spring they were more than starlight. They were the sunshine keeping me alive. I poured myself back into my old loves: the Arthurian legends, the Tristan romance, and Merlin folklore. Simultaneously, I devoured every book on bacteria, fungi, microbiology, botany, and ecology I could find.

The stories and myths I loved so much had not appeared out of thin air. They had sprouted from a world that could create flowers alongside flesh-eating maggots, forests, and volcanic vents. I wanted to plant human stories back in their wilder soil, to see how our gods and goddesses had originally functioned when they were still connected to a more-than-human root system. I'd done this with Jesus in my novel, planting him back in his ecological and historical context and watching him transform from the starved figurehead of patriarchy back into the anti-imperial storytelling healer. Now I tried to do it with other popular myths, to see if I could dig up forgotten root systems of vitality below the monocrop of human supremacy.

I'd done more than a decade of therapy. I had spent years investigating "my stories": somatic, psychological, genetic, ancestral . . . But lying on the floor, filled with grief so viscous and gray I could scarcely breathe through it, I wondered what it meant when our stories always led back to us. Was that really the best destination to orient toward? What if initiation—the story so many healers and lightworkers and mythologists tell—was a bad story? So many of my friends and loved ones had not survived. What assurance did I have that I would? What reason did I have to believe that there was another season coming for me? Another type of time?

"I" statements are human statements. I am the most important species. My individual healing is the most important concern. But if we were going to heal the harm we'd enacted on the biosphere, we were going to have to switch to a different type of statement. Maybe questions were a good place to start, rather than from the hubris of an answer.

What am I not seeing? What do I need to see? How can I be of service?

Merlin's words came back to me. "Learn something. Something that isn't about you."

The best thing for anthropocentric dread, for individual anguish, for heartbreak, for illness, is to interrupt our individuality. When we cannot walk, cannot move, cannot leave our beds, we do not need to find a tree or landscape or butterfly to be. We can be a mote of dust. A potato bug vaulting across the room. The yellowjacket tapping his armored body against the closed window. Sometimes the answer is not to problematize our wounding, but to slip through it like a doorway into otherness. Other minds. Other types of anguish. Other animals and insects going extinct. Birds singing out courtship songs to mates that will never arrive.

I vomited. I wheezed. I lay on the ground. I canceled doctor's appointments. I received another rejection of my novel. There was no point. Everything was a nocebo, instructing me on how to decay, how to fall apart.

There were no cures. There was nothing but bad news I didn't want to hear.

I tried to lose myself in obsessive research. Fungal systems. The evolution of roots. Ivy. Vines. Soundscape ecologies. Amphibious gender-flipping. Woodchuck's territorial behavior. The evolution of eukaryotic cells. Extinction events. Eagle mating behavior. When the physical pain got exquisitely intense, I would imagine myself lengthening into my last name: "strand." Fungal strands. A silvery webwork of mycelia eating and feeling with its whole filamentous fabric. I imagined that every part of me had a reaching hand, a probing hypha. I imagined how delicious and helpful it would feel to be so embodied, so coordinated by appetite and desire. So intuitively tactile and curious.

I lay on the floor of my apartment, watching the full moon rise framed by the window, and I realized that if I was going to die before I could find wild, real love and make babies and write all the long, romantic novels I'd planned on writing, I was going to have to let myself become a mouth for a story bigger than just me.

"Make me an instrument. Blow through me."

Was there healing beyond the human? Beyond the hope for a cure or a happy ending? Was there something wilder and more symbiotic beyond my narrow ideas of well-being?

That night I had a very strange dream. I was in a dark forest filled with all my wild Hudson Valley kin. Amber-hued chanterelles, blushing trillium, ivy curling over my feet, tufts of pigweed on the side of the path, berry-laden juniper trees standing like blue flames against the dim crepuscular light. Witch's butter glowed on branches, and honey fungi bloomed from the cleft trunk of an old maple. A blue darning needle stitched a sapphire thread between two beech saplings. Behind a tangle of wild rose bushes, something flashed like a bone. A white stag. He rounded the vegetation and stared at me with carnelian eyes.

"It's time to let them tell the stories." I heard the voice in my own mind, but it belonged to the albino stag. I knew at once he meant the fungi, the insects, the plants.

"Okay," I whispered. "Where do I start?"

"With men."

The dream ended with that riddle.

The next day, as I sipped my morning coffee and puzzled over the dream, I had a bodily sense that something was rising in me. A vegetal tide. Some fungal infection was hijacking my nervous system. It wasn't until midday, walking down at the river, that all these threads started to braid together into something green and muscular. My years of research into the magician rabbi Yeshua, known as Jesus, while writing my Magdalene novel. Jesus's deep connection to other dying and resurrecting vegetal gods like Dionysus and Orpheus and Osiris. My lifelong fascination with fungi and my long-dormant idea of myths being the fruiting bodies of underground mycorrhizal systems. My love of invasive species. Fermentation. Microbial anarchy. My deep passion for the Arthurian myths. My research into Tristan and Isolde for my next novel. By the time I'd looped back to my apartment, I could conceptualize an entire project. I thought it would be an essay about rewilding myths of the masculine with an ecological lens. Something I'd write privately, for myself, to save myself. Something to throw myself fully into with the hope that it might, like a boat, carry me to a safer shore.

I had a lot of reasons to be angry at men at that moment. I also had a lot of reasons to love them. Some of the people I loved most in the world were men. And these men were suffering from the unfortunate conflation of masculinity and patriarchy. I also knew that if I lived long enough, and found the right partner, I might have a son someday. Didn't I need to understand magical boyhood and fertile masculinity to welcome it into the world someday through the vehicle of my own body? What stories would I want to give my son? If the curtains were dropped during quarantine, if all hope seemed lost, why not risk doing something strange, something goofy, something totally outside "the plan"?

I typed up a brief synopsis and a series of questions I wanted to live inside. As a relatively private person, I'm not sure what inspired me to post this piece of writing to my small social media community. But for some reason I did. I expected no response. I hoped maybe one or two people might have research suggestions. I desperately wanted to puncture the sterility of my isolation. I left my computer. I headed to the woods.

Hours later, when I checked my phone, I gasped. My piece had been reposted hundreds of times. My inbox was filled with messages.

It was as if a pipe burst in me. Within a day, it was clear this was not just an essay. It was a series of essays drawing on all the research—science, ecology, and mythology—I'd directed toward my fictional projects. Suddenly the writing wouldn't stop. I'd be driving to a hiking trailhead and have to pull over. I'd open my Notes app, frantically emailing myself a whole essay. These essays arrived fully formed. Writing them often felt like taking dictation at the side of the highway, in the middle of the night, halfway through my morning run. I felt like I was infected. I was possessed. I couldn't stop.

The first draft—every major essay of the book—was written in under fifteen days. Fifteen days that saved my life. I've experienced inspiration before and mad writing bouts. I always write a lot—with freelance jobs, poetry, books, essays, and long-form fiction projects all unfolding simultaneously. But fiction projects, while they are born from the spark of inspiration, take years to finish and are supported by diligence and dailiness. I treated my novel writing like hygiene. I had to write every single day to complete such a huge undertaking. I plotted, planned, revised, and reworked. Yes, I was deeply in love with my novel, but I tended to that love carefully, slowly, methodically.

This was something entirely different. It was almost anguish. Close to madness. It was all-consuming. But it was also saving me, giving me energy and purpose out of thin air.

Where does art come from? Is it ontologically primary to our own minds? Or does it arrive externally? When we try to explain that slippery moment of creative conception, we often refer to a docile muse. But in reality, creative expression is something stickier, weirder, and more uncomfortable. I am speaking of those spasms of the soul that Spanish poet and playwright Federico García Lorca famously characterized as the *duende*, or "goblin," as it could be loosely translated into English. For García Lorca, the angel sweetly "guides and grants," and the muse gently "dictates and prompts." Both influences come to us externally, herding us like velvet-mouthed sheep-dogs into creativity.

But the *duende* is different. It pulses up from the feet and the roots. It is an internal surge, but its origin is in the ground. It penetrates and infects us with "the spirit of the earth." This is no gracious angel. No. García Lorca explains that the *duende* "is a force not a labour, a struggle not a thought." It is the art that gurgles, arrives on tides of bile, and "won't appear if he can't see the pos-sibility of death, if he doesn't know he can haunt death's house . . . the *duende* delights in struggling freely with the creator on the edge of the pit. Angel and Muse flee, with violin and compasses, and the *duende* wounds, and in trying to heal that wound that never heals, lies the strangeness, the inventiveness of a man's work."

As I typed into the night, my eyes glazed, my heart fluttering, I thought that I was not compelled by a muse. The muse was the companion of romanti-cism—of financial security, inheritance, and languor. The muse was a privilege and an abstraction. The muse was the world at a remove.

No. This felt much closer to the *duende*. The *duende* was the dissolu-tion of dualism—"not form but the marrow of form." It smeared the boundary between ground and feet, body and mind. Philosopher Andreas Weber asserts, "Life has a tendency to transform all available resources into a meshwork of bodies." This meshwork of bodies' goal is aliveness of the whole, and not alive-ness of the individual. An aliveness that "in its innermost core carries the plea that there be more life, not that I am fine. Putting the desire that there be life first might even provoke my own destruction."

That spring, I wanted to stay alive. But not as an isolated subject, mildew-ing in her lonely apartment. I wanted to weave myself back into the risky alive-ness of the whole biosphere. Weber tells us that to be alive is to be "enmeshed" in a "mess that must be constantly negotiated." To be alive is, as García Lorca explains it, to "invite" the transformative and terrible power of the *duende* to the edge of the wound to dance. The *duende* does not care if we live or die, but it cares deeply about "aliveness," generally. It uses us as a channel of "gesture and dance." It spasms and deforms and surges through us.

Art is transformative. But no one ever said it was safe.

Within a week of sharing these essays online, three thousand people had read the work. I was dumbfounded by this, but I was also too obsessed with the actual writing to give it much notice. However, as I continued to freely offer these essays online, another thousand showed up. And then another thousand. These were writers, scientists, poets, gardeners, therapists, mycologists, Tarot readers, herbalists, farmers, healers, educators. People who were incredibly supportive and interested in the work. And who provided crucial feedback and helpful research directions in real time as I wrote the book. Most of all, I found their outright enthusiasm and belief in the project and my writing to be miraculous. After months of rejections from publishers, being in direct relationship with readers was deeply nourishing and refreshing. Why spend years trying to shave down my maximalist, bawdy writing for some sterile, imaginary audience? Why not offer my wildest version of myself and see who else showed up to join the party?

"When are you eating or sleeping? Is this good for your health?" Hannah asked me worriedly. "You've written a book in under a month."

"I don't know if it's good for my body. But I don't know if it's about me—my body or myself—at all," I replied with wonder and a tinge of horror. "It reminds me of those ants that get infected with the fungus."

I explained to Hannah that I felt like the carpenter ant of the tribe Campono-tini that becomes infected with the fungus *Ophiocordyceps unilateralis*, popularly known as the zombie fungus. Once infected with the spores of the fungus, the ant's nervous system and body become an extension of the fungal need to reproduce. With great precision, the infected ants ascend up plants to a specific altitude and microclimate, around ten inches from the ground, and perform a "death bite" into the central vein of a leaf on the north side of the plant. They do this almost always at solar noon. Extraordinarily, fossilized remains of leaves show us that the "death bite" of the infected ant goes back at least forty-eight million years. Once latched on, the fungus erupts from the insect, producing a fruiting body from the head of the ant that releases spores. Infected ants in a lab, once dissected, showed that the fungi colonized the body and musculature of the ant and did not, in fact, take over the brain.

Using the power of imagination, we can try to conceive of the experience of a hijacked consciousness. What does it feel like to still have your mind, but to feel it being compelled, chemically and bodily, toward a purpose not specifically tailored to your own life and needs? We've all had times in our lives when intuition and circumstances compelled us to make choices that seemed absurd. In these moments, we say we are guided by "God" or "ancestors" or "madness." And, when such a moment regards making art, we say we are inspired. We are serving the godhead, Hermes, the imaginal realm, the collective unconscious, the "aliveness" of the world.

What does it mean to become a channel for another species? Another strange type of reproduction? What does it feel like? Is it terrifying? Is it pleasurable? Does it feel like death? Or does it feel like art? Does it feel like both? I think it might feel like *duende*.

Human stories are not the only stories. Human art is a small portion of the world's art. Human stories, when they assert their sterile primacy, directly impinge on the aliveness of the whole. They are used as the inspiration behind clear-cutting, colonialism, ecocide, and monoculture.

What does it mean to be an artist in an age of extinction and ecological collapse? What does it mean to be a storyteller when you have come to the end of all your personal stories? I think it means inviting the *duende* to dance at the edge of the wound. I think it means opening the door to another species. Yes, I wanted to tell stories, but they no longer needed to be my stories. They didn't even have to protect my body and promote my own aliveness.

I wanted my stories to promote the aliveness of the whole Earth. I wanted them to surge up from the ground into my feet. The *duende* showed me that to be a channel of good art was to allow for a radical and risky transformation. This transformation was not personal. It wasn't even human. The carpenter ant and the *Ophiocordyceps* fungus beg us to ask what it means to become the artistic and creative vehicle for another species.

García Lorca quotes a Spanish ballad at the end of his essay: "The lips I kissed you with / I've given to earth below." Only when we surrender to "struggle" and dance with something that wants to create "through" us and not "for us" can we open to what García Lorca calls "the endless baptism of freshly created things."

Confronting climate collapse, a pandemic, and my own failing body, I had to wonder if that was the creative imperative of this moment. How could I become the vehicle of another species' narrative urgency? How could I creatively and dynamically contribute to the vitality of the whole world, perhaps even at the cost of my own personal narrative?

I wrote and wrote. And I stayed alive. I made it through another day. New friends showed up from oceans away. I wove together fungi and Greek gods. Insects and folklore. Science and storytelling. I wove myself back into community at a time when I desperately needed community to survive.

In a miracle totally outside of my expectation, a new reader-turned-friend passed along my writing to an editor at the independent publisher Inner Traditions. Just a month out from its conception, I sent him the project, still in a state of disbelief. He bought the book the next day.

I walked, shaking slightly, around my neighborhood, watching goldfinches wing mating dances through the bushes. The gilt scrawl of feathers hovered in the air like a message written in sunlight. I wept. I knelt in the grass near the river and said thank you to the puffballs and ducks and doves and purple loosestrife that greeted me every morning at the end of my run.

But to return to the metaphor of the carpenter ant with a fungal infection, the infection doesn't end when you want it to. It ends when it has used you up for its reproductive act.

Within days I was writing again. Another book. And then another. True to the psychic's prediction, I sat at my dining room table typing, day in and day out, my time only punctuated by swims in my favorite river, runs, and research.

"You should take a break," suggested my friend Ilana during a late-night phone call. "You've already sold a book! You wrote *The Flowering Wand* in . . . like a month!"

"You see, this is keeping me alive," I tried to explain. Every day when I woke, I could taste the anguish, the inability to imagine a future. I could feel the tremble of absolute physical and practical uncertainty. And then, every day, I would try to offer some medicine to the world. For so long I'd sought medicine for my ailing body and my glitchy nervous system. What would it look like to offer medicine in return?

Usually right after dawn, I would feel something flare in my brain. Why does the *Wolbachia* bacteria harm some insects and not others? How can I explain what it's like to develop intimate kinship within a circumscribed ecosystem? How do hummingbirds migrate so far without stopping? What does storytelling that explodes human narratives look like? What kind of healing is available to someone with an incurable illness? How can I make my body, my life, my work into a home for other beings, good soil for other thinkers to come and plant their seeds inside? Each day, I would try to offer some tiny kernel of magic. And people would reach back, openhearted and openhanded, weaving me into their ecosystems. Telling me I wasn't alone.

The psychic was right about my writing. She was also right about chicken and turkey. I became allergic to both a year out from her initial prediction, just as thousands of pages of writing were pouring out of me. The writing was a ladder out of despair. A thread of spider silk, shot into the sky to help me balloon out of my isolation.

I thanked all the beings that held me during that season of rejection, illness, injury, and uncertainty. I grieved those loved ones I had lost, who would never live to see the writing they inspired. I drove to the local reservoir. Its foundation poured over the valley of the Munsee Lenape and the original European settlers. The reservoir holds 122.9 billion gallons of water, with a shore length of forty miles. On most days, it displays a crystalline mirrorscape of the Catskill Mountains. As I walked along the shore for miles, my skin shivered back into being. A bald eagle screamed somewhere over the emerald reflection of Overlook Mountain. A rivulet of sweat snaked between my breasts. My hips swayed like a spoon in a mixing bowl, stirring me back into the material of myself. My nerves anastomosed and sparked, sending my mind, green as a plant and alive with light, back into the tips of my fingers. I picked a blue star of chicory. The curved edge of a stone kissed into the heel of my foot. And then I felt it. The anguish. A splinter of magma in the pith of me. Pain almost as old as my name, almost as old as my body. My breath twitched in my throat, hitching above my lungs. A memory, gummy with shame, began to overlap with the present moment. Then it happened. A laugh bubbled in me. Laughter so loud it scared the geese off the shore and into the water. Laughter that quickly melted into tears.

The pain arrived because it knew the land was big enough to hold it. The reservoir's wide lap of water said, "Come sit. Swim. Flow. Feel this. I will mellow it. Diffuse it. I am safe enough to hold you while you feel this." This lesson was fundamental. Yes, my nervous system needed to be regulated; this pain needed to be felt and acknowledged. At the same time, I needed to pay close, sensual attention to the ecosystems and landscapes that gently coaxed me into safety.

"Oh," I realized, taking in the fabric of the reservoir, ducks floating across the reflection of mountain summits, the bright zest of pine trees threaded through the low, spicy scent of sunbaked grasses. My body, like the wide expanse of the reservoir, the generous heave of the wildflower-festooned hillside, was finally big enough to hold the pain. Safe enough to diffuse and melt and mix it into something tastier, stranger, sturdier. Safe, but not as in safe from death or harm. Safe as in completely present and embodied. I was safe to fully occupy and exult in the sensory range of every one of my 37.2 trillion cells—viral, bacterial, fungal, human, and otherwise. I felt safe enough to let a feeling oscillate and swell.

Make me a lap of safety for the mountains and rivers and mushrooms and black bears and elm trees and dragonflies. Make me into a place where other beings can finally come back into their bodies, I prayed.

When I returned home, feeling raw and prickly with relief that I had written myself into survival, I received a call from my editor.

"I want to buy *The Madonna Secret.* Your Magdalene novel."

The answer to my prayer wasn't on human time. Its deferral had left open space for me to reach out to anarchic collaborators—human and more-than-human. It had compelled me to write other books and challenge my assumptions about who my art was about and who it was supposed to serve.

"Yes. Thank you. Thank you," I finally answered, my voice woolen with feeling. I wasn't just thanking him. I was thanking Rondout Creek. The Hudson Valley. The Animate Everything. My whole body was a gesture of gratitude, opening its arms up to the whole prickling, stinging, singing, feral world.

It wasn't Jesus the miracle worker who had finally arrived to spit in my eyes and heal me. It was the entire world. The fungi and woodchucks and black mold and mountains. And maybe that had been the lesson all along, the one I'd ignored as I researched my novel *The Madonna Secret*.

"It is I who am the all. From me did the all come forth, and unto me did the all extend. Split a piece of wood, and I am there. Lift up the stone, and you will find me there."

Suddenly I realized this "I who am the all" wasn't a human being or a deity. It was an ecology: the center of a cedar log, the glistening grub under a slab of bluestone. It was my questioning eyes, seeking something in the undergrowth, the dirt, the shallow river water.

The "I who am the all" beyond my human ideas of healing was the overlap between my body and the body of the world.

CHAPTER 19

Becoming Supracellular— The River That Runs Both Ways

I STARTED GOING TO THE RIVER LIKE I USED TO GO TO THE DOCTOR'S office, with an openness and humility that some bodily ease or healing might arrive that I couldn't predict.

Down by the river, I would sit and sometimes think I could smell the moment when the tide reversed and the estuary injected its salt response into a freshwater question. The air bristled, the wake of a passing motorboat cutting crisp Vs in the water. The salt in the air acted like salt in a soup, enhancing the flavor of the honeysuckle, the locust blooms, the sun-toasted cedar planks tilted against the boat-building shop.

The Hudson River is called *Mahicantuck* by the Munsee Lenape people, which means "The River That Runs Both Ways."

The ocean refluxes into the river. The river back into the ocean. Is it, then, still a river? Or is it a brackish finger probing into the landscape?

One summer morning I squinted, as if trying to mark the spot in the water where opposed currents intertwined like the snakes of the caduceus. The water surface, spangled with willow frond reflections, kept its secret. But at my feet I spotted something else: the velveteen dome of a mower's mushroom poking up from the grass. I bent down, noticing how the diminutive parasol structure disappeared into the fine-grained soil. I knew that although this fellow looked lonely, he was really less of a fellow and more of a swarming festivity belowground.

Mushrooms are the reproductive flourishes of fungal lifeforms that live in soil (or wood) as threadlike, filamentous webs called mycelium. Mycelium is composed of long tubes of hyphae. One network might have thousands of different hyphal tips, all capable of forking, fusing, foraging, and creating increasingly complex connections with other fungal systems and vegetal lifeforms.

I lightly pressed my finger to the mushroom, imagining my mind slipping like a yolk from the egg of my brain, into my arm, then strained through my finger into the damp body of the mushroom. Deeper still, below the fruiting body, my consciousness dove on mycelial threads into the underworld. It held tight to a roving nucleus. It traveled through a chain of opening and closing doorlike pores called septa.

If I had entered an animal cell, I might have found myself profoundly confined, abiding by the strict rules of inner and outer, with organelles bolted to the floor. But here in this mycelial network, I was not confined to one node. I could wander through the whole web. My ride was only possible because fungi are biologically unusual, confounding standard ideas of the "cell" and the self.

In 1665, Robert Hooke was the first person to observe a microorganism under a microscope. It was his observations that, over the next two hundred years, informed the concept of the cell as a fundamental unit of multicellular lifeforms. The concept of the cell as a stable and foundational unit, while it applies to most of us, is not universally true. Many plants and filamentous fungi employ a type of cellularity that is much closer to verb than it is to noun. While hyphae are commonly referred to as fungal "cells," that term is misleading. A classical cell can be envisioned as a discrete bundle of protoplasm with one nucleus, neatly bounded by plasma and an extracellular wall. One bead in a necklace. But fungal hyphae behave differently. They create "supracellular" networks. Hyphae are separated by cross walls called septa. However, these septa possess pores that open and close, creating a fluid passageway through a hyphal thread. For mycelial fungi, there is no discrete bead on the necklace. The necklace becomes a flume through which organelles and cytoplasmic material flow. A single hypha can, at one time, house multiple nuclei. And, given fungi's proclivity for promiscuity, those nuclei may not even carry the same genome as the original mycelial network. Fungal webs can fuse, exchanging nuclei and promoting genetic diversity.

I reached the end of a hyphal tip, bouncing on a plush organelle called the *Spitzenkörper* that sits at the head, and screamed as it cleaved beneath me, splitting off in two directions. A nucleus collided with me from behind, then another ramified. The pressure passed my mind through the needle of another mind. I let myself fork and divide.

Whenever I wanted a cure or an answer—whenever I was terrified by irresolvable panic and nausea—I resisted trying another elimination diet or boutique nutritionist or trauma therapist. I needed to try something new.

So instead, I wandered down to the river. I sat looking out at the river, imagining myself not as a patient in a sterile hospital—but as a completely different species. A hummingbird. A sturgeon. The wet-eyed opossum under the barberry bush. The barberry bush itself. The *Wolbachia* bacteria pinwheeling through the colorless blood of the monarch butterfly. The exercise necessarily failed. But I found that the empathy muscle it strengthened within me was crucial. There were bumblebees drugged on pesticide, flailing on the ground beside me; ducks with arteries clogged from being fed breadcrumbs; hummingbirds struggling to find nectar-filled flowers in a sea of manicured lawns. I was not singular in my suffering. My illness was not genetic. It was ecological. It was shared. And if any of us were to heal, I had to understand it would be a communal project, not a singular achievement.

In an age when anthropocentrism is fueling mass extinction and ecocide, it seems vitally important to practice thinking like other beings. Or even, when we feel ambitious, trying to think alongside the deep time oscillations of entire ecosystems as they evolve.

We have behaved like ordinary cells for too long, pretending there is no movement from the inside to the outside or vice versa. We have believed, for too long, that our minds belong to us as individuals. But advances in everything from forest ecology to microbiology show us we are not siloed selves, but relational networks, built metabolically by our every biome-laced breath, thinking through filamentous connectivity rather than inside one neatly bounded mind. I think of the spider who, sitting like the iris inside a lacy eye, tugs and flexes and tightens its grip on different strings, creating an interrogative experience with web and with world. Scientists have likened this behavior to the activity of a brain itself as it sifts through and reacts to stimuli. Each tug is a question, each returning vibration a reply. In this way, spiders can sense which parts of their web attract more flies and focus their continued silk production on these areas. They can tell when prey has been caught immediately; and studies have shown that when webs are deliberately damaged, spiders perceive the damage and locate the spot, where they hurry to make repairs. Even more strangely, extended cognition researcher Hilton Japyassú has shown that cutting a part of the silk dramatically shifts and disorients the behavior of the spider, seemingly imitating the effects of a lobotomy. This begs the question, Where is the spider's mind? Is it inside the spider's actual brain? Is it in its spinnerets or legs? Is it in the web itself?

As cognitive philosopher Evan Thompson describes:

> Part of the problem, however, comes from thinking of the mind or meaning as being generated in the head. That's like thinking that flight is inside the wings of a bird. A bird needs wings to fly, but flight isn't in the wings, and the wings don't generate flight; they generate lift, which facilitates flight. Flying is an action of the whole animal in its environment. Analogously, you need a brain to think, but thinking isn't in the brain, and the brain doesn't generate it; it facilitates it. The brain generates many things—neurons and their synaptic connections, ongoing rhythmic activity patterns, the constant dynamic coordination of sensory and motor activity—but none of these should be identified with thinking, though all of them crucially facilitate it. Thinking is an action of the whole person in its environment.

Thinking, then, is constituted less by an organ and more by a relational process.

At the start of quarantine, I was mourning my inability to respond to expensive trauma therapy. I could not keep my brain in my body. I fled into dissociation to escape physical pain and psychological distress. I was certain this "failure" was also impacting my ability to address my connective tissue disease. If I couldn't properly *be* in my body, how could I possibly understand how to heal it?

But during my time at the river, I began to strongly suspect that the idea of a single brain in a single body, operating smoothly and cleanly, was a human fiction.

My mind was definitely not just in my body. It was in my entire web of relations—fungal, geological, microbial, vegetal, ancestral—that interwove my specific ecosystem. An ecosystem I was created and sustained by with each gulp of oxygen, each grateful exhalation of carbon.

In the mornings I began to practice a new prayer.

Scarlet tanager. Woodcock. Yellow-throated vireo. Thimbleweed. St. John's wort. Black locust. Honey locust. King bolete. Cayuga soil. Schist. Bluestone. Turkey tail. Mountain lion. Coywolf. Trillium. Columbine. Mountain laurel. The Shawangunk Mountains. Esopus Creek. The Millstream. Sturgeon. Purple loosestrife. Wolf spider. Chanterelle. Osha. Phlox . . .

The litany lasted about an hour, or as long as it took for me to boil the water for my pour-over coffee, watching streams of tangerine dawn stripe across my living room. Sometimes the prayer would spill into my early morning run. But by the time I was done summoning and sending thanks to every being I knew in a twenty-mile radius of my home, I was surrounded by a world of witnesses.

The prayer got longer, and my mind got bigger. More insects and stones and animals were added.

My days still begin with this prayer—within an interspecies household. And my decisions during the day that unfold from the prayer—practical, creative, and spiritual—are made with the knowledge that I exist only through my rela-tionships. Everything I do is ecological. When I use the word ecological, I root back to the original etymology: Greek *oikos* for household. I am not a noun on an empty page. I do nothing alone. I am a syntactical being, strung together by my metabolism and needs and desires to thousands of other beings. Together we are all a household, and every choice we make, whether mundane or explo-sive, takes place within the networked household of relationships.

I did not arrive at this practice intellectually. It was a lifeline. Anyone who has been seriously ill, or has had a near-death experience, will know that it cuts the metaphysical chaff. Illness and injury and mental anguish act like a bottleneck. You are squeezed through, pressurized, and simplified. Only the most intrinsic beliefs, prayers, and ideas travel with you to the other side. Growing up, my par-ents gave me beads and taught me Tibetan Buddhist, Zen, and Catholic prayers. I found these repetitive vocalizations to be steadying. But I often struggled with the abstraction of the Christian prayers and the language barrier that existed between me and the Buddhist mantras. Drawn to study, understand, and reinter-pret the words, I was increasingly cognitive about prayer, rather than embodied.

While sitting at the river, a more-than-human mantra emerged. As I sum-moned these beings, I petitioned my extended web for help. How best may I act? How may I act knowing you are watching me tenderly and curiously? What stories need my attention? What songs want to be sung? Who needs my help today? And whose help can I receive?

The potent thing about creating a council of beings you live alongside is that, unlike an abstract human god, they actually show up. The heron does, in fact, dissect the sky, providing a symbol of incisiveness at just the moment when we need to make a decision. The ground really does provide a soil womb for the food that we will eat and metabolize into music, laughter, dance, heated breath on a windowpane, lovemaking. The fungi really do hold the forest together and provide a medicine that heals our brains and rewires our immune systems. These are the guardian angels that have roots instead of wings. They are attached to place, and the more you summon them, the more they will show you that there is a miracle in every footstep, a deep abiding embrace in every biome-laced breath of fresh air.

Anything we do to harm ourselves harms other animals and trees and insects. Anything that nourishes other beings may ultimately nourish us. And when we are suffering, when we are very scared, we do not need to remember a single prayer, or say a holy word. Our body, a doorway poured through with matter, a spider-webbing of relatedness, is prayer enough. Every second we stay present with our connectivity to our ecosystems is a sacred, somatic, lived epiphany.

If we pray, we must ask ourselves: Do our prayers have roots? Do our gods sometimes grow fur? Do our holy words sprout leaves? Does our spirituality connect us to our situated ecosystems?

Sitting at the river, I waited to see who would weave themselves into my web. I gathered counsel as I would wildflowers. I picked the ones that showed up brightly, insistently, and demonstrated that they noticed me just as much as I noticed them. I gathered counsel as I would pick up a few flat stones to skip across the river. I gathered counsel as I would stars—without my hands, held only as a flash of light, in the prismatic blink of an open eye.

Each morning as I summoned my web, I imagined that I was like a mycelial network belowground, opening up the septa pores in my branching hyphae. I am opening myself up to a "supracellular state" whereby my mind can pass through my threads of relation into the minds of woodchucks, black bears, chanterelles, and juniper trees.

Given that most ecosystems are experiencing anthropogenic disruption, this extended cognition is not always painless. As I sought counsel from the river, a few miles away my favorite lake was "managed" by the local land conservancy. This involved cutting down more than three hundred trees, some of which were sentinel elders I had visited with questions and care for years. The management program decimated the local beaver population and the diverse array of wildflowers that had clung like a technicolor crown around its shoreline every summer. Now, every morning, when I go to summon that part of my mind, I find a blank. I think of the spider with its cut web and disoriented behavior. Part of my web has been cut. I cannot flow through my whole web of consciousness. My thinking becomes disorganized. When those trees were cut down, when those eagle nests were dislodged, where did that part of my mind go? It feels equivalent to the loss of a neurological function after brain injury. I've lost the ability to use my left hand. To distinguish faces. To recover certain words.

Some mornings I sat at the River That Flows Both Ways and thought of the countless Munsee Lenape who died right on these banks, slaughtered by the Dutch. I imagined that frayed spot of the web. I felt their absence in my extended mind. I opened my septa up to the nucleus of their void. If nuclei can flow both ways through open-door cells in a mycelial network, maybe time can also flow both ways, refluxing backward from the future like the ocean sending its vein of brine back down into the Hudson and also flowing from the distant past. Could the Munsee Lenape who died here still reach me? And then, leaping forward, I asked the guardian angel of my own self. *What next? How do we bear this?*

Each morning, I gather my council and I summon the supracellular not because I want to go on an adventure, but because I earnestly want to think better. And I have a hunch that thinking better means leaking outside of the bounded cell, the individualized flavor of consciousness. In a similar vein, the Welsh Mabinogion's legendary bard Taliesin recounts:

> *I have been a blue salmon,*
> *I have been a dog, a stag, a roebuck on the mountain,*
> *A stock, a spade, an axe in the hand,*
> *A stallion, a bull, a buck,*
> *A grain which grew on a hill,*
> *I was reaped, and placed in an oven;*
> *I fell to the ground when I was being roasted*
> *And a hen swallowed me.*
> *For nine nights was I in her crop.*
> *I have been dead, I have been alive.*

Whenever I read this poem, I think of how all poetry, all mysticism, all great wisdom comes from a willingness to leak into the minds of other beings. To be a salmon. A stallion. A grain. To know that while we may superficially function as individuals, we are really part of a long-term project in supracellularity whereby all our physical matter flows and recycles and recombines. To be a better salmon, be a man for a while. To be a better man, be a river. To be a better river, let yourself be invaded by the nucleus of a distant ocean.

If a cursory study of somatics shows that we think with our entire body, then how much better could we think if we thought with our entire web of wild kin? How much more healing could we access if we involved all our relations, not just human experts?

I want to think and feel and weep and grieve and heal with my whole multispecies, polynucleated mind. I want to let the yolk of my small desires slide into otherness. I want to nucleate a symbiotic quest for a better future. Throw open all the doors in my cells. Let my river run both ways.

CHAPTER 20

The Body Is a Doorway

THE WEEK BEFORE THE RELEASE OF MY FIRST BOOK, *THE FLOWERING Wand*, I took stock of my life.

I had been gifted with book deals, exciting creative collaborations with peers, a supportive community, and a generous, loving readership that showed up for my events and classes with enthusiasm and empathy. I had exciting new friends I'd met through my writing—spread out across the globe. Scientists, philosophers, activists, teachers, farmers.

But the story of healing and completion I'd put so much time and money toward was somehow more distant than ever before. Suddenly, I was not a person. I was a "platform" online, expected to offer wisdom and answers I most certainly did not possess. This level of visibility made me extremely anxious. With serious spinal issues, I already had a difficult time sleeping, waking every half hour or so when I'd accidentally shift position and impinge a nerve. Now, when I woke, I'd stay awake, ruminating on the hundreds of interactions I'd had with complete strangers online that day. I'd always imagined being an author as a largely invisible role, allowing me to hover quietly behind my fictional stories and characters. Social media, though, required that I be present as a recognizable brand beside my books, which in turn required a level of exposure for which I was largely unprepared.

This anxiety of constantly being seen kindled the fire of autoimmunity and kidney issues. A bout of Covid destabilized my already fragile vasculature, sending me into a mast cell disease flare. I couldn't eat anything safely. Vitamin deficiencies accumulated. A group of strangers reposted an interview with me about the origins of patriarchy, and I received thousands of angry messages from men critiquing my appearance and personhood. As someone who had long struggled with shame and body dysmorphia, I immediately felt my blood curdle. Old, intrusive thoughts I was sure I'd "healed" were suddenly blaring at full volume in my brain.

You are unlovable. You are disgusting. You are dirty.

I turned my phone off. I wished I could turn my brain off. I tried to send my brain into the chestnut tree behind my home, the blue heron streaking down the river, the river itself. But it kept clicking back into the human audience hidden behind my phone's screen.

Somehow, even after years of therapy and trauma work, I was more hypersensitive than ever. Activated and glitchy. A hermit crab without a shell. It didn't feel like my body was keeping the score. Keeping the score implied a closed unit, one that could accumulate and quantify pain and selfhood.

My body wasn't a scoreboard. My body was a doorway.

For survivors of early trauma and abuse, that doorway tends to stay open. Wide open. Hypersensitivity (both neurological and physical) has been tied to early trauma and sexual abuse time and time again. To return to the 2019 study published in the *Journal of Rheumatology* I'd encountered while researching PTSD, women with the highest incidence of childhood abuse were at a threefold greater risk of developing lupus than those who had not experienced abuse. Survivors are also at an increased risk for developing serious autoimmune illness, chemical sensitivity, and allergy disorders. The correlations between early abuse and illness, disability, and neurodivergence are too many to list. The takeaway would seem to be that childhood experiences of trauma register not only emotionally, but physically.

While I didn't understand the science of trauma as a child, I understood that I processed the world differently than my friends did. I seemed to notice more. More bugs. More smells. More texture. More noise. More micro-expressions on adults' faces. More birdsong. More temperature fluctuations. I was aware that something terrible had happened to me and that I was quite good at keeping it hidden. But I didn't connect my radical hypersensitivity to the abuse I was desperately trying to forget. I just knew that, for better or for worse, I was highly attuned to my surroundings.

Yes, I watched doors. I constantly monitored adults around me and scanned rooms for signs of danger. But I was also transfixed for hours by dirt spangled with mycelia, air scintillating with dust, slugs leaving behind starlight-slick stories on the porch. I could read the breathing patterns of our cats and dogs, finding myself keyed into the smallest fluctuations in their well-being. Blue was more blue. I could feel a cat's purr in my belly. Frog song vibrated below my tongue. The blooming lilac was so bright a smell that it almost made a sound. A song. Life was often agonizing. But much to my confusion, it also seemed more available to me than it did to others. Why was this?

Sensory gating is the neurological process whereby we filter out "redundant" stimuli from our sensual experience to create a homogenized reality. We learn to anticipate a certain reality and unburden our brain of constant sensory analysis, only picking up the colors and sounds and sights that we have been conditioned to believe will help us survive. This process of sensory pruning, while necessary for daily functioning, has been tightened by colonization. Research at MIT, in particular the work of Michael Halassa, shows that on a second-to-second basis we receive an outrageous amount of sensory data. Yet we manage to hear our name in a crowded room and spot a friend's face in a sea of people. Contrary to what we might think, though, these stimuli don't show up more "brightly." They show up because we learn to "dampen" and gate out the other sensory information we deem to be redundant. As a child, we learn from our parents and our social environments what information is redundant. And as that sensory information gets classified as "non-goal-oriented," we stop noticing it. Children see the world as magical not because they are naïve, but because they are simply more neurologically open to it. They haven't been taught yet to "gate" out the aliveness of the more-than-human world.

An adult, by virtue of their maturity, doesn't live in the real world. They live in a world where the gates have been raised and locked against magic and mystery.

One strange aspect of early abuse is that it often keeps these gates from fully closing. In fact, in many cases of trauma, those "gates" are opened even wider, showing us that we are permeable and open to danger. This knowledge of threat creates a physiological need to remain "hypervigilant." *Any* sound or smell or movement is potentially crucial to our survival. Our bodies believe that if we gate out sensory stimuli, we potentially put ourselves at risk of abuse or harm again. If we learned to close our sensory gates, we might miss a vital warning. It's the equivalent of keeping our eyes open our whole lives for fear of ambush. This is one of the physiological reasons why so many survivors of childhood abuse experience a constant alertness to their surroundings that is characterized as hypersensitivity. Yes, we remain alert to danger, but we also slowly wear out our bodies by never giving them a chance to sleep, relax, stand down, and repair.

While I was up at night, my heart racing, I thought about how sensitive I was to everything from online trolls to minor changes in air pressure. For years I'd characterized this hypersensitivity as a symptom of my trauma and a fire kindling my autoimmunity and poor health. My inability to "solve" it was going to use up all my physical stamina. It was going to turn me into ash or, at the very least, make me incapable of functioning like other normal people.

But that was an old web—an old story. I shot up my silk. I ballooned into a different possibility. What if that miracle mind I envied in the ancient people who populated my novel was the product of "wider gating"? They believed more was possible, and so *more* was possible. More healing, more miracles, more sentience in the stones and grasses and mountains.

The night before the launch of *The Flowering Wand*, I paced my apartment, the waxing moon following me from window to window. When I finally got into bed, I was still pacing, albeit with my brain instead of my body.

Where was I? Where had I landed? What had I lost and gained since I had gotten ill, and earlier than that, since I had been abused? What would my life look like if those problems suddenly evaporated?

I wanted to be okay with being totally healed and having no explanation or pill to prove that it had happened. I wanted to be okay with *never* getting fully better and still finding joy and pleasure in my life.

Despite years of medical treatment and psychotherapy, I'd never really considered what a normal version of me might feel or act like.

As I drifted into sleep, the thought crossed my mind.

Is a "healthy" Sophie someone who I really want to be?

The banging in the dream was the thump of a woodpecker's beak probing the oak tree. A hungry percussion. *Bang. Bang.* I groggily peered through the door viewer at whoever was demanding entrance into my home in the middle of the night.

Her face was flush, appearing pinker still in contrast to her artificially platinum hair. Her lipstick was smudged into something resembling a scar.

"Come on! Let me in! I forgot my keys."

"Your keys? This is *my* apartment. I don't even know you."

And yet I recognized her. I inched the door open, gagging as I was hit by the strong stench of saccharine alcohol and vanilla-laced perfume.

"Ugh!" She flung her bag into the corner and slammed the door behind her. "It took you forever."

But in fact, it took me only a second to realize that this was not a stranger. This wild, unceremonious invader was—although an inch taller than me, although stinking drunk, although pinker, plushier, bigger all around, as if she'd received a second longer attached to the balloon pump—most decidedly . . . me.

"I need carbs . . . now. Or I'll be a mess tomorrow," she mumbled as she disassembled my kitchen drawer by drawer. I trailed behind her, dumbstruck. She located a stale box of gluten-free crackers and started to eat them without a plate, a corona of crumbs collecting around her booted feet.

"I usually take my shoes off," I suggest, but she's cackling with her mouth full.

"*I usually take my shoes off,*" she parrots in a dopey voice. "Oh, shut up with that sanctimonious bullshit. You are even less fun than I expected. Do you really only have crackers here?"

"Look. What do you need? Why are you here?"

"I need to sleep. And then I need to get this article on dating done for my boss tomorrow. And I need you to give me the space to do that," she answered curtly.

She eats everything in the house and then falls asleep on the sofa with her shoes still on, her antic perambulations around the apartment memorialized by muddy boot prints. She sleeps till noon the next day. I've been up since four, and have already written an essay, caught up on emails, and continued work on a book proposal. She showers for an hour, leaving the bathroom smelling like synthetic grapefruit and ovulation. Her body is so robust, so flush with brightly oxygenated blood, that it feels offensive to this quiet little corner I have cultivated—my orchids, windowsill altars, and old books in tremulous piles.

"Why are you working so hard?" she scolded me. I explained all my books, my projects, and the intense sense of urgency my sick body gifted to me.

"God. I mean . . . I want to write a book. Maybe I'll go get an MFA," she mused while clipping her nails onto the floor. "I wonder what I'll write about."

Her lack of urgency and purpose leaves me stunned. I have never once wondered what to write about. I have never once felt I could defer an idea for even an hour.

It takes several days for me to realize how much she sheds. Crumbs, potato chips, tumbleweeds of hair that her long mane can spare to lose, nail filings so healthy they could be used as a mouse's scimitar, candy wrappers, cigarette butts.

She smokes in the house the first day I leave her alone. We have a scream-ing match when I return. From then on, she compromises and smokes out the window. She lives on sugar and coffee. She talks loudly to friends on the phone while I try to resolve medical debt online, try to schedule an appointment with a new nutritionist, try to get my medical records faxed from one hospital to another. When these conversations end, she tells me she hates these people. She tells me about her job writing beauty and wellness articles for online fem-inist magazines and how idiotic she finds her peers. Her job pays her to attend spas and wellness retreats, then write snarky tell-all reports with pastel graph-ics afterward.

I try to normalize the situation, given my knowledge of family systems and trauma therapy. We must include all versions of ourselves. We must inte-grate the parts that we have exiled and bring them back into wholeness. Is she the manifestation of my trauma? I should be empathic. I should work harder to understand her. Several weeks into her stay, I cook us a beautiful dinner. Salmon and broccoli. But she stands me up, staying out until midnight, telling me she's reconnected with an ex-lover—a married man.

"Why? You're too old for that!" I exclaim, still going to the fridge to retrieve her cold dinner, getting her a glass of water. Feeling sympathy perhaps because she looks like me. She is me. "Don't you want partnership? A family? A romantic collaborator?"

"Yuck!" she responds both to me and to the food. "I'm too young for that. I prefer having lovers. I want a life worth writing about. I'm not ready to be tied down to something yet."

"A life worth writing about is not necessarily an easy life. It's soothing, if unsayable, to be simple and undramatic. It can be good to be tied to something," I try carefully, feeling my own longing uncurl and rearrange itself in my chest like a drowsy cat. "It feels good to care for other people. And to know that their care keeps you alive. It's what trees and fungi do. It's what animals do. We all do our best living in symbiotic community."

Her eyes are glazed and blue with the light of her phone. "I mean, I get it. I'm really lonely."

"Are you?" I probe. "I'm not. I guess, I long for a partner, but I feel held by all my friends. And by the mountains and the trees and the river . . ."

"I have friends," she sniffles, still not looking up from her phone. "I just don't like them very much."

I can't get rid of her. And I can't clean up after her. She emits a toxic miasma of teenage locker room and tobacco smoke that adheres to surfaces like cooking grease. It's a virile smell. Loathsome. I feel as if it could impregnate my very pores with demon spawn. She watches long French movies in the living room, ashing into my monstera plant. She never cooks, yet manages to leave behind half-eaten food everywhere. She makes fun of my early bedtime, my discussions of impending environmental collapse, my friends, my exercise and physical therapy routines, my dedication to work.

I juice parsley. I watch videos about EMDR and psychedelic-assisted trauma therapy. I do a Holotropic Breathwork session alone in my bedroom while she makes out with a shaggy-haired barista in the kitchen.

It isn't until she steals my phone and calls my ex, Jason, and meets up with him for dinner that I really lose my shit.

"He said you were just too sick for him. Too intense. Too focused on your work," she taunts me. "He told me you were uptight and radical and crazy."

I narrow my eyes, finally sharpened into certainty.

"Look," I say to her, to myself. "I know you are me. That you're some version of me. But I've decided I don't care what the trauma therapists say. I don't think I can integrate you into my life. I don't think this is working."

To my surprise, she smiles, revealing polished, straight teeth.

"But I'm the person you're trying to get back to all the time. I'm the person you're trying to find and to remember how to be."

The world tilts. My body, prone to postural tachycardia, knows to sit down, to lean into the vertigo rather than resist it.

"I'm confused. What do you mean?"

She sits beside me so that the comparison is unavoidable. Our bodies are mismatched tuning forks, one prong straight, the other bent, disharmonic. She has better posture, better color. Her skin is candlelit. Her hands are manicured, free of bubbled veins and tissue-paper scarring.

"Haven't you ever wondered what you'd be like if you hadn't been abused as a child? If you hadn't been traumatized? Haven't you ever wondered what you'd be like if your genetic illness had never turned on?" She draws my hand to her face, stroking her own velveteen softness with my fingers.

"I'm the Well You. I'm the Healthy You. I'm the 'You' without trauma. I'm the person you could have been and could still be if you fixed yourself. If you finally worked hard enough to heal yourself."

Suddenly, I understand. She is the version of me with the gates up and locked. She has all her senses pruned to fit into our culture and keep out the bumptious and risky aliveness of the world.

My veins stiffen into a vasculature of wood. I feel planted, vegetal, inhuman. My hand against her human face is not a hand. It is a sheen of mildew. The obdurate green of undergrowth. The lacquer of lichen on a tombstone.

I retract from her sunshine. Her lonely and immaculate selfhood. I retract back into the root system I share with the many beings I depend on to keep my disabled, nonnormative body alive. The salamanders and wildflowers. The mountain streams and honey fungi.

"Get out," I say. "*Get out.*"

"I am the healthy you. I am your wellness. I am your origin and your goal," she insists. "If you reject me, you are rejecting healing and wholeness and abundance! You'll never be complete!"

It takes me a long time to say it. I muster it with every microbial cell of my chimerical body as I push her toward the door.

"If this is wellness, I don't want it. If this is healing, I refuse it."

I wake up from the dream drenched in sweat. And I wake up into the realization that, for my whole life, I've been haunted. Not as I had always believed, by trauma or by the abuse or by a disease defect in my genes. I have been haunted by the idea that there was another version of me. A well version. A normal version. An untraumatized body. A Garden of Eden body free of trespass, somehow walking alongside my hobbled form, taunting me with her agility and ease.

I never strongly considered that to be well inside systems of oppression that snare most bodies is not necessarily a marker of canniness or ingenuity. It is not necessarily a marker of good character or revolutionary verve. It is not a good predictor of someone's ability to survive climate change or social collapse.

How can we be well inside of an Earth we are actively harming? And if we are well at the material expense of ecosystems, is that really health?

I want to suggest that we are all haunted. Not by flashbacks and memories. But by an imaginary idea of wholeness. By the idea that there is a normal body that renders our body deviant. That there is another version of us—a healthy version—that somehow escaped the fire, slipped loose the noose of generational trauma, violence, and illness. That we must spend our every waking hour, our hard-earned money, our dedicated spiritual and physical focus, striving toward this other us.

We do not bring in priests to exorcise this ghost. Instead, we make it our Holy Spirit. We sacrifice our lives, our time, our money, and our attention at the altar of a body that never existed.

A version of us we might, if we met them, not even want to be.

The morning following the dream, as I brewed my coffee, I was reminded of the research I'd done on the concept of sin as I was writing my book about the Magdalene. I was suddenly struck that the popular idea of trauma had become conceptually similar to the ancient idea of sin, in its original Hebraic formulation, meaning "to miss the mark." The traumatized nervous system was a dead end that forked off from a straight highway. A deviation. A wrong turn. A wrong self.

The way we talk about trauma easily reveals its theological undertones. In fact, the cataphatic impulse to name everything as trauma rearticulates the medieval impulse to circumscribe God through intellectual acrobatics. Just as medieval theologians pored over scripture, seeking God, so we have become paranoid readers of our own bodies, taking any symptom as a sign that might lead back to the genesis, the original traumatizing event, the God we can only see through the bubbles he creates on the surface of the ocean.

The hunger to locate and explain trauma might be a hunger for a god of matter. A god of bodies. A god who cares little for our abstract ideas of good and evil. A god who uses our own bodies as instruments. A god big enough for the chaos and collapse to come.

We strive toward the healed body like we strive toward Eden. But as we walk toward Eden, we find we are not actually walking toward a utopian garden, but into the molten wound of a crater. The Chicxulub crater to be exact, created when an asteroid hit the Earth, causing an extinction event that decimated the dinosaurs and killed 75 percent of all life. An event that opened up the real estate, the ecological niches, that protomammalian life would rush to fill. It was that crater that created the space for us to evolve and, finally, produced humanoid bodies.

We are the product not of a garden but of an impact. An extinction event. We are the children of the crater. The bodies produced by collision and eruption.

The well body and the Edenic utopia function similarly. They are advertised as universal but are always partial. They are always produced by some other being's dystopia.

Wellness is built from unwellness. Utopia depends on and produces dystopia. Blood pressure stabilizers, diabetic drugs, and antidepressants keep our bodies upright while also polluting river water. A medication is produced by context, and no substance we produce stays in its correct place for long. It leaks physically and ontologically, producing hells when it was created to stabilize anthropocentric normativity.

For beings that date the beginning of the universe to a Big Bang, should we not expect that we feel the Bang? Is that original combustion, the detonated hurl of one body against another body, the making of bodies by slamming bodies together, not in our very matter?

We are matter conjugated—created by collision and impact and interpenetration. This is the calculus of world-building. It is also language we would readily identify as relating to trauma and trespass.

As I got ready for my book launch, excited to see friends and family who had traveled upstate for the event, I brushed out my hair and peered into the mirror. Here were my strange veins and ghostly pallor. Here was my body's frank refusal to be well. And yet it was this frank refusal that had put me in a position to write a book that attracted readers and collaborators. It was my unhealthy body that drew in the support of these friends and family members. The ways my body misbehaved made me into a hub of necessary community. It reminded me that I was never an individual. I was always a product of others.

What is health *really*? What unwellness is our wellness built from? What dystopias do we unwittingly produce when we fixate on personalized completion? What beings, what possible futures and worlds, have been sacrificed to produce our medicine? And what is our healing really for?

In biology, one species' lack is not always a disadvantage. Rather, it can be read as an invitation to horizontal gene transfer, body-sharing, and symbiotic collaboration. When plants first arrived on dry land over four hundred million years ago, they were hobbled by a lack of roots. They could not access the nutrients of the soil. But early mycorrhizal fungi reached up and acted as a surrogate root system for these prehistoric plants. This physical merger was permanent. Ninety percent of plants today still depend on mycorrhizal fungi to weave them into a wider radius of nourishment and cross-species communication.

Trees with hardy mycorrhizal systems can send nutrients and messages to their kin, and they can receive warnings about incoming parasites. The fungi, in turn, receive translated sunlight from the trees, a symbiotic gift of sucrose. Trees that open their bodies to otherness tend to survive. That decision that a tree makes to open up is not a safe one. It is hard to classify it as healing. But it holds the potential for survival.

What if there was a difference between healing and surviving?

For so long I'd believed that health would look like my complete indepen-dence—freedom from reliance on medicine and suffering and family support. I'd believed that health was an individual pursuit. During the pandemic, I'd watched as the cultural fixation on the language of trauma made us all para-noid readers of our own bodies. We were all keeping careful score rather than joyfully playing a game that cared little for individual players or winners.

I held my newly published book up to the window as I watched the river curl like a silver tongue through the dappled foliage of the valley. A dove was cooing in the eaves. A child's laugh rose like sonic steam from the merriment of the holiday shoppers on the street below. Medicine.

This book was not a pill. Not an expensive therapy. Not an answer to my incurable genetic condition. But it was an object with weight and heft. A collec-tion of words I would not have produced had I not been sensitive to microbes and fungi and soil and starlight. An ecosystem of stories I would not have been forced to grow out of my own body had I been well. This book that was launch-ing my career and tying me into feral, far-reaching community was produced by my weird body, my "incorrect" nervous system.

My incorrectness had left me open to love and joy and unexpected mira-cles and stories.

My incorrectness was a doorway to the very material interdependency that our human-centric culture tries to ignore.

I'd known I was exhausted. I'd believed I was exhausted from years of illness and years of trying to metabolize the abuse my body refused to either expel or integrate. But I finally could see it clearly. My real exhaustion was with the paradigm that said my sensitive body and my sensitive nervous sys-tem were a problem that had to be fixed. Yes, the early abuse made me hypersensitive. It could probably be connected to my body's illness later on. But my hypersensitivity had never discriminated between human and more-than-human stimuli. And this was my saving grace. While I scanned a room for danger, I also let my eyes take in the gestalt of ecosystems. I noticed minute shifts in cloud formations. I could read the silver-flipping twist of leaves to predict the exact moment when a storm would hit. I could taste the milky-rust flavor of mycorrhizal systems below my feet as I walked through a forest. I was able to notice more. Particularly the very small and the very unacknowledged: molds, mushrooms, tadpoles, pond scum, voids of birdsong where the year before there had been a frenetic chorus.

For so long I'd viewed comfort and relaxation and ease as the goals that medical and psychological treatment were supposed to provide. By reading popular self-help books and following social media psychology accounts, I learned that we were supposed to create safe spaces and healthy boundaries. We needed to clean up our attachment styles and remove triggers from our environments. But over time, I'd seen that the more zealously we defended our safety and our comfort, the smaller and more sterile our worlds became. We canceled people with ease, like an overactive cultural immune system, ultimately destroying our own vital cells.

Trauma does not belong to an individual. It is a web that includes someone. It is not an object that can be removed. Your body's innate ability to dance with harm and with discomfort is not always a problem. It is a relational tactic. A nonconsensual opening to both the good and the bad, the human and the nonhuman.

I walked through my front door holding my book, holding my glitchy heart. And I finally stopped defending the doorway of my own body.

Let it in. The love. The wonder. The pain. The uncertainty.

What if my traumatized body was not so much a scorekeeper as a doorway, acting like an aperture, capturing pictures of horror as well as imprinting cosmic light from distant galaxies? What if the body was a doorway open to more than human stories? Just as I realized my connective tissue disease mapped directly onto my love of underground fungal connective systems, so could I understand my trauma to be less of a mortal wound and more a compass pointing out of anthropocentrism. What if the shape of our wounds, the exact flickering silhouette of our hypersensitivity, was the shape of the doorway into another being's pain and experience?

I'm done, I whispered like a prayer before heading into the church where my book launch was beginning. My phone was buzzing in my pocket like a bumblebee, reminding me of the flower, the pollen, the friends waiting for me in the field of a more feral future.

I knelt in the frosty dust near an old apple tree that grew beside the parking lot. My body's aches and pains were ritual enough. They were my sacred way of understanding the tree's own body adjusting to winter, to dryness, to probing wind.

If I can't close my sensory gating, then open me wider. Dilate me like a cervix so that I may be the birth canal for stories that are not about human beings and human progress. Let me become a doorway for viruses and ecosystems and fungi and dove song. Let me become a doorway so big and so open that a new way of being can emerge, one not tied to the fiction of human supremacy.

May I be a doorway that is equally aware of the agony and ecstasy and is allowed to wildly swing out of the window of tolerance, achieving both the valleys and peaks that our culture has denied us. Let me exceed the graph. Let me swing past wellness into something wilder and less predictable and more beautiful.

We could say the climate itself is out of its window of tolerance. How, then, can I ride these nervous system oscillations in wild solidarity? How does the body of an abuse survivor act as an expert barometer for shifting ecosystems and temperatures and weather patterns? It is important to note that the temperate conditions human beings consider optimal are a rarity in the history of deep time. What if the window of normalcy that trauma survivors are expected to reenter isn't normalcy at all? What if it's just an anthropocentric model that gates out the wily and often ecstatic?

I stopped worshipping at the altar of penitential healing that day.

I vowed to be incorrect.

I would let my joints dislocate, cracking open space for fungal incursions. I would choose to take the wrong path. I would hobble myself into holiness. Stumble my way to the sacred. I would finally honor my body as a material refusal to participate in this ecocidal culture. I would tie my roots to other roots permanently.

Let us join hands and then let our hands melt together, permanently, terrifyingly fused. Let us honor our wounds as invitations to risky collaborations we might otherwise not attempt. Let us acknowledge that to be correct is to be isolated. To be incorrect is to be relational. Survival is never safe. It is always a breach. A break in the skin.

I did not want to heal; I wanted to survive.

I want us *all*—the entire biosphere—to survive.

CHAPTER 21

Let Me Be Wrong

A WIND, SLENDER AND INSISTENT AS STARLIGHT, ACUMINATED BY THE nearby river, whips through my hair, traces the curve of my skull, and makes me keenly aware of my own skeleton. The brushstroke bones that keep me moving, keep me upright. I bend over, seeking shelter in the dried mugwort patch from last summer, watching as my small dog shuffles across the ground. Often he's nose-led. I've learned to read his shape, register his desire in the tug of the leash up my arm, arrow-pointed toward some crumb, some effervescent spray of pheromone tucked in the cleft of a tree stump. But then there's the moment he begins to circle, his body turning into curlicues of cursive, nose to tail, spine like a seashell. His eyes are practically glazed. It's almost a trance. He circles and circles. Bends into a horseshoe, then pauses, shivering against the shape as if to test it. Tries again. Until—there—the perfect spot. He shits.

If you're a dog owner, you're familiar with the strange ritual a dog needs to perform to find the right spot, and the correct orientation, to finally take a poop.

I wait. And I wait. For a cure. A miracle. A medicine. A romantic partner. I wait for pain relief and physical ease. I wait for an answer. For a placebo that convinces me to wake up the potential in my body for joy and regeneration.

I wait in the open doorway of my body for these unanswered prayers, and other things blow through.

Authors and writers and musicians I admire arrive at my doorstep as intimate friends and collaborators. This small dog arrives. He is the color and size of a well-toasted cinnamon bun, and he is plagued by life-threatening ailments. I spend months concerned with his medical care and health, grateful to be distracted from my own body's failings. He grows into a companion of anarchic whimsy and incredible sweetness.

While romantic love and physical healing don't arrive, I take great pleasure in my dog's slow growth, his sturdiness, his magical poop peregrinations.

The more uncertain I feel in my own life and my own body, the more I piggyback on this ritual, letting it become my own little absurd punctuation to the strange syntax of each day. We go outside and we skim across the grasses like a metal detector looking for treasure. These mini-quests stabilize me in the midst of paradox.

My books are taking flight. The Magdalene novel is born. The miracles it delivers are more oblique than the ones contained within its pages. I am not miraculously healed by its publication. But I *am* rewoven into celebratory community.

My world is expanding after the bottleneck of pandemic isolation: the overabundance of friends and collaborators is my own Cambrian explosion of new forms, flowers, ways of being.

How can I have so much friendship and love in my life and still be decaying?

My kidneys continue to malfunction. My bone marrow starts to fail, and no one has a good explanation for why. An anaphylactic reaction to a hornet sting destabilizes my immune system, and for months afterward my vision degrades dramatically in both eyes, doubling then blurring. What I initially misinterpret as an ocular migraine stretches into a semipermanent impairment with no sign of ending. I pass another birthday and look back at what I've lost and not yet regained.

In the Gospel of Thomas, a text that arguably predates the New Testament, we get a wilier Jesus, more concerned with riddles than he is with spiritual certainties. While writing my Magdalene novel, it was to this strange text that I often returned, and to one "riddle" in particular.

That which you have will save you if you bring it forth from yourselves. That which you do not have within you will kill you if you do not have it within you.

Had I missed something? What was killing me? Something I hadn't yet written? Or something I needed to open the door wider to receive?

When will my clear eyesight come back, I wonder? My health? My working gastrointestinal tract? My hope? What more am I going to lose?

I have lost my hope that we get anything back.

There is no return journey to the kingdom of the well.

Taking my dog, Baba Ghanoush, outside is a life-sustaining ritual. And the best thing is that these rituals cannot be intellectualized, and they cannot be forgotten. No matter how sick and sad and burnt out I am, I have to go outside into the chill clarity of sky and rain and often starlight. My little dog teaches me how to read topography not with my eyes, but with my entire body. I let my brain leak down my arm into the leash and into his determined furriness. Slowly, he teaches me to find the acupuncture points in the landscape that need to be activated with a dense package of dog-translated matter.

Curious about his poop dance, I did research, unearthing a 2013 study published in *Frontiers in Zoology* that showed dogs are one of the many mammals that spontaneously align their body axis in relationship to the Earth's magnetic field during a certain behavior. Foxes use magnetoreception on the hunt. Many canine species use it to return home. Birds use it to navigate long distances as they seasonally migrate. In a study conducted with various dog breeds over a series of years, it was shown that dogs predictably aligned themselves with the north-south axis before urinating or pooping. The dogs were sensitive to small geomagnetic shifts and had more ease in excreting during calm geomagnetic conditions. It's unclear what the sensory experience of this is like for the dogs. But we can imagine. Is it a tingling sensation? The full-body exhalation when you find the position of relaxation in bed after a long, upright day? When a subluxed joint finally slips back into place?

I find myself wondering how good it must feel to know exactly where to shit. To be able to feel the invisible wiring of the world pulling me into place. In a culture in which we are abstracted from our waste physically and metaphorically, we are constantly anxious. What populations are made responsible for my trash? What environments are impinged by the exhaust from my commute?

What if we knew, in a deeply physical sense, where to put our shit? Where to feed it?

I remember long camping trips with the anarchist wilderness group I participated in as a teen during which I would dig my shit hole each morning. It was an incredible feeling, looking through the fallen and tumbled bluestone, the roots bubbling up like serpent sea monsters in a soil ocean, for exactly the right spot.

To find the correct spot to shit is also to find the correct spot to be vulnerable. How rarely do we ever know with our whole body that we have found the right spot to surrender? To let down our guard? To release our waste? Our fears? Our threadbare identities? Another study I read on animal behavior said that dogs make eye contact with you when they shit because they know they are exposing themselves to predators. They are trusting you to keep an eye out while they take care of business. It makes me think that the search for the right axis is like a ritual against harm. *If only I am aligned, I won't be eaten while I poop.* It reminds me of a certain flavor of internet pop spirituality. "You need to find alignment. You need to come back into the right frequency or vibration."

I wanted to recover an instinct for surrender and safety. I desperately wanted a guiding principle or divinity to make my decisions for me. Maybe that's why I'd spent years studying ancient healers and miracle workers. When we have known loss and violence and incurable pain, when we have spent years trying to heal the aftereffects of these ruptures only to find ourselves wearier and more defeated than before, sometimes all we want is someone else to tell us what to do. We want someone to give us the right placebo: *you are healed. Stand up and walk.*

Tell me how to live my life today, I want to plead with the world. *I do not know which shoes to wear. I do not know which way to walk. I obviously do not know how to avoid pain.*

Baba, my dog, licks my feet when I lie on the ground, stitched to the present by nausea and fear. His bark never fails to shatter my solipsism. Life is not deferred. It does not belong to a future me or future you or future us. It is not a given, and it is not perfected.

Life is provisional and entangled and impossible to see from an imaginary God's Eye objectivity. It is messy and canine and it is *now.* When I wonder if I will truly navigate this life alone, if I will ever know a pain-free body again, I go outside with my dog, and I ask him to teach me where to put my shit.

How do I do the simple things with such grace and precision that I find myself aligned with forces both too immense and immaterial for me to ever grasp in my sensory frame?

Human hubris will never fix the problems we have created for the Earth. So often our solutions in any moment are so shortsighted they end up creating more ecological harm down the road. But we are *here* on Earth. We must have a role. A role that, like the dog circling through magnetic fields and a bumblebee following desire into a flower, does not always appear to us in its full complexity. We need to learn where to put our shit. How to become useful to our entire extended web of kin. How can we accept our blinkered perspective with grace and bodily purpose?

I want to know where to put my shit. I want to align with the tides of the universe such that they dance me into place. I want my agency to choose not to be relinquished, but to be rerooted deeper than my intellect, in the place where my gut knows it is safe to stand still and surrender.

Baba takes me out of myself, into my larger self: my extended ecology that flows on roots and spores and curlicues of wind through the Hudson Valley. We go on meandering forest walks, stepping off the path, bushwhacking through duff and bracken. Lower to the ground, scent-led, he redraws the world with his nose as an undulating smellscape. His tail is the furry extension of his nose hairs, registering excitement or wonder in a certain odor. I feel my body respond sympathetically, my own heartbeat hitching when we reach a dark patch of soil that was recently unearthed by another being's curious hooves. Baba leads the way off the path, off the sterile trajectory of my human narrative.

He leads me. He keeps me moving blindly, dumbly, into a succession of moments that often have no syntax, no uniting sense.

But Baba doesn't cure me. We do not move toward a tidy resolution.

He leads me in circles and circles. Finally, he shits.

And then, an hour later, we do it again.

I want so desperately to give you a happy ending. I want so desperately to paint a picture of me buxom and rosy-cheeked, sitting under an apple tree studded with golden planets, a child—my child—on my lap, another in my belly. A partner beside me. A house with clean hardwood floors and open windows. Years of health behind and ahead of me. Romance, family, partnership, ease.

But I do not want to lie.

I want to offer the sobriety I have so desperately needed from other writers and artists and have so often failed to receive.

It doesn't get better. And sometimes, it gets worse.

I never planned to write about being sick. I worried—and still worry—that labeling myself as sick is the kind of self-capture our capitalist culture so readily encourages. Is writing a book about being sick a nocebo? Does it convince my body that it must continue to live into disease? Simone Weil famously wrote, "Attention, taken to its highest degree, is the same thing as prayer. It presupposes faith and love. Absolutely unmixed attention is prayer."

I worry I am praying to being sick when I write about being sick.

But my body is bigger and wilder than even that superstition. I get sicker when I write. And I get sicker when I *don't* write about illness. My pain doesn't have a logic or a single story. I can't game it. I can't escape it. And yet I try, like Homer's Penelope, to unweave my shroud each night.

I get snarled in the threads of my life as I write about it. Maybe I'm not really unweaving. I'm knotting. Tangling.

I don't care if I'm tied to this life incorrectly. I just want to stay here—hobbled, tangled, uncertain—for a little bit longer.

What if I'm wrong about everything?

As I write about illness, other sick friends die, some with the same conditions as me. They are pressed incomplete into these pages, calyx and stem but no flower. They will never be able to see their names in the acknowledgments of this book, years in the future.

I feel a similar combustion of meaning when I think about our ecocidal culture, our warming planet, the fraying webs of symbiotic extinctions.

Top climate scientists are clear. We have already driven off the cliff. We are floating in thin air, wheels spinning, hands pretending our steering wheel still works. Even if we halt our worst extractive behavior, it is too late to prevent massive population dislocation, death, and collapse. We must proceed humbly and carefully from this sober reality. Our best human solutions have created our biggest ecological problems.

I cannot bear this, I think. I must bear this, I know. I cannot understand this. And yet I must live inside it.

I don't want to finish this story and end this book. I've been waiting for a better ending. I wanted to bring you flowers, hope, a cure, a solid answer.

Can I write myself a miracle? A story so compelling it awakens my body? Your body? The vitality of species dwindling into extinction?

I don't have my miracle or my cure. But I am here. I am still here. And that is a gift.

I am here with a handful of dirt, a vision of the mountains caught briefly in the twin bowls of my cloudy eyes. I am here flanked by woodchucks and black mold and glyphosate and phlox and roses.

Here I am: incomplete and unraveling. Tangled and torn. A howl, a moan, an unsated hunger for answers, for pleasure, for ease, for love.

I run into an acquaintance in the grocery store as I try to decide what food is not going to kill me today. My safe foods are dwindling again. Most things make me vomit or burst out in hives.

"Congrats on all your success with your books! You're really glowing. I'm so glad you are feeling better."

"Thanks . . ."

I swallow back bile. I nod. I take care of her own discomfort with my illegibility. My pain. I erase the complexity of my experience to pacify someone else's inability to stay with pain and sorrow.

I am not feeling better, I want to say to her. *And I may feel worse. But I am feeling with every part of me. Can you feel with me?*

I keep walking in circles with my dog. Seasons unstitch themselves from their normal colors, flowers, migrations. Everything is early. Everything is late. I keep not arriving.

Summer is here with a sun flat and blank as a copper penny. The air we take for granted makes itself visible as a blushing thickness that breaks and ripples like a great metallic banner across the Hudson River. On my morning runs I feel like I'm smoking cigarettes as I struggle up hills that, days earlier, had been easy to zip up and down. It took a week for the science to come in. For the migraines and asthma to restrict my movement out of doors. By the time my phone chimes with an "air quality alert," I'm already alert to something between awe and terror constricting both my airways and my poet's heart.

The light is tangerine concentrate. It fills my apartment so curiously, striking itself like flint against the walls, hungry to remake the fire from which it was born in Canada. It is this frantic and colorful display that makes me more keenly aware that light is a cosmos-weary traveler, photons flung from a combusting muscle of matter at the center of our star system.

What does it feel like to finally hit? To make contact and then to bounce? Photon cloaked in smoke, alchemized, solidified, then expelled by screaming forests, what have you felt? Was it terrible? Delicious? Both?

The climate apocalypse that the global south has been familiar with for years finally reaches the sterile lawns of suburbia, the glittering cityscapes of capitalist denial. It is a summer when disasters leak. Fires send long-distance messages. Ashen trees tattoo themselves into our lungs. Floods consume this sediment of cinders and flush it into towns, washing away homes. People die. But many more animals and birds and plants die.

And it is terrible. And it also stopped me in my tracks. *Red in the morning, sailors take warning*, I think every morning as the smoke-filled days fill with light like blood. The smoke *bodies* the air, giving it flesh. I cannot avoid breathing this dense smog. But I can eat it. Eyeful after eyeful of outrageous sunrises and sunsets.

What do we call this terrible thing that also compels us to stop? We have always been drawn to fireworks, meteors, volcanoes. The expanding shore beckoning us before the tidal wave. Is it in our nature to turn toward the eclipse, willingly erasing our own eyesight?

When I gazed at the sky, jaundiced with storm before the tornado watch told me to take shelter this past July, I thought, "Terrible. Beautiful."

When I look in the mirror at the rosy hives on my cheeks, the incorrectly healed scar luminous and silky as a slug streak beneath my left eye, at the filigree of blue veins surfacing from my chest, I think, "Terrible. Beautiful." What kind of augury can I practice by reading these signs? Do they predict my death? My decay? My transformation?

Or are they written in a language of matter simultaneously too microscopic and cosmic for my narrow human literacy?

This is the season of illness that never ends. This is the sun that never sets. This is the beauty that is also a siren, calling us to jump off the ship into the rocks. Light that wears a skin of trees, a smoke of blood, a kiss from a sun that will explode someday.

This is not an ending. It is a circlet of air cut by a hawk's flight in the sky. A nautilus shell discarded by a fleshy creature in search of a bigger container. A wall of smoke preventing me from seeing what horrors and beauties lie ahead.

Let me walk past the end of this sentence, this page, this typed word, into worlds wilder, less human, more generous than I can individually author. And if I die, let it not be seen as a failure. And if I live, let it not be mistaken for success.

Let me stumble and love and howl and dance and fail and dream and eat. Let me keep changing shape.

Here, world. Let me be wrong. Let me live long enough to write this story again someday differently.

ACKNOWLEDGMENTS

HUMAN BODIES ARE SWARMS OF MORE-THAN-HUMAN ALIVENESS: we contain more microbial and fungal cells than we do human cells. We are never truly singular beings. We are polyphonic, multispecies celebrations. And books are no different. My name may be on the cover of this book, but it wouldn't exist without hundreds of people, plants, animals, microbes, and ecologies that have held, nourished, and grown me.

It is impossible to thank the hundreds, if not thousands, of beings that should be thanked. I'm going to do my best while also gesturing wildly out at the entire Hudson Valley and my entire library of dog-eared books, saying, "All of them helped. Every word. Every bird. Every poem. Every stone."

First, I want to acknowledge that I never intended to write a memoir about illness. And I would never have attempted such a thing had I not tentatively shared some thoughts about trauma and ecology and illness with my social media community early on during the Covid-19 quarantine and received encouragement from early readers, asking for me to share more and inspiring me to give voice to experiences in my life I had kept quiet for much too long. These early supporters and readers of my work are part of my bedrock. And I am thankful for the community of readers who support me through my Substack and who have helped this project to bloom. I'm so grateful you took the time to read and comment on the essays that eventually inspired this book.

Second, my friends are my root system. They keep me steady in strong winds and they tie me into forest-wide networks of support. They challenge me. They make me laugh. And they have helped me survive years of physical uncertainty. They have driven me to the ER. They have brought me flowers. They have sent me funny texts from whole continents away, managing to brighten long, gray days at the doctor's office. And they have helped me think and feel wider, stronger, and wilder. I would like to thank in no particular order David Abram, Lindsay Abromaitis-Smith, Marion Albers, Bayo Akomolafe, HeatherAsh Amara, Chris Baker, Miles and Susie Bellamy, Judith Berger, Sophia Burton, Gracie Coates, Christian Cummings, Veroniqe d'Entremont,

Sean Fitzgerald, Amanda Yates Garcia, Ben Goodman, Marisa Goudy, Liz Grammaticas, Gabrielle Greenberg, Amber Magnolia Hill, Annabel Howard, Lyndsey Harrington, Kat Hunt, Adam Jackson, Kimberly Ann Johnson, Lucy Jones, Christie Jordan, Patricia Kaishian, Coco Karol, Jennifer Keltos, Nora Knight, Henry Kramer, Beckie Kravitz, Alnoor Ladha, Sam Lee, Edith Lerner, Sophie Macklin, Manchán Magan, Seraphina Mallon-Breiman, Katie Martucci, Sophie Mason, Mark Matousek, Cassie and Simon McBurney, Michael McComiskey, James McCrae, Karen Miller, Holly Miranda, Nathan Monk, Greta Morgan, Nicole Nyhan, Amanda Palmer, Mara Pfeffer, Mary Porter Kerns, Mary Evelyn Pritchard, Ricky Ray, Carol Ribner, Fariha Róisín, Dana Ronnquist, Chloe Rovitz, Oceana Sawyer, Susan Saxman, Rebecca Scolnick, Kathy Scott, Daniel Shankin, Maxine Shifrin, Hannah Sparaganah, Mirabai Starr, Michael Steward, Matthew Stillman, Gavin Van Horn, Holly Whitaker, and Devany Amber Wolfe.

Several conversations—public, private, and epistolary—I had with colleagues and friends had a profound influence on the ideas in this book. I would like to thank cross-pollinations with Andreas Weber, Ayana Young, Bayo Akomolafe, Manchán Magan, Anthea Lawson, Alexander Beiner, V (formerly Eve Ensler), Amanda Palmer, David Abram, Alnoor Ladha, Oceana Sawyer, David Zilber, Holly Whitaker, Patricia Kaishian, Willow Defebaugh, Fariha Róisín, brontë velez, Greta Morgan, and Mary Evelyn Pritchard.

I want to thank the group of girls from Onteora High School I mentored in writing from fall 2018 to spring 2019.

There have been incredible groups and communities that have supported the ideas encapsulated by *The Body Is a Doorway*. In particular, I would like to thank Science and Nonduality (SAND) for collaborating with me on a course called The Body Is a Doorway in winter of 2023 based on this book. I would also like to honor Robert Howe, who offered such wisdom during that course and passed shortly after. And deep gratitude to the generous and lovely community members at SAND who have been such supporters of my work, in particular thanks to Zaya Benazzo, Maurizio Benazzo, Lisa Breschi, Sara Kasprowicz, and Stacy Simone. Other conversations that were crucial to this book happened thanks to the generosity of Amanda Palmer, Graveside

Variety, Tim McHenry and the Rubin Museum, Melina Roise at Bard College, Lou Sagar at the Alchemist's Kitchen, and the team at advaya, with special thanks to Ruby and Christabel Reed.

Thank you to *Art Papers*, *Spirituality & Health*, the Center for Humans and Nature, *Where the Leaves Fall*, *Wimblu*, *Atmos*, and *Braided Way* for publishing early glimmers of the ideas that made it into this book.

All books are written using other books. This book is a product of every writer I have ever admired and every story that has ever reignited my faith in the beauty of the world. I want to thank The Golden Notebook in Woodstock—my favorite bookstore—and I would like to thank their amazing team, Jacqueline Kellachan, Drew Broussard, and James Conrad. Thank you for keeping me in books and providing such crucial support for my own work!

There are thinkers and writers I must single out as having had a profound influence on this book. In particular, I am deeply indebted to Lynn Margulis, Thomas Halliday, Nan Shepherd, Susan Sontag, Audre Lorde, Emanuele Coccia, Gaston Bachelard, and the artist Ana Mendieta, whose *Siluetas* series accompanied and inspired me throughout the writing of this project.

I thank the ecosystem that grew me, held me, and made me and this book possible. Thank you to the Rondout in Kingston. Thank you to Tivoli Bays and the blue herons and hawks and morels and foxes of that terrain. I thank the Mahicantuck River, Rondout Creek, Cooper Lake, Overlook Mountain, the Comeau, Esopus Creek, the Ashokan Reservoir, the wall of the Manitou, the gullies and lakes and rivers and ancient bluestone. I thank the Munsee Lenape. I thank the ghosts of the glaciers that once carved the shapes that now embrace me in my home. I thank the black mold, the mugwort, the mycorrhizal systems, the ghost pipe, the mountain lions, the rattlesnakes, and the phlox flowers. I thank the woodchucks and the peonies and hummingbirds. I thank Cornell Park and its chestnut tree heart.

This project exists thanks to the encouragement and wisdom of my wonderful agent, Leslie Meredith. Thank you so deeply for believing in me, Leslie, and for helping me to bring this story into the world. Your guidance is impeccable.

A big, wide, owl-hoot cry of gratitude to my brilliant editor, Shannon Fabricant, who saw me and this project early on and took a chance on us. Thank you so much to Amber Morris and Duncan McHenry for your editorial help. And thank you so deeply to the team at Running Press.

I wouldn't be here were it not for my family and for their spiritual and practical support. This has been such a long, hard journey. Your love has kept me alive, kept me joyful and laughing, and kept me writing. I love you all so much. Thank you to my mom and dad: Perdita Finn and Clark Strand. Thank you so much to my brave and profoundly funny brother, Jonah Strand. Many thanks to my oldest friends who happen to also be my cousins: Adam and Daniel Finn. And to the animal kin that raised me: Fuji, Oliver, Sputnick, and Rosamund. And to the tiny tornado of mischief dog that saved me, Baba.

SELECTED BIBLIOGRAPHY

Abram, David. *Becoming Animal: An Earthly Cosmology.* New York: Random House, 2010.

Abram, David. *The Spell of the Sensuous.* New York: Random House, 1997.

Adler-Bolton, Beatrice, and Artie Vierkant. *Health Communism.* New York: Verso, 2022.

Bachelard, Gaston. *The Poetics of Space.* Boston: Beacon Press, 1969.

Bone, Eugenia. *Mycophilia: Revelations from the Weird World of Mushrooms.* New York: Rodale, 2011.

Boyer, Anne. *The Undying.* New York: Farrar, Straus and Giroux, 2019.

Bringhurst, Robert. *Everywhere Being Is Dancing: Twenty Pieces of Thinking.* Berkeley: Counterpoint, 2007.

Bringhurst, Robert. *The Tree of Meaning: Language, Mind, and Ecology.* Berkeley: Counterpoint, 2007.

Brown, Adrienne Maree. *Emergent Strategy: Shaping Change, Changing Worlds.* Chico, California: AK Press, 2017.

Brundrett, Mark C. "Coevolution of Roots and Mycorrhizas of Land Plants." *New Phytologist* 154, no. 2 (2002): 275–304.

Buhner, Stephen Harrod. *Plant Intelligence and the Imaginal Realm: Beyond the Doors of Perception into the Dreaming of Earth.* Rochester, Vermont: Bear & Company, 2014.

Candeias, Matt. *In Defense of Plants: An Exploration into the Wonder of Plants.* Coral Gables, Florida: Mango Publishing Group, 2021.

Chemaly, Soraya. *Rage Becomes Her: The Power of Women's Anger.* New York: Simon and Schuster, 2018.

Clark, Andy. *The Experience Machine: How Our Minds Predict and Shape Reality.* New York: Pantheon, 2023.

Cleghorn, Elinor. *Unwell Women: Misdiagnosis and Myth in a Man-Made World.* New York: Random House, 2021.

Coccia, Emanuele. *Metamorphoses.* Cambridge, United Kingdom: Polity Press, 2021.

Cooke, Lucy. *Bitch: On the Female of the Species.* New York: Basic Books, 2022.

Deacon, Terrence W. *Incomplete Nature: How Mind Emerged from Matter.* New York: W. W. Norton and Company, 2011.

Erickson, Bruce, and Catriona Mortimer-Sandilands, eds. *Queer Ecologies: Sex, Nature, Politics, Desire.* Bloomington: Indiana University Press, 2010.

Febos, Melissa. *Body Work: The Radical Power of Personal Narrative.* New York: Catapult, 2022.

Febos, Melissa. *Girlhood.* New York: Bloomsbury, 2021.

Frazer-Carroll, Micha. *Mad World: The Politics of Mental Health.* London: Pluto Press, 2023.

Ghosh, Amitav. *The Great Derangement: Climate Change and the Unthinkable.* Chicago: University of Chicago Press, 2016.

Griffiths, David. "Queer Theory for Lichens." *UnderCurrents: Journal of Critical Environmental Studies* 19 (October 2015): 36–45.

Grusin, Richard, ed. *Anthropocene Feminisms.* Minneapolis: University of Minnesota Press, 2017.

Halliday, Thomas. *Otherlands: A Journey Through Earth's Extinct Worlds.* New York: Random House, 2022.

Haraway, Donna J. *Staying with the Trouble: Making Kin in the Cthulucene.* Durham: Duke University Press, 2016.

Haskell, David George. *Sounds Wild and Broken: Sonic Marvels, Evolution's Creativity, and the Crisis of Sensory Extinction.* New York: Random House, 2022.

Hawksworth, David. "Lichenization: The Origins of a Fungal Life-Style." *Recent Advances in Lichenology* 2 (January 2015): 1–10.

Kaishian, Patricia Ononiwu. *Forest Euphoria: A Queer Bestiary.* New York: Spiegel and Grau, 2025.

Kenrick, Paul, and Christine Strullu-Derrien. "The Origin and Early Evolution of Roots." *Plant Physiology* 166, no. 2 (October 2014): 570–580.

Kimmerer, Robin Wall. *Braiding Sweetgrass: Indigenous Wisdom, Scientific Knowledge, and the Teachings of Plants.* Minneapolis: Milkweed Editions, 2013.

Kolbert, Elizabeth. *Under a White Sky: The Nature of the Future.* New York: Crown, 2021.

Leduc, Amanda. *Disfigured: On Fairy Tales, Disability, and Making Space.* Toronto: Coach House Books, 2020.

Levine, Peter A., with Ann Frederick. *Waking the Tiger: Healing Trauma.* Berkeley: North Atlantic Books, 1997.

Lewis, C. S. *On Stories: And Other Essays on Literature.* New York: Harcourt Brace Jovanovich, 1981.

Lorde, Audre. *The Selected Works of Audre Lorde.* New York: W. W. Norton and Company, 2020.

Lovelock, James. *The Revenge of Gaia: Earth's Climate Crisis and the Fate of Humanity.* London: Penguin Books, 2007.

Margulis, Lynn. *Symbiotic Planet: A New Look at Evolution.* New York: Basic Books, 1998.

Marya, Rupa, and Raj Patel. *Inflamed: Deep Medicine and the Anatomy of Injustice.* New York: Farrar, Straus and Giroux, 2021.

Murphy Paul, Annie. *The Extended Mind: The Power of Thinking Outside the Brain.* New York: HarperCollins, 2021.

O'Rourke, Meghan. *The Invisible Kingdom: Reimagining Chronic Illness.* New York: Random House, 2022.

Róisín, Fariha. *Who Is Wellness For? An Examination of Wellness Culture and Who It Leaves Behind.* New York: HarperCollins, 2022.

Salmón, Enrique. *Iwígara: The Kinship of Plants and People.* Portland: Timber Press, 2020.

Sheldrake, Merlin. *Entangled Life: How Fungi Make Our Worlds, Change Our Minds, and Shape Our Futures.* New York: Random House, 2020.

Shepherd, Nan. *The Living Mountain.* Edinburgh: Canongate Books, 2011.

Shlain, Leonard. *The Alphabet Versus the Goddess: The Conflict Between Word and Image.* New York: Penguin Books, 1998.

Shotwell, Alexis. *Against Purity: Living Ethically in Compromised Times.* Minneapolis: University of Minnesota Press, 2016.

Simard, Suzanne. *Finding the Mother Tree: Discovering the Wisdom of the Forest.* New York: Alfred A. Knopf, 2021.

Solnit, Rebecca. *Recollections of My Nonexistence.* New York: Random House, 2020.

Sontag, Susan. *Illness as Metaphor and AIDS and Its Metaphors.* New York: Doubleday, 1990.

Stamets, Paul. *Mycelium Running: How Mushrooms Can Help Save the World.* New York: Penguin Random House, 2005.

Stengers, Isabelle. *Cosmopolitics I.* Translated by Robert Bononno. Minneapolis: University of Minnesota Press, 2010.

The Mabinogion. Translated by Sioned Davies. Oxford: Oxford University Press, 2008.

Tolkien, J. R. R. *Tolkien on Fairy Stories*. Edited by Verlyn Flieger and Douglas A. Anderson. New York: HarperCollins, 2014.

Tsing, Anna Lowenhaupt, Heather Anne Swanson, Elaine Gan, and Nils Bubandt, eds. *Arts of Living on a Damaged Planet*. Minneapolis: University of Minnesota Press, 2017.

Tsing, Anna Lowenhaupt. *The Mushroom at the End of the World: On the Possibility of Life in Capitalist Ruins*. Princeton, New Jersey: Princeton University Press, 2015.

van der Kolk, Bessel. *The Body Keeps the Score: Brain, Mind, and Body in the Healing of Trauma*. New York: Viking, 2014.

Weber, Andreas. *Enlivenment: Toward a Poetics for the Anthropocene*. Cambridge, Massachusetts: MIT Press, 2019.

Weber, Andreas. *Matter and Desire: An Erotic Ecology*. White River Junction, New York: Chelsea Green Publishing, 2017.

Wilk, Elvia. *Death by Landscape*. New York: Soft Skull Press, 2022.

Wong, Alice, ed. *Disability Visibility: First-Person Stories from the Twenty-First Century*. New York: Random House, 2020.

Woolf, Virginia. *On Being Ill*. Ashfield, Massachusetts: Paris Press, 2012.

Yong, Ed. *An Immense World: How Animal Senses Reveal the Hidden Realms Around Us*. New York: Random House, 2022.

Yong, Ed. *I Contain Multitudes: The Microbes Within Us and a Grander View of Life*. New York: HarperCollins, 2016.

Yunkaporta, Tyson. *Sand Talk: How Indigenous Thinking Can Save the World*. Melbourne: Text Publishing, 2019.

INDEX